BOOKMARKS
London and Chicago

MARXISM AND TRADE UNION STRUGGLE THE GENERAL STRIKE OF 1926

TONY CLIFF & DONNY GLUCKSTEIN

Marxism and Trade Union Struggle: The General Strike of 1926
by Tony Cliff and Donny Gluckstein

Published April 1986
by Bookmarks,
265 Seven Sisters Road, Finsbury Park, London N4 2DE, England
and PO Box 16085, Chicago, IL 60616, USA.

ISBN 0 906224 25 X

Printed in Great Britain by A. Wheaton & Co., Ltd., Exeter
Typeset by Kate Macpherson, Clevedon.
Design by Roger Huddle.

Bookmarks is linked to an international grouping of socialist organisations:

AUSTRALIA: **International Socialists**, GPO Box 1473N, Melbourne 3001.
BRITAIN: **Socialist Workers Party**, PO Box 82, London E3.
CANADA: **International Socialists**, PO Box 339, Station E, Toronto, Ontario.
DENMARK: **Internationale Socialister**, Morten Borupsgade 18, kld, 8000
    Arhus C.
FRANCE: **Socialisme International** (correspondence to Yves Coleman, BP 407,
    Paris Cedex 05).
IRELAND: **Socialist Workers Movement**, PO Box 1648, Dublin 8.
NORWAY: **Internasjonale Sosialister**, Postboks 2510 Majorstua, 0302 Oslo 3.
UNITED STATES: **International Socialist Organization**, PO Box 16085, Chicago,
    Illinois 60616.
WEST GERMANY: **Sozialistische Arbeiter Gruppe**, Wolfgangstrasse 81,
    D–6000 Frankfurt 1.

MARXISM AND TRADE UNION STRUGGLE

THE GENERAL STRIKE OF 1926

This book is published with the aid of the **Bookmarks Publishing Co-operative**. Many socialists have a few savings put aside, probably in a bank or savings bank. While it's there, this money is being re-loaned by the bank to some business or other to further the aims of capitalism. We believe it is better loaned to a socialist venture to further the struggle for socialism. That's how the co-operative works: in return for a loan, repayable at a month's notice, members receive free copies of books published by Bookmarks, plus other advantages. The co-operative has about 130 members at the time this book is published, from as far apart as East London and Australia, Canada and Norway.

Like to know more? Write to the **Bookmarks Publishing Co-operative**, 265 Seven Sisters Road, London N4 2DE, England.

CONTENTS

Acknowledgements

Many people have helped in the writing and preparation of this book. Thanks are due to Lynda Aitken, Peter Binns for help with the section on the Coventry Minority Movement, Alex Callinicos, Duncan Hallas, Alasdair Hatchet for assistance with the period 1919–20, Peter Marsden, Sheila McGregor, Penny Packham and Andy Strouthous.

Especial thanks are due to Chanie Rosenberg, who worked so hard in the TUC Library and Public Records Office.

Tony Cliff and Donny Gluckstein are both leading members of the Socialist Workers Party in Britain.

Tony Cliff's earlier publications include **Rosa Luxemburg** (1959), **Russia: A Marxist Analysis** (1963, republished as **State Capitalism in Russia** (1974)), **Incomes Policy, Legislation and Shop Stewards** (1966) with Colin Barker, **The Employers' Offensive: Productivity Deals and how to fight them** (1970), **The Crisis: Social Contract or Socialism** (1975), **Lenin** (four volumes 1975–9), **Neither Washington nor Moscow** (1982) and **Class Struggle and Women's Liberation** (1984).

Donny Gluckstein is the author of **The Western Soviets: Workers' Councils versus Parliament 1915–20** (1985).

INTRODUCTION

THE KEY question for Marxists is how to relate to the working class. In countries where the workers are organised in unions, this question then takes the form of how should Marxists approach trade unionists and their struggles. Nowhere is the problem illustrated better than in Britain.

The history of the British working class is one of heroism and betrayal. There have been tremendous struggles, ranging from Chartism in the 1840s to the great miners' strike of 1984–5. There have also been a succession of catastrophic defeats engineered by trade union leaders and Labour politicians.

The event that best sums up these aspects is the 1926 General Strike. This was easily the biggest single strike in British history. Including the miners, who were locked out by the coal-owners, fully 3½ million workers were involved. The millions who were drawn into this tremendous show of working-class solidarity felt they were caught up in a battle, not just to defend the miners from wage cuts and longer hours, but for the destiny of their class. The time of the General Strike has rightly been called 'the days of hope' of the British labour movement. Everywhere the rank and file responded to the strike call with a vigour and enthusiasm that exceeded all expectations.

The dreadful end of the strike could not have been in greater contrast. On 12 May 1926 the TUC General Council committed an act of black treachery when it surrendered unconditionally, at the very moment that the numbers on strike climbed to a new peak. The betrayal of the General Strike dealt a crushing blow to the labour movement, a blow from which it took decades to recover.

When Rosa Luxemburg wrote her pamphlet **The Mass Strike** in 1906, she argued that if vast numbers of workers go into action this is a challenge to both the economic power of capitalism and the political authority of the state. She showed how, in Russia in 1905, workers had, through their own struggles, transformed their political ideas and acquired the power to change the society around them. In the 1926 General Strike the TUC, aided and abetted by Labour Party leaders, did its best to prevent such developments. Whether in the area of picketing, the movement of essential supplies, or strike organisation, the bureaucratic method prevailed.

Those who were on strike were carefully segregated from those who were supposed to continue working. The government strike-breaking operation was, with one or two notable exceptions, allowed to continue unhindered. Above all, the TUC hotly denied that any political intentions could be read into their actions.

That trade union bureaucrats should behave in this way is not, perhaps, so surprising. They have never behaved very differently. What is remarkable, for a strike of such magnitude, is that the bureaucracy had almost total success in limiting the strike and engineering its defeat. Local strike organisations sometimes asked the TUC to clarify its instructions, because these seemed so non-sensical. But once explained, the TUC's instructions were practically never challenged. The contrast between the potential of this mass strike and the historical reality is one of the chief issues for socialists.

To understand the unquestioned authority of the bureaucracy during the General Strike, we must look at the British Communist Party, at that time an avowedly revolutionary organisation. Although the Communist Party possessed a limited membership, it had the confidence of substantial numbers of trade union militants. The party should, on the face of it, have acted as a small but serious alternative source of authority to the TUC General Council. Tragically, until the end, the party did not attempt to counter the general direction that the bureaucrats imposed on the strike by word or deed. It did not act as a revolutionary party.

Yet when the Communist Party had been founded in 1920 it had pledged to apply the lessons of the 1917 revolution in Russia, and to build a mass socialist movement in Britain. As part of the Communist International it could draw on the experience of the Bolsheviks in fulfilling this task. Furthermore, in its trade union work it could learn from recent movements in Britain which had overcome the conservative influence of union officials — the war-time shop stewards' organisations and the Unofficial Reform Committee in the South Wales coalfield.

The British Communist Party made pioneering efforts towards building a Marxist party in Britain. Its debates on trade union strategy, unofficial strikes and so on, though they often led to false conclusions, raised many important points which are relevant for socialists today. Although many of its initiatives proved misconceived, as much can be learnt from the mistakes as from the successes.

The Minority Movement, which was set up by Communists in 1924, is a good example. It grew out of a campaign to stop the retreat, a collapse in union power that had been continuing since the miners were left to fight alone on 'Black Friday', 15 April 1921. The Minority Movement quickly attracted the support of a large number of militant trade unionists. But it failed to prepare its membership politically, and in 1926 made no attempt to counter the orders of the union officials during the General Strike.

On the political field the notion of an independent revolutionary party in sharp opposition to reformism, which had been central for the Bolsheviks in Russia, was replaced for the Communist Party in Britain by an effort to act as a left ginger group in the trade unions and Labour Party.

Much of this degeneration can be traced back to the rise of Stalinism in Russia and in the Communist International. In its early days the Communist International had been, under the influence of Lenin and Trotsky, an invaluable guide to revolutionaries. In those years its discussions on trade unionism, though marred by insufficient experience in this field, raised far-reaching questions about the nature of revolutionary intervention.

One outcome of these early debates was the Red International of Labour Unions, which sought to win unions to Communism and away from the reformist federation of unions based in Amsterdam. The Red International of Labour Unions ran into problems because its founders did not understand Western trade unions. But the situation became far worse when the group around Stalin gained pre-eminence in the Communist International. Now the policy was to seek unity between the Russian trade union leaders and reformist bureaucrats in Europe, and this had serious consequences for the political direction of the British Communist Party.

Underlying all these issues is the nature of unions themselves. We offer here a comparison between trade union traditions as different as the Russian and the British in order to highlight some of the basic characteristics of trade unions. To this is added a study of the writings of Marx, Engels and Lenin on trade unionism.

As the epitome of trade union bureaucratic methods, the 1926 General Strike raised problems these thinkers did not deal with. Why does a trade union bureaucracy emerge, and how is its behaviour governed? What is the relationship between trade unionism and Labour Party politics? How important is the division between left-wing and right-wing union officials?

In order to establish guidelines for the work of revolutionary socialists in the trade unions, we must answer these questions. Our first principle must be that of Marx, that 'the emancipation of the working class is the act of the working class itself'. Socialists must therefore always take as their central focus the activity of rank-and-file trade unionists. But to apply this principle in times of retreat for the workers' movement, when a general lack of confidence in the working class leads to a low level of activity, calls for an understanding of complex strategies. In this the experience of the early years of the British Communist Party and the General Strike can be invaluable.

The events of 1926 are not just of historical interest. They are vital for socialists today. The problems we face in the mid-1980s are substantially the same as those of sixty years ago. The names of government ministers and trade union leaders may have changed, but the task we face — to build a mass revolutionary socialist party and to overcome the influence of the trade union bureaucracy in order to release the power of the organised working class — is the same.

PART ONE:
SOCIALISTS AND THE TRADE UNION MOVEMENT

Chapter One

TRADE UNIONS IN RUSSIA AND BRITAIN

TRADE UNIONS are deeply affected by the situation in which they operate. This is clearly shown if we compare the history of unions in Russia and Britain — one the home of the world's first workers' state, the other the first haven of mass reformism.

Trade union experience in Russia was very meagre. Before the 1905 revolution unions hardly existed. It is true that in 1901 a police chief called Colonel Zubatov organised a sort of union. In Petrograd it was called the Society for Mutual Aid for Workers in Mechanical Industries. Similar societies were founded in other cities. But when, after two years, these began to get out of hand, they were liquidated. The only authentic union established was that of the printers, founded in 1903.

However in 1905, under the impact of the revolution, a limited legalisation of trade unions took place. At the same time shopfloor organisation mushroomed as *starosty* (shop stewards) appeared, along with strike committees and factory commissions. The latter were directly elected by the workforce and 'began to take charge of all matters affecting the internal life of the factory, drawing up of collective wage agreements, and overseeing the hiring and firing of workers.'[1]

The revolution also gave a massive impulse to the organisation of trade unions. But

even at the time of the 1905 revolution only a tiny proportion of all industrial workers in Russia — some 7 per cent, or 245,555 in absolute figures — belonged to trade unions. The unions which existed were tiny. 349 out of a total of about 600 had less than 100 members; 108 had a membership in the range of 100–300; the number of trade unions with over 2,000 members was only 22. During the period of reaction, 1908–9, they ceased to exist altogether. In later years they picked up, but only to a limited extent. Nationwide trade unions did

not exist at all. The few local unions that there were had a total
membership of scarcely more than 20,000–30,000 throughout the
country.[2]

In the period of reaction after the defeat of the revolution very few
of the factory commissions or the *starosty* survived.

In the conditions of Tsarism, where unions were virtually
illegal, there was no economic or political space for a successful
reformist strategy to be pursued by a trade union bureaucracy,
since up to the February 1917 revolution the unions had a shadowy
existence at best.

After February 1917, however, they grew rapidly. 'By October
there was a total trade union membership of about 390,000 in
Petrograd . . . Petrograd had one of the highest levels of unionisa-
tion in the world.'[3]

Unlike the British, the West Europeans or the Americans, the
Russians built industrial unions. In the West many of the unions
were organised on craft or at best trade lines. The term 'craft union'
denotes a narrow, exclusive union of workers possessing a specific
skill in common; the term 'trade union' means that workers of
several related trades are covered; the 'industrial union' is a body
which embraces all workers in a branch of industry regardless of
their jobs.

In Russia the first national conference of trade unions in June
1917 decided in favour of industrial unions.

> There was pressure from some quarters for 'trade unions', but Men-
> sheviks and Bolsheviks united to quash this . . . The only major union
> to reject the policy of industrial unionism was the woodturners' union
> — a 'trade union' rather than a strict craft union.[4]

At least 90 per cent of trade unionists in Petrograd, the Russian
capital, were therefore members of industrial unions.

In Britain the rise of rank-and-file organisation independent of
the trade union bureaucracy — the shop stewards' movement —
took place generations after the establishment of the unions. In
Russia shopfloor delegates, the *starosty*, rose at the same time as the
unions or even preceded them. Furthermore, the factory committees they created were, from the beginning, the bastions of
Bolshevism. Already in June 1917 the Bolshevik Party had a secure
majority on the Central Council of Factory Committees.

In Western Europe it had become customary for workers and

their organisations to see a division between the fight against the state, for political change, and trade union struggle to win economic improvements from employers. In Russia no such separation existed because of the repressive action of the Tsarist regime:

> attempts at home-grown reformism never got very far, however, for the simple reason that even the most 'bread and butter' trade union struggles foundered on the rock of the tsarist state; all efforts to separate trade unionism from politics were rendered nugatory by the action of police and troops. In this political climate trade unions grew up fully conscious of the fact that the overthrow of the autocracy was a basic precondition for the improvement of the workers' lot. It is true that there was a powerful moderating tendency in the trade unions represented by right-wing Mensheviks such as those involved in the Workers' Group of the War Industries Committee, but even this tendency was verbally committed to a brand of socialist trade unionism which would have seemed dangerously radical to the 'business' unionists of the AFL in the USA* or the Liberals of the British TUC. It is thus important to bear in mind when analysing the conflict between 'left' and 'right' in the Russian unions in 1917, that even the 'right' was fairly radical by Western standards since it was committed to socialism albeit at some indefinite time in the future.[5]

Russian unions arose at the same time, or even following, the establishment of the *soviets*, the workers' councils. In Britain we have had trade unions for generations, and not yet a *soviet*. The *soviets* also expressed a fusion of economic and political demands that was common to the whole of the Russian labour movement. 'The close link . . . was summed up in the words of one spokesman of the 1905 Soviet: *"Eight hours and a gun!"* shall live in the heart of every Petersburg worker.'[6] From this slogan it can be seen that the Soviet organised both workers' economic struggles against the employers and the political struggle against the regime.

The influence of the revolutionary left — the Bolsheviks — made itself felt in every working-class organisation during 1917. Their control of the Petrograd factory committees was matched in May 1917 by a majority on the Petrograd Council of Trade Unions. Only the skilled labour aristocrats of the printers' union resisted in the capital. Outside Petrograd, however, Bolshevik support was

---

*The American Federation of Labor was the main union federation in the USA, consisting of skilled men and dominated by the right wing.

smaller, but significant. At the All-Russian Trade Union Conference of June 1917 the Bolsheviks had 36.4 per cent of the delegates.
In September, at the Democratic Conference, 58 per cent of all
trade union delegates sided with the party. By October all the trade
unions in major industries supported the Bolsheviks except for the
important railway workers' association, the postal and telegraph
union and the printers.

The experience of Russia was poles apart from that of Britain,
where the beginnings of trade unionism were to be found as far
back as the end of the seventeenth century. Permanent unions were
in existence a few decades later: '. . . one of the earliest instances of
a permanent trade union that we have been able to discover occurs'
in the tailoring trade in 1720, wrote Sidney and Beatrice Webb.[7] In
1894 they reported that unions 'existed in England for over two
centuries.'[8] Of today's unions a number have existed continuously,
with only changes in name and composition, for one and a half
centuries — although eighteenth-century trade clubs and societies
were, unlike modern unions, local bodies and much more concerned
with mutual aid than their counterparts are today.

By the First World War British trade unionism had already
passed through four main phases. In the first half of the 19th
century many trade unionists were inspired by the utopian socialism
of Robert Owen and the demands for democratic rights embodied
in the People's Charter. After 1850 the conservative 'New Model'
craft unions took centre stage. Their dominance was briefly challenged by the 'New Unionism' around 1889 and more seriously
during the 'Labour Unrest' of 1910–14. At each stage the social
conditions of the time played a role. The turbulent changes and
economic instability of the early industrial revolution encouraged
militant trade unionism and revolutionary politics. The economic
boom of the mid-century undermined this movement. Unlike the
general trade unions of 1830–1834, the 'New Model Unions' were
narrow and conservative in outlook. As the Webbs commented:
'The generous but inescapable "universalism" of the Owenite and
Chartist organisations was replaced by the principle of the protection of the vested interests of the craftsman in his occupation.'[9]
This stamped the British labour movement with a deep-going
sectionalism.

The fact that British industry was not challenged by any other
country during much of the nineteenth century meant that the
capitalist economy remained healthy. This gave employers much

leeway for accommodating the demands of organised groups of skilled men. Although the craft unions had again and again to fight bitter battles against the employers to achieve economic security, when seen in a broad historical context, craft unionism inflicted grave damage on the working class, women and men alike. To the extent that it influenced the working class as a whole it created a tradition of narrow-minded conservatism. Under its influence skilled workers felt no need to generalise their struggle or overthrow the system.

Sectionalism became deeply entrenched in the British labour movement. To give a couple of illustrations: while Russian unions from their inception recruited both men and women, and in Germany women became members of the engineering unions some two decades after its foundation, in Britain, where hundreds of thousands of women worked in engineering, it took until 1943 — 91 years after the founding of the Amalgamated Society of Engineers — for women to be allowed into its successor, the Amalgamated Engineering Union (AEU).

The loss of Britain's industrial monopoly in the 1880s, and the consequent attacks on wages and conditions, encouraged a wave of union building from 1889, when 'New Unionists' attempted to batter down the sectional barriers. But when the wave receded the craft and trade unions still dominated the scene. Still today there are only a few pure industrial unions in Britain — the National Union of Mineworkers being the most important.

Along with sectionalism a powerful trend in British trade unionism was a hostility to open class struggle. The post-1850 'New Model' unions, for example, turned their backs on strikes:

> The Stonemasons' Central Committee repeatedly cautioned their members 'against the dangerous practice of striking . . . Keep from it,' they urge, 'as you would from a ferocious animal that you know would destroy you . . . We implore you, brethren, as you value your own existence, to avoid in every way possible, those useless strikes . . .'
> A few years later the Liverpool lodge invites the support of all the members for the proposition 'that our society no longer recognises strikes, either as a means to be adopted for improving our condition, or as a scheme to be resorted to in resisting infringements.' . . . The **Flint Glass Makers' Magazine**, between 1850 and 1855, is full of similar denunciations. 'We believe' writes the editor, 'that strikes have been the bane of trade unions.'[10]

William Allan, who as secretary of the Amalgamated Society of Engineers was one of the most important union leaders of the century, told a Royal Commission in 1867 'that all strikes are a complete waste of money, not only in relation to the workmen, but also to the employers.'[11] Even when forced to use the strike tactic, such unions made sure it was restricted to economic goals. In contrast Russian workers struck for the overthrow of the state.

Another feature in Britain was the complete separation of the economic struggle from politics. This dated from the decline of Chartism. The National Conference of Trade Unions of Easter 1845 decided 'to keep trade matters and politics as separate and distinct as circumstances will justify.'[12]

In Russia we saw how shop stewards appeared in strength at the same time as the founding of the unions. In Britain the shop steward began as 'a minor official appointed from the men in a particular workshop and charged with the duty of seeing that all the trade union contributions were paid. He had other small duties.'[13] This limited function was performed by Amalgamated Society of Engineers stewards after 1898, but it was only during the First World War that shop stewards came to play an important role in the labour movement.

Unlike the Russian trade unions, those in Britain were dominated by bureaucracy. Already in the 1850s the full-time official appeared in the arena. As the Webbs wrote:

> During these years we watch a shifting of leadership in the Trade Union world from the casual enthusiast and irresponsible agitator to a class of permanent salaried officers expressly chosen from out of the rank and file of trade unionists for their superior business capacity.[14]

The Webbs, being Fabians, welcomed the appearance of what they called 'the Civil Service of the Trade Union world', because its influence was conservative. In the old craft societies full-time officials were a small proportion of the members and were usually elected to their positions. However it was typical for officials of the New Unions from 1889 to be appointed, and with the massive growth of organisation at this time, and especially during the 1910–14 Labour Unrest, the bureaucracy developed into a clearly-defined and distinctive group. Trade union membership rose from 1,436,300 in 1894 to 3,918,809 in 1914 but the number of full-time officials expanded at an even faster rate. By 1920 they numbered some three or four thousand.[15]

Writing in their **History of Trade Unionism** (1894) the Webbs said:

> The actual government of the trade union world rests exclusively in the hands of a class apart, the salaried officers of the great societies. This Civil Service of the Trade Union world [was] non-existent in 1850.[16]

They describe well the way the officials became a 'class apart':

> Whilst the points at issue no longer affect his own earnings or conditions of employment, any disputes between his members and their employers increase his work and add to his worry. The former vivid sense of the privations and subjection of the artisan's life gradually fades from his mind; and he begins more and more to regard all complaints as perverse and unreasonable.
>
> With this intellectual change may come a more invidious transformation. Nowadays the salaried officer of a great union is courted and flattered by the middle class [in the language of those days, this meant the capitalists]. He is asked to dine with them, and will admire their well-appointed houses, their fine carpets, the ease and luxury of their lives . . .
>
> He goes to live in a little villa in a lower-middle-class suburb. The move leads to dropping his workmen friends; and his wife changes her acquaintances. With the habits of his new neighbours he insensibly adopts more and more their ideas . . . His manner to his members . . . undergoes a change . . . A great strike threatens to involve the Society in desperate war. Unconsciously biased by distaste for the hard and unthankful work which a strike entails, he finds himself in small sympathy with the men's demands, and eventually arranges a compromise on terms distasteful to a large section of his members.[17]

Another feature of British trade unionism which did not apply to the Russian situation was the integration of union officials into the state. The Webbs noted:

> In 1890 trade union organisation had already become a lawful institution; its leading members had begun to be made members of Royal Commissions and justices of the peace; they were, now and then, given such civil service appointments as factory inspectors; and two or three of them had won their way into the House of Commons. But these advances were still exceptional and precarious. The next thirty years were to see the legal position of trade unionism, actually in

consequence of renewed assaults, very firmly consolidated by statute, and the trade union claim to participation in all public enquiries, and to nominate members to all governmental commissions and committees, practically admitted. Trade union representatives have won an equal entrance to local bodies, from Quarter Sessions and all the elected councils down to pensions and food and Profiteering Act committees; an influential Labour Party has been established in parliament; and most remarkable of all, the trade union itself has been tacitly accepted as a part of the administrative machinery of the state.[18]

This integration reached a peak when the state felt itself most threatened:

> . . . it was during the Great War that we watch the most extensive advance in the status, alike of the official representatives of the trade unions and of the trade unions themselves, as organs of representation and government. It is needless to say that this recognition was not accorded to the trade union world without a *quid pro quo* [a favour in return] from the trade union movement to the government.[19]

The trade union movement in Russia came into existence with the revolutions of 1905 and 1917. In Britain the rise of trade unions was very much part of the 'normal' expansion of capitalism. The 'New Model' unions rose during the 1850s amid industrial expansion that for a quarter of a century was greater and steadier than in any other previous period.[20] The rise in unions was not smooth. It paralleled the movement of the economy but the peaks and troughs were more marked. The spring tides of trade union organisation in 1872–3, 1889–90 and 1910–1918 were interspersed by employers' offensives that cut the size of union membership in 1875–79 and 1892–3.

So trade unionism is not a fixed form. In Russia it showed itself capable of uniting masses of workers and joining them in the revolutionary struggle for power. In Britain it proved equally capable of sowing sectional divisions among workers, whether on the grounds of skill, industry or sex, and in so doing it limited class conflict to the narrow circle of wage demands. The Russian unions avoided the dangers of bureaucracy and brought forward leaders who were able to serve as an effective channel for the demands of the rank and file. Britain produced a layer of officials who were a block on workers' struggles.

Chapter Two

MARXISM, BUREAUCRACY AND THE TRADE UNIONS

OFTEN WHEN people write about the trade unions — and this includes many Marxists — they present them as static and outside the changing stream of history. There are many and various kinds of trade unions. They change all the time. But basically their nature and mode of operation is determined by whether they are an outgrowth of a revolutionary period, or of 'normal' capitalism.

What Marx and Engels wrote on unions during the Chartist movement and up to 1848 was radically different from what they wrote two, three or four decades later. There is far more detailed discussion about the role of the trade unions in their earlier writings than in the latter.

In 1844 Engels wrote in **The Condition of the Working Class in England** that unions try to abolish competition among workers; but competition is 'the vital nerve of the present social order.' Hence the trade union struggle leads inevitably to the struggle against capitalism as a system: it seeks 'to abolish not only one kind of competition but competition itself altogether, and that they will do.'[1]

Strikes are guerrilla actions against capitalism that can lead to total war against the system. 'The incredible frequency of those strikes proves best of all to what extent the social war has broken out all over England,' writes Engels. Strikes are skirmishes, 'they are the military school of the working men in which they prepare themselves for the great struggle which cannot be avoided . . . and as schools of war the unions are unexcelled.'[2]

The same argument, that the trade unions do change from organising resistance against capital to the final assault on capitalist power, appears again and again in Marx and Engels' early writings. Marx, in **The Poverty of Philosophy** (1847) stated:

If the first aim of resistance was merely the maintenance of wages, combinations, at first isolated, constitute themselves into groups as the capitalists in their turn unite for the purpose of repression, and in face of always united capital, the maintenance of the association becomes more necessary to them than that of wages. This is so true that English economists are amazed to see the workers sacrifice a good part of their wages in favour of associations, which, in the eyes of these economists, are established solely in favour of wages. In this struggle — a veritable civil war — all the elements necessary for a coming battle unite and develop. Once it has reached this point association takes on a political character.[3]

In **The German Ideology**, completed shortly before this, Marx and Engels had written:

> . . . even a minority of workers who combine and go on strike very soon find themselves compelled to act in a revolutionary way — a fact [one] could have learned from the 1842 uprising in England and from the earlier Welsh uprising of 1839, in which year the revolutionary excitement among the workers first found comprehensive expression in the 'sacred month', which was proclaimed simultaneously with a general arming of the people.[4]

This refers to events connected with Chartism. When parliament rejected the first Chartist Petition in July 1839, the Chartists made a call for a general strike ('sacred month'). At the beginning of November 1839 a rising of miners took place in South Wales which was crushed by police and troops. In August 1842, after the second petition was rejected by parliament, spontaneous actions of workers took place in many industrial centres in the country, which turned into a general strike — the first in history.

> At its height, the General Strike of 1842 involved up to half-a-million workers and covered an area which stretched from Dundee and the Scottish coalfields to South Wales and Cornwall. It lasted twice the length of the 1926 General Strike.[5]

Until the 1905 strikes occurred in Russia, the 1842 strike had involved more workers than any the world had seen. It started in a comparatively small area of south-east Lancashire, in Stalybridge. It engulfed towns and industrial villages east of Manchester, and then Manchester itself. From there it spread to the rest of Lancashire and to Cheshire and Yorkshire. Soon it was reaching out to

Lancaster, Norwich, Carlisle and other towns so that it eventually stretched from Dundee to Somerset and South Wales.

The methods the workers used to spread the strike were those of mass flying pickets. They called them 'turn-outs': workers of one factory would march to another factory and turn out its workers.

The strike blended economic and political demands.

> It raised the sights of the trade union and labour movement. From demands of an every day, trade-union character, limited to individual trades, it went forward to pose class aims. Its unification of wage demands with the demand for universal suffrage raised working-class struggle to the level of class struggle for the revolutionary transformation of society.[6]

In the conditions of the time the workers' demand for universal suffrage meant a revolutionary challenge to the capitalist social system. As the Lord Chief Justice stated during one of the trials of strikers in 1842: 'If those who had no property should have powers to make laws, it would necessarily lead to the destruction of those who had property.'[7]

The formal organisation of the strike foreshadowed the *soviets* of 1905 and 1917. Trade conferences were established to unify the various trades and groupings of strikers. These were organised in all parts of the country. The situation in Manchester was described thus:

> There were the general mass meetings with thousands attending, followed by mass meetings of particular trades: loom weavers, mechanics; the trades conferences of certain trades — the power loom weavers, the mechanics, the various trades and mill hands; then finally, the general trades conference. Each stage led to a higher one, leading to the central trades conference.[8]

The trades conferences were more than the usual strike committees: they

> organised and ran communities, outfaced local magistrates and army commanders, issued permits to work, ensured policing, collected and distributed food, and brought together mass meetings by which entire populations were involved in determining the course of the strike.[9]

Two decades after those events Marx and Engels saw the trade unions as having a far narrower horizon, oriented on narrow and short-sighted goals, incapable of facilitating the march to socialism.

In **Wages, Price and Profit** (1865), Marx wrote:

> At the same time, and quite apart from the general servitude involved
> in the wage system, the working class ought not to exaggerate to
> themselves the ultimate working of these everyday struggles. They
> ought not to forget that they are fighting with effects, but not with the
> causes of those effects; that they are retarding the downward move-
> ment, but not changing its direction; that they are applying palliatives,
> not curing the malady. They ought, therefore, not to be exclusively
> absorbed in these unavoidable guerrilla fights incessantly springing
> up from the never-ceasing encroachments of capital or changes of the
> market. Instead of the *conservative* motto, '*A fair day's wage for a fair
> day's work!*' they ought to inscribe on their banner the *revolutionary*
> watchword, '*Abolition of the wages system!*'
>
> . . . Trades unions work well as centres of resistance against the
> encroachments of capital. They fail partially from an injudicious use
> of their power. They fail generally from limiting themselves to a
> guerrilla war against the effects of the existing system, instead of
> simultaneously trying to change it, instead of using their organised
> forces as a lever for the final emancipation of the working class, the
> ultimate abolition of the wages system.[10]

Then in 1871, at the London Conference of the First International, Marx stated:

> . . . in England, the trade unions have existed for half a century,
> and the great majority of the workers are outside of the trade unions,
> (which) are an aristocratic minority. The poorest workers do not
> belong to them; the great mass of workers whom economic develop-
> ment daily drives out of the countryside into the cities remain
> outside the trade unions for a long time and the wretchedest (part of
> the) mass never gets into them . . . The same goes for the workers
> born in the East End of London: one out of ten belongs to the trade
> unions. Peasants and day-laborers never join these (trade-union)
> societies.[11]

During the preparations for the conference, Engels had written to
an Italian comrade along the same lines. In England, he wrote,

> The trade-union movement, among all the big, strong and rich trade
> unions, has become more of an obstacle to the general movement than
> an instrument of its progress; and outside of the trade unions there are
> an immense mass of workers in London who have kept quite a

distance away from the political movement for several years, and as a result are very ignorant.[12]

The differing statements of Marx and Engels on the trade unions between 1844–47 and 1865–71 reflected changes in the nature of the unions themselves. The later craft unions were dominated by bureaucracy, imbued with bourgeois ideas, supported the Liberals or Conservatives and depended for their survival on the defence of sectional interests in battles against other workers. They were not the same as the unions that participated in the 1842 general strike or supported Chartism.

The same pattern appears in Lenin's writings. One finds that at a time of revolution, he sees a much more direct tie between the economic, trade union struggle of workers and the political struggle than there is at other times. Thus the actions of workers in a spontaneous strike movement in the Putilov Works in Petrograd at the beginning of January 1905 were a demonstration for Lenin of workers' 'revolutionary instinct':

> One is struck by the amazingly rapid shift from the purely economic to the political ground, by the tremendous solidarity and energy displayed by hundreds of thousands of proletarians — and all this, notwithstanding the fact that conscious Social-Democratic [meaning here revolutionary socialist] influence is lacking or is but slightly evident.[13]

Later, during the 1905 revolution, Lenin wrote that 'the working class is instinctively, spontaneously, Social-Democratic'[14] — again meaning revolutionary socialist, for this was before the majority of the Social-Democratic parties showed their reformist colours.

Rosa Luxemburg agreed. Writing in the heady days of this first Russian revolution she too stated that the struggle for economic reforms could spill over spontaneously into revolutionary action, but that this could happen 'only in the sultry air of the period of revolution.'[15]

At other, non-revolutionary times Lenin emphasised the great distance between trade union consciousness and revolutionary consciousness:

> the spontaneous development of the working-class movement leads to its subordination to bourgeois ideology . . . for the spontaneous working-class movement is trade unionism . . . and trade unionism means the ideological enslavement of the workers to the bourgeoisie.[16]

Without the intervention of the revolutionary party the workers could not cross the abyss between the fight against individual capitalists and the fight against the social system.*

It is clear that trade unions which grow in a revolution are *qualitatively* different to those that rise in 'normal' times. Complications arise when the 'normal' trade unions, with their sectionalism and bureaucracy, enter a pre-revolutionary or revolutionary period, as we shall see. But first let us elaborate on the character of unions in non-revolutionary times. These organisations both unite and divide workers. The theoretical maximum unity trade unionism could achieve would be a single organisation covering the entire working class — the 'One Big Union' which was the dream of some socialist activists. But this never had the prospect of becoming reality, for the very name *trade* unionism implies sectionalism.

If the aim of all organised workers was the abolition of the wages system, then of course their common interests could be expressed through one body. But the task of trade unions is different. It is to defend workers' interests *within* capitalist relations of production, within the wages system. The unions exist to improve the terms on which workers are exploited, not to put an end to exploitation. As workers in various industries earn different wages, work under different conditions, the unions unite workers into distinct groups and keep each group apart from one another. The geography of trade unionism matches the geography of capitalism. Here there are low wages, there an increase in track speed or unsafe working conditions. In no way could the same negotiations with the employers cover teachers and miners. Hence there is no place for teachers in the miners' union or miners in the teachers'.

---

*Writers on Marxism and the trade unions have often noted the contrast between Marx's attitudes in the 1840s and 1860s, or Lenin's views before and during the 1905 revolution. However these differences have often been inadequately explained. Examples of this weakness are A Losovsky's **Marx and the Trade Unions** (New York 1936) and R Hyman, **Marxism and the Sociology of Trade Unionism** (London 1971). The latter talks of Marxists such as Marx, Lenin and Trotsky as having either an 'optimistic' or 'pessimistic' approach. But the explanation for the difference between Marx in 1848 or the 1960s, for example, is not his mood, but the change in the class struggle itself. In 1848 the British unions were a threat to the survival of the capitalist system. In the 1860s they were not. The change was not in Marx's emotional or intellectual make-up, but in the consciousness and fighting strength of the class. It is this that determines the nature of the trade unions.

The role of the bureaucracy is rooted in the narrow economistic and sectional nature of the trade unions. A division of labour emerges between the mass of workers and the person who spends his or her time bargaining with the employers. The union official is a mediator between workers and employers. It is this role which reinforces his or her authority within the union. These are the managers of discontent.

> The effect . . . is to isolate him from those he represents. He is removed from the discipline of the shop floor, from its dirt and dangers, from the immediate conflicts with the foreman and manager, from the fellowship of his workmates, to the very different environment of an office. Even if he is not paid more than his members, his earnings no longer depend on the ups and downs of capitalist production — they no longer involve working overtime, nor are they vulnerable to short-time or lay-offs. If a plant is closed, the official who negotiates the redundancies will not get the sack. Constantly closeted with management, he comes to see negotiation, compromise, the reconciliation of capital and labour as the very stuff of trade unionism. Struggle appears as a disruption of the bargaining process, a nuisance and an inconvenience, which may threaten the accumulated funds of the union. Organisation becomes an end in itself, threatening even the limited goal of improving the terms on which the worker is exploited.[17]

Basically the bureaucracy balances between the two main classes in capitalist society — the employers and the workers. The trade union officials are neither employers nor workers. Union offices may employ large numbers of people, but, unlike a capitalist employer, it is not this that gives the union official his or her economic and social status. On the other hand the union official does not suffer like the mass of workers from low wages, being pushed around by the employers, job insecurity and so on.

The trade union bureaucracy is a distinct, basically conservative, social formation. Like the God Janus it presents two faces: it balances between the employers and the workers. It holds back and controls workers' struggle, but it has a vital interest not to push the collaboration with employers and state to a point where it makes the unions completely impotent. For the official is not an independent arbitrator. If the union fails entirely to articulate members' grievances, this will lead eventually either to effective internal challenges to the leadership, or to membership apathy and organisational disintegration, with members moving to a rival union. If the union bureaucracy strays too far into the bourgeois camp it will lose its base. The bureaucracy has an interest in preserving the union organisation which is the source of their income and their social status.

The trade union official balances between different sections of the union's own membership. He keeps in check the advanced sections of the union who are the more active and rebellious by relying on those who are more passive, apathetic or ignorant. The official also strengthens his hold on the union by juxtaposing it to other unions. The presence of many different unions in an industry — and therefore the difficulty of organising totally united action — provides the officials of each with a convenient alibi for their own inactivity.

The pressure from employers and state on the one hand, and rank-and-file workers on the other, does not remain in equilibrium. The relative strength of the internal and external forces bearing upon the union shifts and fluctuates. In certain periods the pressure from below is of overriding effect; in others the pressure from the capitalists and the state predominates. On occasion both sets of pressures may be comparatively weak, allowing a large measure of autonomy to the trade union bureaucrat. At other times both may be powerful and the bureaucracy appears trapped between irreconcilable forces. But the bureaucracy always tries to pursue its own needs and so in no case can it be trusted to truly represent those it speaks for.

Of course the bureaucracy is not homogeneous. Union officials in different industries find themselves under varying pressures from below and above. Again, ideologically, union officials are not the same. The division between left and right-wing union officials is significant. Splits in the bureaucracy — between unions or within a union — can weaken its conservative influence.

The *fundamental* fact, however, overriding all differences between bureaucrats, is that they belong to a conservative social stratum, which, especially at times of radical crisis — as in the 1926 General Strike — makes the differences between left and right-wing bureaucrats *secondary*. At such times *all* sections of the bureaucracy seek to curb and control workers' militancy.

When we say that the trade union bureaucracy has a dual role, that it vacillates between the employers and workers, we have also to be specific about the parameters of this vacillation. Elsewhere Tony Cliff deals with this:

The union bureaucracy is both reformist and cowardly. Hence its ridiculously impotent and wretched position. It dreams of reforms but fears to settle accounts in real earnest with the state (which not only refuses to grant reforms but even withdraws those already granted) and it also fears the rank-and-file struggle which alone can deliver reforms. The union bureaucrats are afraid of losing their own privileges *vis-à-vis* the rank-and-file. Their fear of the mass struggle is much greater than their abhorrence of state control of the unions. At all decisive moments the union bureaucracy is bound to side with the state, but in the meantime it vacillates.[18]

This does not mean that all trade union officials are born bureaucrats from the start. Indeed many win popularity and rise to high office in the unions through their earlier effectiveness as working-class fighters. And this does not apply just to left-wing union officials.

Ernest Bevin was one of the strongest right-wing figures in the trade union movement in the 1920s and 1930s. He played a central role in the 1926 General Strike and its sell-out. Yet even Bevin had established his position by past militancy. His biographer records that during the pre-war Labour Unrest:

> Bevin played a leading part in making Bristol a stronghold of the Dockers' Union . . . Elected to the Trades Council by the dockers, he put new life into the trade union movement throughout the city.[19]

His national reputation was based on two achievements in 1920: leadership of the Council of Action to prevent British military intervention in Soviet Russia and his defence of workers' rights at the 'Shaw Inquiry' into dock labour: 'The position which he won as the "dockers' King's Counsel" opened the way for him to carry through the amalgamation which set up the Transport and General Workers' Union'.[20]

Whatever militant past a union official may have, if he or she acts as guardian of the union apparatus and mediator between workers and bosses for a prolonged period, the habits of bureaucratic thinking must inevitably creep in. Indeed, a militant past may provide just the credibility needed to make a bureaucrat's control of the union all the more effective.

The most important lessons concerning the relationship between the trade unions and the struggle for socialism have been learned in the process of struggle itself — including in particular the 1926 General Strike. Before looking at the General Strike itself, it is useful to set these out here.

Today, as in 1926, the trade union question is the most important issue for revolutionary socialists in Britain as well as in the majority of the old capitalist countries. Socialists who see as their aim the leading of the working class to power can carry out this revolutionary mission only by winning the majority of the working class and thereby their mass organisations, primarily their trade unions.

But the revolutionary party is not the same as a trade union. It does not recruit, like a union, on the basis of separate industries or trades. It is a minority, defined by the common political outlook of its members, who are bound by unity of action and organisation. Unions work by a different set of criteria. For them the larger the mass of their membership, the better able they are to fulfil their task effectively. As Trotsky wrote:

> The trade union embraces broad masses of workers, at different levels. The broader these masses, the closer is the trade union to accomplishing its task. But what the organisation gains in breadth it inevitably loses in depth. Opportunist, nationalist, religious tendencies in the trade unions and their leadership express the fact that the trade unions embrace not only the vanguard but also heavy reserves. The weak side of the unions thus comes from their strong side.[21]

Thus when revolutionaries approach the trade union question they have to bear the following points in mind. In normal conditions the working class is far from homogeneous. It is only in periods of revolutionary upheaval that the class can achieve a common goal and common socialist consciousness. In such situations, although many unorganised workers may join unions, there is no guarantee that unions will be the chief or the leading mass collective organisations. Trade unions may be supplemented or even supplanted by new organisations — the workers' committees or *soviets*, which are better adapted to leading a struggle for power.

From this one could draw the conclusion that since the mass of workers can be consciously revolutionary only at the time of revolution, the task of the Marxist party up to that point is to limit itself to pure propaganda and abstain from partial struggles of the trade union sort. This is obviously false, since a revolution does not appear spontaneously, but is itself a product of class struggle. Therefore the workers will have to fight countless limited and indirect battles within the system before they are ready to over-throw capitalism and the system itself is weak enough to be finally defeated. Equally it is only through such struggles that the party can be built to the point where it is able to lead the revolution to a successful conclusion.

If one rejects the limitation of Marxist action to propaganda alone and decides for intervention, what choices are there? The party can encourage the self-activity of the rank and file; or the workers can be used as a ginger group to pressurise union leaders to act on their behalf. The latter choice is dangerous. To believe that pressure from below can force union leaders on to a revolutionary path is to misunderstand the nature of the bureaucracy, to spread illusions in it, and to blunt workers' consciousness and action. Trade union leaders may be induced to obey some wishes of the rank and file, but they will never be able to substitute for the collective action of the masses. The self-activity of the workers is therefore paramount.

In leading workers' struggles, the revolutionary party must have its priorities clear. It must start from the basic contradiction under capitalism: the contradiction between the proletariat and the bourgeoisie. It must also take into account a secondary contradiction — that between the trade union bureaucracy and the mass of workers — and a third: the division inside the bureaucracy because of its dual nature. Pulled in different directions by the force of the two major classes in society — the bosses and the workers — arguments develop among the bureaucrats.

These arguments open the door to common action between a revolutionary party leading sections of the rank and file, and the trade union bureaucracy — both the left wing and sometimes the right. This common action can be useful in developing the working-class struggle, for although even the most left elements of the bureaucracy remain unreliable and unstable, a temporary alliance of revolutionaries with them can weaken the hold of the bureaucracy as a whole. A revolutionary party must know how to exploit the division between left and right bureaucrats, between those who are prepared to make militant speeches (even if they will not act upon them) and those who are openly wedded to conciliation at all times. Through using this division the independence, initiative and self-confidence of the rank and file may be strengthened, on one condition: the party must make clear that the rank and file *cannot* trust the left officials or put their faith in radical rhetoric. The party must always remind trade unionists that even if bureaucrats put themselves at the head of a movement of insurgent workers, they do so in order better to control that movement.

An alliance with left bureaucrats is only a means to broad *action*. Even the best and most radical speeches should never become a substitute for the action of the mass of workers themselves. Such an alliance, like every other tactic in the trade union field, must be judged by one criterion, and one criterion only — whether it raises the activity, and hence the confidence and consciousness of the workers.

To raise the power of the rank-and-file workers one has to fight for internal democracy in the unions. The degree of internal democracy varies considerably from one union to another. Issues such as the content of the union rulebook or the organisational tradition of the union are important. Therefore the revolutionary party must propose radical safeguards against the bureaucracy: for the regular election of officials and the right to recall them, for their wages to be dependent on the wages in the industry, and so on. Nonetheless the best trade union constitution in the world can remain no more than a scrap of paper if it is not based on the *activity* of the members.

Revolutionaries cannot be indifferent to the tendency of the trade unions to be incorporated into the capitalist state — a tendency sometimes accentuated by crisis, as during world wars. The fact that *complete* independence of the unions from the bourgeoisie and its state cannot be achieved without revolution does not mean that the level of this dependence cannot be pushed back here and now.

The improvement of workers' conditions within capitalism — not the overthrow of capitalism — is the common guideline of trade union activity in normal times. In reality unions tacitly accept the framework set by the system and tend either to exclude political issues from discussion or to support reformist political parties that do not challenge the present order of society.

This tendency cannot be ignored by revolutionaries, whose approach to trade union work differs markedly from that of reformists. The latter argue that they are for gradual change and against revolution. But because they wish to improve conditions under capitalism they can move forward only when the system is healthy enough to grant concessions. When the economy is in decline reformists prove themselves very poor fighters for reform, and often undermine what gains have been made in the past. Revolutionaries, by contrast, are for both reform and revolution. They are fighting for gains inside capitalism and for overthrowing capitalism. It is through struggle within the system that workers' consciousness of their own interests is built up. This prepares elements in the class for the time when, inevitably, the system falls into crisis and revolutionary leadership is necessary.

The relationship between the fight for reforms and revolution was well expressed in the slogan of the Petrograd Soviet in 1905: 'Eight hours and a gun!' The demand for a shorter working day was wedded to a challenge to the armed force of the Russian state. Rarely have the mass of British workers made such a direct connection between reform and revolution, but this does not mean that here and now Marxists should not fight to politicise workers' struggles and the unions.

The revolutionary party must strive to transform the unions into *socialist* organisations. This must be fought for even though it can be consummated only at the time of revolution. The campaign to raise politics in unions should go on here and now, and if one cannot win over the trade union movement as a whole, or even an individual union, one can convert a minority to socialist ideas — whether it be the branch activists, a section of a union or individuals in a workplace.

A revolutionary party puts emphasis on the activity of the trade union members. It consistently adheres to the idea that the working class cannot change society unless it changes itself in the struggle — that socialism will come from below. But this does not signify that in the meantime, prior to the revolution, the party does not fight for changes in the personnel of the trade union machine. One cannot denounce the leadership of a trade union unless one is ready to challenge it and replace it. However for a revolutionary to stand for office in a union, especially full-time office, a clear and definite rule must apply. First of all it must be understood that the decision to become a shop steward, trade union branch official, member of a trades council or its secretary, depends on whether, by doing so, it assists the *activity* of the rank and file, or removes obstacles to this. Union office cannot substitute for this activity. The decisive factor in looking for any union position, therefore, is the possibility of raising the level of combativity of the workers one represents.

The aim of the revolutionary party is to mobilise the working class, and as a by-product to gain influence over the mass organisations of the class, above all the trade unions. But this cannot be fully achieved except at the time of a revolution. It is a mistake to think that the mass of trade unionists can be won, or the official apparatus substantially remoulded rapidly to reflect changes in workers' consciousness *before* the turmoil of revolution. Such a false position could lead either to a propagandist view of union work (trying to win workers to Marxism without intervening in struggle) or to accommodation with the bureaucracy (trying to conquer or influence the top positions).

This does not mean that revolutionaries wait with folded arms till the glorious day comes along. Intervention at every stage is a vital necessity. To the extent that revolutionaries win influence over a number of workers, this must reflect itself in changes in the physiognomy of the union, and in the selection of new leaders. The risk of being sucked in by the machine is great, but abstentionism is not the answer. Instead there must be collective control by the party over the individual and his or her subordination to the party cell in the workplace or the local party branch. There must be a constant effort to control all union officials, and above all those who belong to the party.

In any case, whether the union official is a member of the revolutionary party or a left official supported by the party, the struggle for the election of any official should supplement and not supplant the activity of the workers. Elections in the union should enhance the power of the rank and file, and not substitute for it.

The revolutionary attitude to *all* union officials should follow the line expressed by the Clyde Workers' Committee in November 1915:

> We will support the officials just so long as they rightly represent the workers, but we will act independently immediately they misrepresent them.[22]

Trotsky also put it well when he wrote:

> 'With the masses — always; with the vacillating leaders — sometimes, but only so long as they stand at the head of the masses.' It is necessary to make use of vacillating leaders while the masses are pushing them ahead, without for a moment abandoning criticism of these leaders.[23]

Above all a revolutionary party should never forget that the fight for socialism has everything to do with the daily battle at the workplace, against the boss and the bureaucrats, and very little to do with what happens away from it, whether in the electoral field of the unions, or even more so in that of parliament.

Chapter Three

LENIN'S CONTRIBUTION ON TRADE UNIONS

THE STRENGTH of Lenin and the Bolsheviks was that they were able to enrich Marxist theory with their own experience and struggles. But their contribution to trade union questions did not go beyond the most general level. Before 1917 **What Is To Be Done?** was the only well-known work of Lenin dealing with the economic struggle. Lenin later insisted that the pamphlet, written in 1901–2, should not be seen out of the context of a definite historical milieu and the debates in which it was an intervention. Nevertheless it was very clear about the difference between the political work of the revolutionary party (at that time called Social Democracy) and the current function of Western trade unions. In regard to the latter Lenin wrote:

> all they achieved was that the sellers of labour-power learned to sell their 'commodity' on better terms and to fight the purchasers over a purely commercial deal . . . Social Democracy leads the struggle of the working class, not only for better terms for the sale of labour-power, but for the abolition of the social system that compels the propertyless to sell themselves to the rich. Social Democracy represents the working class, not in its relation to a given group of employers alone, but in its relation to all classes of modern society and to the state as an organised political force.[1]

In the years between **What Is To Be Done?** and the First World War Lenin returned to the issue of trade unionism. Again party/union relations were under debate, but this time Lenin wished to rebut the idea that unions should be neutral on political matters. The argument first arose in Germany's Free Trade Unions. These had been set up by German Social Democrats but were now clamouring for an end to 'political interference'. After much wrangling the following division of labour was agreed upon at a Congress of the Second International held in 1907:

> Both the political and economic struggle of the working class are
> equally necessary for the complete liberation of the proletariat from
> the shackles of ideological, political and economic servitude. While it
> falls to [the parties of] Social Democracy to organise and lead the
> political struggles of the proletariat, so it is the task of union organisa-
> tion to co-ordinate and lead the economic struggles of the working
> class.[2]

When this debate surfaced in Russia it was inevitably fairly
abstract since no mass trade union movement existed after the 1905
revolution was smashed. The debate therefore turned on ideal
party/union relations rather than real ones. The Bolshevik position
was strongly against trade union neutrality or the concept of a
division of labour between economic and political organisations.
Lenin quoted approvingly a resolution passed by his organisation
in 1907 which stated the following:

> The Congress reminds party units and Social Democrats active in the
> trade unions, of one of the prime tasks of Social-Democratic activity
> in them, namely that of promoting the acceptance by the trade unions
> of the Social-Democratic Party's ideological leadership, and also of
> establishing organisational ties with it.[3]

This position is the correct starting point for revolutionaries in
the unions. They are not there merely to be good trade unionists,
nor to preach from the sidelines, but to struggle for ideological
leadership.

However this general position does not clarify the complications
that arise when a conflict of interest emerges between the trade
union bureaucracy and the rank and file. There are dangers of too
great a concentration on official influence at the expense of the
grass roots, or an abstentionist approach which leave the rank and
file under the tutelage of the officials. These are issues we shall take
up later.

When, on the outbreak of hostilities in August 1914, the
leaders of the trade unions, together with those of most Social-
Democratic and Labour parties, abandoned their internationalist
rhetoric and backed a bloody imperialist war, Lenin looked for an
explanation of the catastrophe. He found it in the theory of the
aristocracy of labour, first sketched by Marx and Engels in relation
to the British trade unions.

Lenin's theory had very great strengths. It focussed on the devastating effect of the treachery of leaders and the importance of organisation. It tried to explain why it was that those workers who had enough class consciousness, sense of solidarity, and confidence in their own strengths to *organise* — in other words those who ought to have led the working class forward — were not playing the role of vanguard. This stress on leadership and organisation was necessary at a time when many socialists were abandoning both of these principles and adapting to the rightward lurch of the trade union and reformist bureaucracies.

In 1915, in an article entitled 'The Collapse of the International', Lenin explained reformism, or to use the word he coined, 'opportunism', thus:

> The epoch of imperialism is one in which the world is divided among the 'great' privileged nations that oppress all other nations. Morsels of the loot obtained as a result of these privileges and this oppression undoubtedly fall to the share of certain sections of the petty-bourgeoisie and to the working-class aristocracy and bureaucracy.[4]

How big was the section of the working class which received 'morsels of the loot'? Lenin says: 'these strata . . . form an insignificant minority of the proletariat and of the toiling masses.'[5] And in line with this analysis Lenin defines reformism as 'an alliance between a section of the workers and the bourgeoisie, directed against the mass of the proletariat.'[6]

The economic foundation of the tiny 'aristocracy of labour' was to be found, according to Lenin, in imperialism and its super-profits. He wrote on 6 July 1920 in a preface to his book **Imperialism, the Highest Stage of Capitalism**:

> Obviously out of such enormous super-profits (since they are obtained over and above the profits which capitalists squeeze out of the workers of their 'own' country) *it is possible to bribe* their labour leaders and an upper stratum of the labour aristocracy. And the capitalists of the 'advanced' countries do bribe them: they bribe them in a thousand different ways, direct and indirect, overt and covert.
>
> This stratum of bourgeoisified workers or 'labour aristocracy', who have become completely petty-bourgeois in their mode of life, in the amount of their earnings, and in their point of view, serve as the main support of the Second International, and, in our day, the principal *social* (not military) *support of the bourgeoisie*. They are the real *agents of*

the bourgeoisie in the labour movement, the labour lieutenants of the capitalist class, the real carriers of reformism and chauvinism.[7]

Lenin's assumption, that only a thin conservative crust of the proletariat benefitted from the massive expansion of Western capitalism, was flawed. A capitalist economy works in such a way that its benefits, if any, cannot be confined to a single section of the working class. As Tony Cliff has written elsewhere:

> The first question one has to ask in tackling Lenin's analysis of this: How did the super-profits of, say, British companies in the colonies, lead to the 'throwing of crumbs' to the 'aristocracy of labour' in Britain? The answer to this question invalidates the whole of Lenin's analysis of reformism . . .
>
> No capitalist says to the workers: 'I have made high profits this year, so I am ready to give you higher wages.'
>
> Imperialism, and the export of capital, can, of course, greatly affect the wages level in the industrial country by giving employment to many workers who produce the machines, rails, locomotives, etc., which make up the real content of the capital exported. This influence of the level of employment obviously affects the wages level generally. But why should it affect only the real wages of an 'infinitesimal minority?' Does the increase of employment possibilities, and decline in unemployment, lead to the rise of a small 'aristocracy of labour' while the condition of the masses of the working class is hardly affected at all? Are conditions of more or less full employment conducive to increasing differentials between skilled and unskilled workers? They are certainly not.
>
> . . . Indeed, everything that raises the standard of living of the mass of the workers, unskilled and semi-skilled, *diminishes* the difference between their standards and those of the skilled workers. The higher the general standard of living, including the educational level, the easier is it for unskilled workers to become semi-skilled or skilled. The financial burden of apprenticeship is more easily borne by better-off workers. And the easier it is for workers to learn a skill, the smaller is the wage differential between skilled and unskilled workers.
>
> Again, one can argue that imperialism throws 'crumbs' to workers through the fact that it gets foodstuffs (and raw materials) extremely cheaply from the backward, colonial, countries. But this factor, again, affects the standard of living not only of a minority of the 'aristocracy of labour' but the whole of the working class of the industrial countries. To this extent, by raising general living standards, it *diminishes* differences between sections of this same working class.[8]

An economic analysis was only one part of Lenin's theory. There were also important conclusions concerning trade unions. The fact that the economic roots of reformism go much deeper than a small layer of the working class meant that the effort to build a revolutionary socialist movement in the West was bound to meet with much greater difficulties than were encountered in Russia, that it demanded a hard and prolonged struggle. And of course no mass party, including a revolutionary party, could be completely immune from the influence of ideas current among the masses.

Lenin's theory not only underestimated the strength of reformism, it misjudged its character. In an article written in October 1916, entitled 'Imperialism and the Split in Socialism', Lenin went on to elaborate further the nature of the 'labour aristocracy'. He came perilously close to identifying it in Britain and Germany with the entire union membership, and hence discussing them as sold to the bourgeoisie:

> In the nineteenth century the 'mass organisations' of the British trade unions were on the side of the bourgeois labour party. Marx and Engels did not reconcile themselves to it on this ground, but exposed it. They did not forget, firstly, that the trade-union organisations directly embrace a *minority of the proletariat*. In Britain then, as in Germany now, not more than one-fifth of the proletariat were organised.
>
> Engels draws a distinction between the 'bourgeois labour party' of the *old* trade unions — the privileged minority — and the '*lowest* strata', the real majority, and he appeals to them as *not* infected with 'bourgeois respectability'. This is the essence of Marxist tactics!
>
> We cannot — nor can anybody else — calculate what portion of the proletariat is following and will follow the social-chauvinists and opportunists. It will be revealed only by the struggle, it will be definitely decided only by the socialist revolution. But we know for certain that the 'defenders of the fatherland' in the imperialist war *represent* only a minority. And it is therefore our duty, if we wish to remain Socialists, to go down *lower* and *deeper*, to the real masses.[9]

The identification of trade unionists with 'labour aristocracy' took a more crude form with the writings of Gregory Zinoviev, who was close to Lenin in the years 1910–17. In an article entitled 'The Social Roots of Opportunism' (1915), Zinoviev singled out munitions workers as the most obvious example of those who 'sell their birthright for a mess of pottage' and 'become a tool of reaction':

Yet there can be no doubt as to the existence of a small layer of labour aristocrats to whom the cannon and munition kings do throw a bone occasionally from their rich feast of war profits. This minority made good wages even before the war and has enjoyed still higher wages during the war. All kinds of privileges were granted this minority before the war, also. During the course of the war these privileges have become far more valuable for these aristocrats of labour. It is sufficient to point out that this labour aristocracy *has not been sent to the front in most cases.*[10]

Events utterly confounded Zinoviev's analysis. All over Europe precisely these munitions workers, in factories such as the DMW in Berlin, Putilov in Petrograd or Weir's on Clydeside, spearheaded new forms of industrial militancy in the closing years of the war — leading, in Berlin and Petrograd, to revolution. This was at a time when other sections — 'the lowest strata' — were still quiescent.

Zinoviev's analysis also suffered from over-simplicity, for he saw the roots of the labour bureaucracy as directly in the labour aristocracy:

The worker functionaries very often hail from the circles of the labour aristocracy. The labour *bureaucracy* and the labour *aristocracy* are blood brothers.[11]

The connection between the two was far more complex. Taken as a whole the theory tended to equate the bureaucracy with the labour aristocracy, which in turn was equivalent to the entire trade union membership. All this only obscured the different roles of each group and, if taken to its logical conclusion, would have suggested abandoning work in the existing trade unions. Speaking for the Russians in 1920 Radek admitted that 'at the beginning of the war many of us thought that the trade union movement was finished.'[12]

Lenin's analysis, by counterposing 'a minority, the aristocrats of labour . . . the trade union membership' to the ' "virgin soil" represented by the "lowest mass" of the working class', added to the confusion. One could come to the idea that trade union action which raises wages is in fact a veiled form of bribery. For although this was not Lenin's intention, it would be possible to draw the ultra-left conclusion that the fight for reforms (such as higher wages) is an obstacle to progress since the working class may be bought off by them.

Lenin's study of the origins of reformism was exceptionally valuable for wartime revolutionary socialism in that it cut right through the smokescreen and excuses with which the bulk of reformist leaders hoped to hide their treachery in supporting the war. It showed that they were in fact *serving the capitalist class from within the workers' movement.* At the same time it did not succumb to the despair of many who, shaken by the apparent support of many workers for imperialism, abandoned faith in the working class as the means of revolutionary change.

Finally, the theory served as a knife to cut away the diseased portions of the Marxist movement, thus preserving the health of that principled section which remained. Nevertheless, it was a fairly blunt instrument and was only the most general guide for revolutionaries in Western Europe, who were faced with intricate and complex tactical decisions.

Chapter Four

THE COMMUNIST INTERNATIONAL AND TRADE UNION STRATEGY

IN ITS early years the Communist International was a power-house for the development of Marxism. It was set up by the Russian Communists, who drew on a wealth of experience in many fields. But, alas, trade unionism was not one of these. The result was that in the years leading up to the 1926 General Strike, there was little aid forthcoming for the British Communist Party in overcoming weaknesses in its own trade union policies.

In March 1919 at the first Congress of the Communist International (or Comintern, as it was known), only the briefest references were made to trade unionism. Its manifesto was penned by Leon Trotsky, who suggested that unions would simply be superseded by soviets for the duration of the revolution:

> The old organisations of trade unions having in the persons of their leading summits proved incapable not only of solving but even understanding the tasks imposed by the new epoch . . . the proletariat has created a new type of organisation, a broad organisation which embraces the working masses independent of trade.[1]

It was not clear from the manifesto whether the birth of the soviets meant that trade unions would play a marginal role, or no role at all, in the further development of revolution in the West.

Events proved Trotsky wrong. The trade unions were far from finished, and were enjoying an extraordinary growth in all countries. By 1920 the idea that by simply raising the banner of Communism, revolution would spread, had given way to a more sober assessment of the needs of the moment. Though hopes were still high.

In April–May 1920, Lenin wrote his pamphlet **Left-Wing Communism: An Infantile Disorder**. In this brilliant essay on Marxist strategy and tactics he based his argument on the experience of the Bolsheviks' rise to power. The booklet illustrated how important was flexibility, the ability to advance or retreat, and the need to work for mass support in hostile institutions such as parliament. On trade unions Lenin emphatically warned against the 'childish nonsense' spread by those who argued that Communists should abandon the masses who were now looking to unions by the million.

To refuse to work in the reactionary trade unions, said Lenin, meant leaving the insufficiently developed or backward masses of workers under the influence of the reactionary leaders. Revolutionaries

> must absolutely work *wherever the masses are to be found.* You must be capable of any sacrifice, of overcoming the greatest obstacles, in order to carry on agitation and propaganda systematically, perseveringly, persistently and patiently in those institutions, societies and associations — even the most reactionary — in which proletarian or semi-proletarian masses are to be found . . . We must be able . . . to make any sacrifice, and even — if need be — to resort to various strategems, artifices and illegal methods, to evasions and subterfuges, as long as we get into the trade unions, remain in them, and carry on communist work within them at all costs.[2]

But apart from this most general of arguments there was practically no guidance on how to operate inside the unions. In particular the question of the bureaucracy was barely touched upon.

The second Congress of the Comintern, which opened on 19 July 1920, had a thorough debate on trade unions, for this was now held to be 'the most serious, most important question facing our movement.'[3] Radek led off the discussion. His major concern, like Lenin's, was to combat the strong European current of syndicalism which suggested that workers should quit the mass unions and set up their own narrow revolutionary bodies. It was essential to quash this argument. Radek thought the task ahead was straightforward:

> The problem is this: partial struggles will finally lead the masses of workers to a general onslaught on capitalism. There is no 'new method' in this struggle. If we wipe out the counter-revolutionary tendencies of the bureaucracy in the great mass formations, the trade unions, if we depose them, then these mass organisations of the working class are the organs best able to lead the struggle of the working class on a broad front.[4]

Much of his argument was well-founded. Again, unlike some

others, he was prepared to admit that this was a difficult job:

> Now we come to the question of the practical possibility of transform-
> ing the reactionary trade unions into institutions of the revolution. In
> our theses submitted to the congress we issue the following slogan as a
> general rule for communists: Join the trade unions and struggle in the
> big trade unions to win them. But if we lay down this general rule we
> should not close our eyes to the difficulties.[5]

There might be exceptional circumstances, such as in America
where the Industrial Workers of the World (IWW) had had to work
outside the official union structures because of the intense hostility
of the 'business agent' officials towards unskilled workers, but
Radek repeated that despite this, 'We are therefore laying down
the fight to conquer the trade unions as a general rule.'[6]

The crucial flaw in Radek's analysis was that in correctly
opposing the syndicalists, who called for breakaways from reformist unions, he was completely unrealistic in believing that the union
bureaucracy could be removed or the official machinery wrested
from their control on this side of the revolution. In all probability
the bureaucracy in the West, which has existed for decades, will
only be broken *after* the victory of the revolution. We shall return
to this question later.

British and American delegates to the congress argued against
Radek. Without doubt many of the points made by Willie Gallacher
and Jack Tanner, from Britain, or Louis Fraina and John Reed,
from America, were ultra-left and underestimated the importance
of consistent trade union work. Nevertheless the useful points they
raised concerning the difficulty of combatting reformism in the
industrial field were not at all understood by their Russian comrades. The congress debates convey an overwhelming impression
that both sides were speaking languages incomprehensible to each
other in more than the literal sense. The attempt to draw lessons
from the experiences of Western trade union struggles fell on deaf
ears.

To add to the difficulties we find Zinoviev, the president of the
Comintern, looking at the situation in an entirely Russian way. He
therefore completely misunderstood the reality of trade unionism
in the West. Thus he wrote:

> The Bolshevik Party gave in 1913 during its discussions with the
> Mensheviks the following definition of trade union: 'A trade union is a

permanent union of the workers of one branch of industry (therefore not simply of one industry) that directs the economic struggle of the workers, and in constant collaboration with the political party of the proletariat, takes part in the struggle of the working class for its emancipation, through the abolition of wage slavery, and the victory of socialism.'[7]

It is not clear where wishful thinking began and an appraisal of actual trade unions ended, for Zinoviev also repudiated the Webbs' claim that a union had 'the purpose of maintaining and increasing wages', saying:

Our party has never agreed to this phrase any more than it has to that other which defines a trade union as 'a union of workers having as its aim to assist its members in times of unemployment and to look after their interests by increasing wages.'[8]

If the 'true' union was defined by its struggle to abolish the wages system then there was an unbridgeable gap between this and existing bodies led by notorious reformists. The onward march of the masses would either drive these bureaucrats out or the unions would break into separate revolutionary and reformist wings. This was a prospect which Zinoviev looked forward to as inevitable:

In the course of the proletarian revolution the trade unions will split into sections as the socialist parties have done . . . The Russian trade union movement must take the initiative in founding a Red Trade Union International as the political party has done in the politicial field.[9]

In 1920 Zinoviev acted on this idea, and in April the Russian trade unions issued a call for a new trade union international. This was intended to rival the International Federation of Trade Unions, a reformist body which had been disrupted by the war but had been recently re-established with its headquarters in Amsterdam. It was popularly known as the 'Amsterdam International'. The Russian call was put in these terms:

The old unions are reshaping, within a year we shall not recognise them. The old bureaucrats will be generals without armies . . . Red trade unions should unite on the international level and become a part (section) of the Communist International.

We make this proposal to the workers organised in unions throughout the world. In the trade union movement there is impending that evolution and breakaway which occurred in the political parties of the proletariat. Just as all the most important workers' parties left the Second International, so all honest unions should break with the yellow Amsterdam trade union international.[10]

These expectations of rapid Communist advance were confounded. The first task of the Red International of Labour Unions (RILU) was to woo national trade unions away from allegiance to the Amsterdam International and win their affiliation. But the trade unions in the West retained their cohesion and put up great resistance.

It was established as a general rule that trade unions must disaffiliate from Amsterdam before affiliating to the RILU. But when this did not happen, the rule was altered. In countries where the major trade union organisations remained faithful to the reformist international, individual unions were permitted to affiliate to RILU without severing their connection with the old organisation.[11]

Soon the whole situation was totally confused. Communists were called upon to pursue a policy of working within Amsterdam unions, while also being called upon 'to break every contact with Amsterdam'. These contradictions showed clearly in the resolution of the founding congress of RILU in July 1920. This

denounced 'neutralism' and declared that 'the creation of this centre of the revolutionary trade union movement is the starting-point for an embittered struggle within the world trade union movement under the slogan: Moscow or Amsterdam'. But the resolution of the same congress on organisation condemned slogans such as 'The Destruction of the Unions', or 'Out of the Unions':

This tactic of the withdrawal of revolutionary elements from the unions, and the abandonment of the many-million mass of workers to the exclusive influence of traitors to the working class, plays into the hands of the counter-revolutionary trade union bureaucracy and should therefore be sharply and categorically rejected.[12]

The loose definition of RILU membership made it possible for Communist leaders to give fantastic figures about RILU's membership. This led to a curious method of addition which confused the rank and file with the official machinery, and resolutions in union conferences with the opinion of the rank and file itself. After a mere 15 months in existence RILU was claiming 16 million supporters.[13]

This sum was achieved by simply combining the membership of the affiliated organisations and those that might affiliate at some time. This mathematical procedure is akin to the union block vote system in which bureaucrats claim to cast hundreds of thousands of votes by merely raising their arms. J T Murphy, then a leading member of the British Communist Party, showed how the RILU total was calculated:

> The German comrades claim that there are three million supporters of the Red International in the unions of Germany, although the union movement has not yet been detached from Amsterdam. The British comrades claim a support of 300,000 workers . . . In Italy there is reason to believe the Confederation of Labour . . . will vote in favour of detaching the 2½ million workers from Amsterdam.[14]

In fact the implantation of RILU was far smaller. The 6½ million Russian trade unionists provided a solid core, but none of the other claims of membership stood up to examination. The highest level of official representation that the German Communists achieved at any trade union congress was just over one eighth of the delegates at Leipzig in June 1922 out of a total union membership of 7,895,965.[15] Communist Party influence was much greater in Germany's works councils movement, but RILU did not look to such rank-and-file bodies as its base of support.

The Italian Confederation of Labour never exceeded 2.2 million in membership and while it flirted with RILU for a time, it never actually joined it.[16] Presumably the British figure of 300,000 cited by Murphy referred to the South Wales Miners' Federation, which also toyed with affiliation to RILU but never took the final step. The calibre of the claimed British support must be judged against the fact that membership of the British Communist Party itself hovered around the 3,000 mark at this time.

Later 35,000 Indonesian workers affiliated to RILU[17] and in May 1925 Chinese unions with one million members joined too.[18] Growing support in this part of the world threw light on the differences between trade unions in advanced industrial countries and those in backward countries — the prototypes for each being the unions of Britain and Russia. It got to the stage where, at an enlarged meeting of the Comintern executive during February–March 1926, Zinoviev felt the need to ridicule the suggestion of a British trade union leader that the world should be divided between two trade union internationals — one at Amsterdam for Europe, the other at Moscow for Asia. But the suggestion contained an uncomfortable element of realism: the boast was now often heard that, though Amsterdam might still dominate Europe, the rising trade union movement of Asia turned infallibly to [RILU].[19]

With the exception of France, where right-wing leaders engin-eered a split in the General Confederation of Workers (CGT) and the left had to set up their own confederation (CGTU), RILU succeeded best beyond Western Europe. It often won official support of unions in countries with low industrialisation and repressive regimes which forced workers' economic organisations to ally far more closely with their respective Communist Parties than in the West.*

Persistent rumours that RILU was about to be disbanded illus-trated that it was a far more hollow organisation than it claimed. In February 1922 Zinoviev warned of the need to 'combat vigorously all the forces making for its dissipation'.[20] Again at the Fourth Comintern Congress, Losovsky reported: 'The enlarged executive meeting had put an end to the calls for liquidation.'[21]

But three months later Murphy still had to 'dispose of the notion which has been running through the mind of many party members in this country, as in others, that there is an intention or ever was any intention of winding up the RILU.'[22] The expectation that RILU was about to be wound up had to be put to rest again and again.

Much later, at the Fifth Congress of the Communist Inter-national, Zinoviev made a significant avowal of embarrassment at the existence of RILU (he was too cowardly openly to admit the error and complete fiasco of the enterprise):

> The [RILU] was founded at a moment when it looked as though we could break through the enemy lines by a frontal attack, and quickly win over the trade unions. . . . It was during the time when we thought that we should win over the majority of the workers in the shortest possible space of time. You know, comrades, that after that

---

*In 1925 RILU claimed the entire trade union federations of Russia, China, Java, Greece, Chile, Persia and Egypt; the split federations of Bulgaria and Esthonia, the 'ideological identification' of the Finnish unions and 'not less than half the organised workers' of France, Czechoslovakia, Rumania, Yugoslavia, Japan, Argentina and Australia. The rest were made up of minority movements. (**The Worker**, 15 August 1925)

the movement was on the ebb. All the problems, all the tactical difficulties of the Comintern during these five years are rooted in the fact that the development was much slower than we had expected.[23]

The trouble with the whole concept of RILU was not merely that it was ambiguous, but that it was fundamentally wrong. When Zinoviev had spoken at the Second Congress of the Comintern on the preliminary steps taken to found RILU, he stated that the task was to 'split Amsterdam' and draw the workers away.

> We can now tell every trades union: 'You should leave the Amsterdam International. You have an International of Red Trades Unions, and you should join it.'[24]

British delegate Jack Tanner argued that it was inconsistent to urge the workers to stay in the unions while calling on the unions to split from the international organisation. When Tanner sought to expand his view in the plenary session of the congress, Zinoviev denied him the floor.[25]

As a result of the contradiction in the basic concept of RILU, one finds leaders of the Comintern and RILU arguing for the splitting of reformist trade unions. Thus Radek, in introducing a discussion on trade unions, said:

> We go into the unions in order to overthrow the bureaucracy and if necessary to split the unions. We go into the unions in order to make them instruments of struggle. We shall try to turn the unions into fighting organisations; but if the resistance of the bureaucracy should be stronger than we assume, we shall not hesitate to destroy them, for we know that it is not the form that is most important, but the capacity of the workers to organise, and their will to organise the revolutionary struggle.[26]

An open letter from the Comintern executive to members of the German Communist Workers Party (KAPD) of 2 June 1920 stated:

> The new epoch, the epoch of embittered class struggle which is changing before our eyes into civil war, also changes the 'free' trade unions into a new organisation. Some of these unions we must split. Others will of themselves come over to us, either wholly or in a majority.[27]

It is an inevitable result of the uneven consciousness of workers under capitalist rule that they are divided along political lines, and so by party allegiance, if the alternatives of reform or revolution take organised form. But trade unions cannot be treated in the same way. The Comintern was not calling for breakaway red unions. That stupidity only came with full Stalinism at the end of the 1920s, and had the effect of tearing workforces apart — with disastrous consequences on their collective organisation in the face of the employers. Instead RILU tried to win whole unions to affiliation. But this too ignored the difference between parties and collective organisations such as unions.

RILU was bound to fail because it was attempting the impossible — to be an official mass union body committed to Communist politics *before* a revolutionary crisis made such an organisation possible. Once set up, RILU could pursue two courses. It could recognise the period it was in, and stand as an organisation of the militant rank and file looking to organise the minority with advanced ideas or who were involved in struggle; or it could pose as a conventional trade union body. It turned down the first alternative. But to achieve the second it would have to broaden its platform greatly and abandon much of its politics — in order to win a majority vote from non-revolutionary trade unionists.

That the Communist International could blunder into such a confused position was evidence of a wrong perception of what trade unions are, and their relation to the revolutionary party. Thus the Comintern described the connection in this way:

> The Communist Party is the vanguard of the proletariat . . . Trade unions are mass organisations of the proletariat . . . which unite all the workers of a given branch of industry; they include in their ranks not only dedicated Communists, but also workers who have little interest in politics and workers who are politically backward . . .

So far, so good. But once again we see an enormous leap in logic, for from this we are told that the relation of the unions to the party

> is to some extent like that of the provinces to the centre. In the period before the seizure of power, the truly revolutionary trade unions organise the workers, primarily on an economic basis, to fight for gains which can be won under capitalism. However, the main object of all their activity must be the organisation of the proletarian struggle to overthrow capitalism by proletarian revolution.

The passage continues:

At a time of revolution the genuinely revolutionary trade unions work closely with the party; they organise the masses to attack capitalist strongholds and are responsible for laying the foundations of socialist production. After power has been won and consolidated, economic organisation becomes the central focus of trade-union work.[28]

The ideal — the relations between the Bolsheviks and the Russian trade unions at the time of revolution — is not distinguished from the actual, where the unions were under bureaucratic reformist leadership. So we move from a description of unions as they are, to what they should be, without a word on how the transition from one to the other can be effected. Moreover, if the relation of the unions to the party 'is to some extent like that of the provinces to the centre' then there is no qualitative difference between party and unions. Consequently it is logical to split the unions just as the political organisations of the Comintern had split from the reformist Second International.

The original call for the conquest of the unions was absolutely correct. But the way it was framed led to serious mistakes in judgement. RILU's strategy depended on the hope that, in the short term, unions could be conquered wholesale or substantial sections split off. This excluded the possibility of building a rank-and-file movement which could keep up a consistent challenge to the official machine. Radek, with more extensive experience of Western conditions than many Bolshevik leaders, showed a sensitivity to the value of the rank-and-file movements which had sprung up during the First World War and did not propose to dissolve them immediately. But neither did he advocate a rank-and-file strategy since, like the rest of the Comintern leaders, he telescoped the pace of events:

> When the question is posed as to whether new organisations should be created alongside the trade unions, and what their mutual relations should be, we reply that as long as the unions are dominated by the bureaucracy these new organisations are our bases of support against the trade union bureaucracy. But when communists have become the leaders of the movement, the time has come to let the two streams flow together and to turn the factory committees into trade union organs.[29]

The rejection of a policy of building rank-and-file movements implied a certain expectation about what would happen to union bureaucracies in a revolutionary crisis. Radek accepted that the

tactics of the trade union leaders are tactics of demolishing the class
struggle . . . [But] the general condition of the working class is such
that any thought of reformist tactics, of a gradual increase in the real
wages of the working class, in their standard of life, is a completely
opportunist illusion . . . It is clear in this situation that the tactics of
the trade unions, the objective of communist struggle, cannot consist
in repairing the capitalist edifice, but in working consciously for the
overthrow of capital.[30]

Note how easily Radek, with a grammatical sleight of hand, puts
'the tactics of the trade unions' next to 'the objective of communist
struggles' implying that both are the same.

The reasoning behind this approach — that the crisis is deep
and therefore the trade unions as at present constituted will become revolutionary organs — again undervalued the special role of
the bureaucracy and its deep roots. The mechanical logic behind
Radek's position could be summarised like this: trade union leaders
reared in pre-crisis times will propose reformist tactics. These can
no longer succeed. Therefore the leaders will either themselves
change or be replaced by revolutionaries. The notion that the
bureaucrats might play a central role in defusing the revolutionary
situation that threatened them is absent.

In the West, and especially in Britain, where the trade union
machine has existed and consolidated over decades, in all probability *the victory of the socialist revolution will precede the destruction of
the trade union bureaucracy*, and special methods of organisation will
be needed to prevent the bureaucracy strangling that revolution at
birth. But this was not the Comintern's view. At the Second
Congress Alexander Losovsky, who ran RILU almost as a one-man
show, insisted on the possibility — even more, the imperative
necessity — of transforming the trade unions *before* the revolution:

Before the October revolution we transformed the factory committees
. . . We will yet transform the trades unions before the social revolution, for the trades unions must become the organ of this revolution.[31]

Only the British and American delegates criticised this approach. Louis Fraina, for example, argued that the bureaucracy
was strong enough to hold on to its posts right up to the moment of
revolution, and would be in a position to paralyse the movement
unless an independent rank-and-file movement organised against
it. Therefore the current Communist line was wrong.

We are of the opinion that it is not the tying-down of the bureaucracy that must be emphasised but the liberation of the masses to proceed independently of the bureaucracy . . . I do not quote this as an argument against work in the unions but as an argument against the idea of tying down the bureaucracy. We must fight against this bureaucracy in the unions; it will only be possible to tie them down or finish them off *during the revolution or after it.*[32]

Gallacher raised a valid point about the difficulties posed by a blanket slogan 'Conquer the unions':

It is simply nonsense and ridiculous to talk of conquering the old trades unions with their ossified bureaucracy . . . We have been active in the British trades unions for 25 years without ever having succeeded in revolutionising the trades unions from inside. Every time we succeeded in making one of our own comrades an official of the trades unions, it turned out that then, instead of a change of tactics taking place, the trades unions corrupted our own comrades too. We have often made our comrades into big trade union officials, but we have seen that nothing can be achieved for communism and the revolution through such work.[33]

Unfortunately these arguments were simply ignored.

The inner nature of the Western trade unions eluded the Comintern. The Bolsheviks did not see the contradictory character of these organisations, reflecting on the one hand the collective organisation of workers and on the other the limitations imposed by the subordination of workers under capitalism — such as sectionalism, economism and so on — which were in turn reflected in the trade union bureaucracy. By 1921, when it became clear that the reformist leaders were holding their own, the Third Congress of the Communist International spoke of the need to organise 'communists and elements sympathetic to the communists' into 'cells within trade unions'. But even then such cells were not to work towards independent rank-and-file action so much as

revolutionising the trade unions, ridding them of reformist influence and the treacherous reformist leaders, and transforming them into a genuine stronghold of the revolutionary proletariat.[34]

So capture of the official machine remained the prime target, although the assault would now be better organised. The ultra-left tactic of splitting the unions that had marred RILU's early years was replaced with an opportunist tactic of making alliances with left officials.

This possibility too was contained within the original concept of RILU, since the role of the bureaucracy had never been properly understood. In 1920, as a step towards the foundation of RILU, Zinoviev had signed an agreement with people like D'Aragona and Robert Williams. D'Aragona was an unashamed reformist and leader of the Italian Confederation of Labour. He had no qualms about signing a document which declared 'the duty of the working class is to unite all trade union organisational power in a revolutionary union which works hand in hand with the political organisation of the international communist proletariat' and called for the 'dictatorship of the proletariat'.[35] Yet weeks earlier this same man had used every ounce of bureaucratic power to smash the independent factory council movement in Turin. And just a few months later he did the same to the mighty 'occupation of the factories'. Robert Williams, leader of Britain's transport workers and another signatory, was soon to sabotage the miners' struggle by his betrayal on Black Friday. The pamphlet reporting discussions between Zinoviev and these bureaucrats gave no hint that union leaders were capable of such things. Indeed it was entitled 'Proceedings of the First Conference of the Representatives of the Revolutionary Trade Unions of Great Britain, Italy and Russia'.[36]

Zinoviev was criticised for consorting with such characters. But his defence showed how little he understood the type of 'leader' he was dealing with:

> Should I not reach an agreement with Robert Williams . . . ? Of course. But he stands at the head of the Triple Alliance. Why then do not the comrades in the Shop Stewards' Movement stand at the head of this million-strong union? In this way they show that they are sectarians and not revolutionaries.[37]

Zinoviev's mistake was not that he had reached an agreement with reformist union leaders. It was that the agreement by which RILU was established was not about action but about phrases, phrases which gave the bureaucracy a left credibility at no cost, and which made their sabotage of struggle all the more effective. An agreement for action, or a united front, as it became known, would have been totally different, for it would have opened the way to real progress through the activity and self-education of the rank and file.

Duncan Hallas explains the nature of the united front:

> The tactic starts from the assumption that there is a non-revolutionary
> situation in which only a minority of the working class support the
> revolutionaries. This can be altered only on the basis of a rising level of
> class struggle, involving large numbers of workers, many of whom
> will support reformist organisations. The united front is a tactic
> intended to win these workers to support for revolutionary organisa-
> tions, which it can do under favourable circumstances. It is not a bloc
> for joint propaganda between revolutionary and reformist organisa-
> tions, but a limited agreement for *action* of some kind.[38]

In 1921 the united front became an important part of Comintern
strategy and was supposedly adopted by RILU as well. However RILU
was so confused in its analysis that it found it impossible to apply this
tactic successfully. Furthermore, despite its exaggerated claims of
support, the Red International of Labour Unions was an embarrass-
ing failure. Losovsky and Zinoviev decided to be rid of it.

In November 1922 Losovsky reported that RILU was now
ready to join with the Amsterdam International and end its separate
existence in order to achieve a united front:

> How is unity to be achieved? In all its resolutions the RILU has
> declared itself ready, for this end, to make all the concessions. But it
> goes without saying that unity cannot be realised without minimum
> guarantees . . . We are ready to have unity on condition that both
> reformists and revolutionaries are assured freedom of propaganda.[39]

Losovsky's proposal had nothing to do with the genuine united
front. The essence of that tactic is that revolutionaries do not merge
with the reformists they wish to influence, but that the two act
together. RILU's call for a joint conference without any preconditions imposed no obligations on the reformists for joint action
but 'made all the concessions'.

Unfortunately, in making this turn in 1922, RILU did not
admit that it had been wrong in the past. It did not conclude that
instead of attempting to build a trade union international at an
official level it should encourage rank-and-file movements. RILU's
search for an end to its contradictory existence took it in a different
direction altogether — towards trying to unite with the bureaucrats
who led the Amsterdam International. In pursuing this aim revolutionaries in Western Europe were urged to win over left union
officials in their own countries.

The confused trade union policies of the Communist International had been symbolised by the creation of RILU. At first this had encouraged an ultra-left attitude to union work; later on it opened the door to accommodation to left-talking bureaucrats.

Elsewhere Tony Cliff has written:

> The congresses of the Comintern were schools of strategy and tactics. How effective they were depended not only on the quality of the teachers, but also on the background, the level of preparation and quality of the pupils.[40]

In the case of RILU, in which neither Lenin nor Trotsky played any role at all, being far too overburdened with other tasks, the teachers were not very good, and their weaknesses exacerbated those of the pupils.

The mistakes of the first few years of the Comintern were the mistakes of revolutionaries searching for new tactics in an unfamiliar field. But around 1923 a qualitative change took place. The degeneration of the Communist International and the search for alliances with left union officials was the result of the isolation of the Russian revolution. This gave rise to a state bureaucracy in Russia which put its own self-interest above that of the international working class. This process did not fully take hold until after the Fourth Comintern Congress. Until then the Congresses had been a genuine forum for the debate and development of Marxism. After Lenin's illness in 1923 the Stalinist bureaucracy put a stop to development. This meant that the opportunity to correct and improve on the Comintern's trade union strategy, as had been done in so many other spheres, was lost.

This outcome was not inevitable, as is clear from Trotsky's writings. Though driven from a position of influence in the International, he produced the most lucid and penetrating analysis of trade union bureaucracy in Britain and elsewhere right up to 1926. To this we will return later.

The Communist International in 1926 still had not become a direct tool of Russian state policy, and nor was the CPGB a slavish follower of Moscow. Nevertheless the shift towards wooing left union bureaucrats compounded weaknesses already existing in the British labour movement.

Chapter Five

BRITISH SOCIALISTS AND INDUSTRIAL STRUGGLE

THE FIRST Marxist group in Britain was the Democratic Federation, which was founded in 1880 and changed its name to the Social Democratic Federation (SDF) in 1884. It was very sectarian. H M Hyndman, its leader, believed that socialism would come through propaganda and education which would go on until a majority of workers were convinced it was correct. Anything less than socialism was to be deplored as a diversion from the true path. Thus his attitude to trade union action of any kind was dismissive or downright negative.

The SDF paper **Justice** described the great dock strike of 1889 as 'a lowering of the flag, a departure from active propaganda and a waste of energy.'[1]

'We are opposed to strikes altogether,' wrote Hyndman in April 1903. 'They never were a powerful weapon, and now they are quite out of date.' At the time of the threatened railway strike of 1907 Hyndman wrote: 'We of the Social Democratic Party and **Justice** are opposed to strikes on principle . . . Political action is far safer, far better and far less costly.' Even in 1912, the year of the greatest upsurge the working class had ever known, Hyndman repeated: 'Can anything be imagined, more foolish, more harmful, more in the widest sense of the word, unsocial than a strike . . . ? I have never yet advocated a strike . . . I have never known . . . a successful strike.'

In the name of real socialism the SDF leaders scorned the industrial struggle of workers. Once a strike began, however, the Party would give its support in principle. This usually meant a lecture on the impossibility of making real gains while the capitalist system lasted.[2]

This does not mean that there were not several leading rank-and-file activists among its membership, but because the SDF erected a Chinese wall between the final goal of socialism and trade union activity it remained totally divorced from the real struggles of workers. As an organisation it was doomed to irrelevance. As one member put it:

> Every organisation which has some ideals to translate into life, but is deprived of the possibility for action, is apt to degenerate sooner or later into a mere sect . . . It ends by withdrawing from the world which it despairs of influencing.[3]

One cannot help sympathising with this cry of frustration from one activist about the 'educational road' taken by British Marxism:

> What's gone wrong with Britain? Here we have been preaching socialism for 20 to 30 years till we have everyone converted or nearly . . . The man in the street admits readily enough, that Socialism is the only plan put forward to get him out of that blind alley; he will even agree that Socialism is bound to come if the world is not to go to entire smash; yet he will not join . . .[4]

Thus the main Marxist current before the war was the unwitting victim of the very disease of reformism it wished to cure. Reformists always separate immediate issues, such as a wage demand or the winning of an election, from the final goal of social ownership of production, action for which has to be put off to some indefinite future date. The SDF turned this formula on its head and rejected involvement in existing struggles, and trade unionism in particular. In doing so, the SDF rejected the classical Marxist approach which saw a connection between trade union activity and political mass struggle. Nor did it have anything in common with the Leninist notion that the connection between politics and economics has to be consciously fought for by the intervention of a distinct revolutionary party in all day-to-day struggles.

In 1908 the Social Democratic Federation became the Social Democratic Party. In 1911, after fusing with other small groups, it became the British Socialist Party. It continued to be ineffective, with a paper membership of 11,300 in 1913. The BSP, like its predecessors, continued to focus on the politics of the street rather than the workplace.

Although the SDF chose to ignore workers' struggles they welled up nevertheless. In the 'Labour Unrest' between 1910 and 1914 millions of workers went on strike. The origins of this agitation lay in the combination of many factors which had been accumulating since the turn of the century — economic growth leading to falling unemployment, inflation that cut wages, disappointment with the Labour Party's performance and the conciliatory policies of union leaders. The fact that strike days shot up to more than ten million a year and trade union membership doubled in the period did not perturb the sectarians. The founding conference of the BSP in 1911 made it clear what the majority of delegates felt:

> Their business at that conference was to constitute a political party to work primarily in the political field . . . They were not a trade unionist party. [BSP involvement in union work was] something of an impertinent interference in a field with which they had nothing to do. The industrial field was already provided for.[5]

The BSP had no criticism of the union officials as such, since they rejected the whole union movement as irrelevant. One speaker declared:

> as one who has been on the executive of a trade union he was convinced that there was no possibility of the trade unions striking for socialism. The Socialist Party was not out for the pettifogging reforms which the trade unions were striving for.[6]

The BSP contributed the bulk of the membership of the Communist Party at its foundation in 1920. But these members had practically no understanding of the trade union movement and considered the self-activity of workers to have nothing to do with the struggle for socialism. This attitude was to have important consequences.

Though the Labour Unrest passed the official 'Marxists' by, there was a live revolutionary current fighting in its midst. This went under the label of *syndicalism*. In contrast to the belief that change would come through political education and the capture of the state (state socialism as it was called), the syndicalists saw the immediate class struggle as all-important. Syndicalism gave a voice to genuine workers' struggles, and because these varied from place to place and industry to industry, it too took many forms.

The most important syndicalist current before 1914 was represented by Tom Mann, a recent convert from state socialism, who established the Industrial Syndicalist Education League in 1910. His position was unequivocal:

> The time is now ripe for the industrial organisation of all workers on the basis of class — not trade or craft . . . merging all existing unions

into one compact organisation for each industry, including all labourers of every industry in the same organisation as the skilled workers.[7]

Leading syndicalists such as Mann considered themselves to be revolutionary socialists. They believed that if such a union movement could be created it would have to be:

> Revolutionary in aim, because it will be out for the abolition of the wages system and for securing to the workers the full fruits of their labour, thereby seeking to change the system of Society from Capitalist to Socialist.[8]

Although the framework of trade unionism was to be widened to encompass all workers in an industry, nevertheless the pull towards sectionalism (but with bigger sections) remained. Questions of class politics and the state began to appear increasingly minor to the syndicalists. Between 1910 and 1911 Mann, for example, moved from denials that he was anti-political to proud assertions of the fact. The attitude of the Industrial Syndicalist Education League was summed up in this way:

> Politics, like religion, was a matter for the persons themselves; and it was of no concern to the workers whether other workers were Liberals or Conservatives. All that was necessary for workers was to understand the solidarity of their class.[9]

It did not occur to the syndicalists that anyone who was a Conservative might find it difficult to conceive of working-class solidarity except with hostility. On trade union issues the League saw clearly that the existing unions were bogged down by years of conciliation and bureaucratic domination. They directed their fire principally against the sectionalism of the craft unions and the disunity in action that this could lead to. However there was no underlying analysis of why trade unionism had got into this position, nor of the role of the union officials. The nearest the League came to an analysis was this offering from Mann:

> The unions came into existence by means of men who were partially class-conscious only, and they are composed now of men who are partly class-conscious only. But they are truly representative of the men, and can be moulded by the men into exactly what the men desire . . . And I am for moulding all the organisations . . . We should not say we will have nothing to do with the old organisations.[10]

Another major strand in syndicalism before the First World War was the Socialist Labour Party (SLP). Founded in 1903 as a breakaway from the SDF, it too was marred by sectarianism. It took an even harsher line than the SDF towards involvement in the struggle for reforms:

> The hope of the British proletariat lies in the decay and death of trade unionism, the death of the Labour Party and reformist socialism, and in the birth and growth of Industrial Unionism and the development of a revolutionary political party of socialism.[11]

The Socialist Labour Party took its line from the American socialist Daniel de Leon. Having seen American business unionism at close hand, de Leon called the trade union officials the 'labour lieutenants of capital'. The SLP saw their task as dual in nature. The political party was to destroy the offensive power of the state. But the most important job fell to industrial unions which were to seize control of production from the bosses and institute socialism. They judged that the existing unions could not be adapted for such a task, and while SLP members usually worked within these, they hoped to construct completely new revolutionary unions to take their place. Repeated attempts at forming such industrial unions failed miserably, since their rivals were powerful and well-established.

The SLP clearly recognised the problem of sectionalism and bureaucracy within the trade unions. They sought to wish these difficulties away by setting up their own incorruptible versions. But in Britain, where the best section of the working class was still found in the established trade unions, despite all their failings, this strategy was a sectarian non-starter. During the First World War, however, a number of SLP members were to transform their outlook and take a lead in mass struggles, so that by 1920 this tiny party brought to the Communist Party some of its finest working-class leaders.

To sum up the situation in Britain before 1914, the official Marxist position on the trade unions was abstentionist. By accepting the narrow sectional definition of trade union struggles put forward by the bureaucrats, the BSP implicitly accepted the domination of these bureaucrats over the unions. The main syndicalist currents, on the other hand, offered a demand for bigger and better trade unions, or an appeal for new revolutionary unions in conditions where such a call was doomed to failure.

The disease of reformism had taken its toll on the British revolutionary movement. Although its members were dedicated and courageous, and many syndicalists showed tremendous skills in leading day-to-day struggle, they were crippled by political feebleness. The official Marxists were equally impotent when it came to genuine workers' movements.

The crisis of wartime, however, was to create a totally new situation which offered greater potential for recovery and growth than ever before.

Chapter Six

TWO RANK AND FILE MOVEMENTS

DURING the First World War a militant rank-and-file movement rose among the engineers, traditionally regarded as archetypical labour aristocrats. This was an 'engineers' war', and as producers of vital munitions they had real bargaining power.

There was one factor which prevented engineering union officials from containing militancy in the same way as they had done before the war. The output of armaments in ever greater quantities required the lifting of all restrictions on production, and use of new machinery and work methods, and above all the employment of untrained youth and women on work formerly handled only by craftsmen. This last change was called 'dilution'. To lead an effective fight against such trends the union leaders would have had to call massive strikes and virtually sabotage the supply of arms 'to the boys in the trenches'. This they were not prepared to consider.

The engineering union bureaucrats could choose whether or not to struggle. But engineers in the workshops could not. By withholding the strike weapon the officials had given the green light to an employers' offensive against all the customs and practices that engineers had painstakingly built up to make life a little more bearable under capitalism. Labour aristocrats they certainly had been, with better pay and conditions than many other workers. But now they were forced to fight and in so doing to take the lead in working-class struggle.

The officials had abandoned the membership. There was no alternative but to create an unofficial movement. Based on shop stewards, this came to challenge traditional trade unionism in a way even more fundamental than syndicalism. The first steps towards independent shop stewards' organisation came in February 1915 when Clydeside stewards led an unofficial strike of 10,000 engineers for a twopence-an-hour rise. The leadership of the strike came to form the Clyde Workers' Committee, which during Christmas 1915 was involved in a battle over the terms by which dilution would be carried out. The government fought back and broke up the committee, arresting its leaders and dispersing them around the country. The following year Sheffield set up a Workers' Committee, and by 1917 a national organisation was in existence capable of leading 200,000 workers on unofficial strike. Independent stewards' organisation existed in enough centres for national conferences to be held and a national administrative committee established to link them together.

Syndicalism had, for all its boundless militant energy, remained within the framework of unionism. The shop stewards' movement represented something more. It consisted of assemblies of delegates elected directly from the rank and file on the shopfloor. Regardless of the particular union they were in, or who their employer was, they met together to represent the interests of all the engineers in the local area. In the days when bosses offered no perks, no offices, no facility time to their stewards, but only the threat of the blacklist, these delegates were the direct voice of the rank and file. They spent their time working alongside the people who elected them and experienced the same pressures. Unlike the officials, they were subject to recall should they cease to be representative of the members' wishes, and received no special wages for their work.

The trade union members provided the base of the movement, for organised workers were the only source of collective strength. Shop stewards were also the lowest rung of the union machinery and still had the task of taking subscriptions. Nevertheless when they came together to form 'workers' committees' they were not simply gingering up the union apparatus. Theirs was not an attempt to control the bureaucracy from below, nor an attempt to set up a pure revolutionary union in opposition to the established bodies. The movement's attitude to the officials was deceptively simple and was summed up by the Clyde Workers' Committee's first leaflet, which we have already cited:

> We will support the officials just so long as they rightly represent the workers, but we will act independently immediately they misrepresent them. Being composed of delegates from every shop and untrammelled by obsolete rule or law, we claim to represent the true feeling of the workers. We can act immediately according to the merits of the case and the desire of the rank and file.[1]

The claim to be able to 'act independently' and 'immediately' was no idle boast. The 200–300 stewards who met together every Sunday on Clydeside united the collective power of thousands of engineers. They had shown their influence in the February 1915 strike and were to do so in several victimisation cases soon afterwards.

The Sheffield Workers' Committee, the most powerful of the English shop stewards' bodies, was equally effective. Unofficial action began during November 1916 in defence of a young engineer named Leonard Hargreaves. He had been called up for military service in spite of the exemption engineers had enjoyed till this time. The Sheffield stewards issued an ultimatum to the government setting a deadline for Hargreaves' return. As J T Murphy, then the leading Sheffield steward, recounted:

> There were not less than two hundred shop stewards waiting for the stroke of four on this eventful day. Standing outside the Institute was a fleet of motor cycles with the cyclist shop stewards ready to be despatched to the engineering centres . . . Four o'clock came. The government had not replied. The strike was called . . . At five o'clock the strike was complete. Ten thousand skilled workers walked out of the factories. Then the government got busy with the telegraph wires . . . The third day of the strike saw the capitulation of the government.[2]

The militants who organised such strike action in the middle of world war were socialists and for the most part revolutionaries. Only they dared to lead action that might disrupt the flow of arms. Before the war they had built up a tradition of rank-and-file action and initiative capable of withstanding the combined political and economic attack of government, police, courts, Labour Party and trade union leaders.

With the state and private capital working hand in hand it was possible to show many workers that there was a link between the changes workers were suffering in industry and the political aims of capitalism at home and abroad. There was the chance that economic grievances might be harnessed to a political challenge to the bosses and the state — through a revolutionary party. At the same time, with union leaders openly siding with the bosses, there was a good opportunity to overcome the obstruction formed by the union bureaucracy — by showing that the rank and file could only trust to their own collective strength and independent organisation.

All these possibilities were latent in the wartime situation, as was demonstrated in Germany. There a distinct revolutionary party was gradually to take shape, and out of this the mass Communist Party of the 1920s was to grow. Concurrent with this, engineering stewards' organisation in Berlin became the prototype for a workers' council movement that united the class, brushed the reformist bureaucrats aside and directly threatened state power.

For British revolutionaries to realise the full potential of the times they had to be clear about their tasks. Alas, as we have seen, the tradition of separating politics and economics, typified by the mutual hostility of 'state socialists' and syndicalists, left them ill-prepared. Individual socialists in the engineering workshops moulded workers' militancy into an independent mass movement. But as yet no one had a theoretical grasp of how to connect socialist politics and industrial agitation. The shop stewards' leaders were still in the habit of treating politics as something external to the factories and shopfloor unrest as simply an economic issue.

Jack Murphy, who led the Sheffield Workers' Committee, was typical. As a member of the SLP he was committed to opposing the war and to the overthrow of the state that prosecuted it. But one could never have guessed this from his writings for the wartime stewards' movement. Its best-known publication was Murphy's **The Workers' Committee**, a widely-read pamphlet of 1917. This contained a carefully thought-out plan for a national network of stewards' organisations that would rise up as a rank-and-file alternative to the officials, an important development on the strategy of pre-war syndicalism. Yet in the pamphlet there was absolutely no discussion of the war. Doubtless Murphy was right to point out that:

> None of the strikes which took place during the course of the war were anti-war strikes. They were frequently led by men like myself who wanted to stop the war, but that was not the real motive. Had the question of stopping the war been put to any strikers' meeting it would have been overwhelmingly defeated.[3]

Skilled engineers would not automatically dissociate themselves from nationalist ideas or labour aristocratic pride. But if anything opened the way for arguments in that direction it was the extreme situation of the war and the abject failure of traditional reformism to defend workers' wages and conditions in the face of an all-out attack by the state.

Murphy, Gallacher and the other leading stewards showed great talent in pioneering a mass movement which, for the first time, posed an organised alternative to official methods. But further progress depended on political leadership — the knitting together of that minority who through their experiences had come to understand the system as a whole — in other words it depended on building a revolutionary party. But this was not done. Gallacher, for example, might speak on anti-war platforms at the weekend, but at work he saw himself as a steward, a spokesman for rank-and-file opinion at a time when the majority were generally *not* against the war.

Even in terms of a healthy rank-and-file movement, political leadership was essential for long-term success. Take the question of craft sectionalism, which was under attack through the government's promotion of 'dilution'. Gluckstein has written elsewhere:

> From their strong bargaining position, metalworkers could fight this in two different ways: either as a threat to the privileges of the elite of skilled men, or as the first phase of a war against the hard-won rights of *all* trade unionists.[4]

The elitist argument might mobilise the engineers' sectional strength and delay defeat for the duration of the war, but once exceptional conditions ceased to operate in the industry, the ruling-class attack would be redoubled. The only hope for a successful long-term resistance lay in generating a class-wide agitation for militant trade unionism.

May 1917 saw the biggest strike of the war. It came after three years of mindless slaughter and the February revolution in Russia. The 200,000 engineers who stayed out for three weeks followed the lead of the national shop stewards' movement. The strike was sparked off by the spread of dilution to work unconnected with the war effort. The issue was not that workers should refuse to sacrifice themselves to aid imperialist war, but whether a few private firms could join the profit-making jamboree. No one but skilled engineers were directly concerned and when the unofficial leaders were jailed the strike crumbled.

An opportunity to link politics and mass militancy came in early 1918. The Bolsheviks had taken power in Russia, and withdrawn from the war. It was at this very point in time that the British army began baying for yet more men and insisting on wider powers of conscription. The stewards' national administrative council put an ultimatum to the government demanding it scrap the new conscription laws and consider the Bolshevik peace proposals. But the threat of action was undermined by political confusion. **Solidarity**, the paper of the English stewards, carried the ultimatum in its columns, but the same issue stated:

> If only we could be certain that the German workers would follow suit, we would have no hesitation in calling for an immediate policy of 'down tools and damn the consequences'. But we are not in touch with our fellow workers in Germany . . . It may be that the German workers would be willing to do the bidding of their warlords . . . by attempting to invade these islands. In which case, they would get the surprise of their lives.[5]

With such weak leadership coming from their own newspapers, it was no surprise that the rank and file hardly responded with enthusiasm to suggestions for a strike. In the end the same weaknesses that defeated the Clyde strategy against dilution — the lack of a consistently revolutionary party and the habit of divorcing workplace issues from political ones — wrecked the chances of a strike against conscription.

Tragically, at the very moment **Solidarity** voiced its fear of German workers, 400,000 German engineers struck against the war, only to find themselves isolated internationally.

The refusal of **Solidarity** to extend its spirit beyond the shores of Britain came directly from the syndicalist split between politics and economics. Because the stewards failed to link the fight in the workshops to wider political questions it meant they were able to maintain militancy on workshop issues, but, by default of a political fight, bourgeois ideas prevailed. So instead of a strike for workers' unity on an international scale many skilled engineers took up the labour aristocratic chant: 'Don't take me, I'm in the ASE' (meaning the Amalgamated Society of Engineers).

The lack of a clear revolutionary leadership condemned the stewards' movement to sectionalism in another way — by restricting their activity to the engineering industry.

These were not the only problems. The central body of the movement was never designed to give leadership. It was only established after much opposition during a 1917 conference of stewards:

> Finally, G Peet set the conference at its ease by assuring it that the national committee would be 'an administrative committee' and not an executive committee and all matters would be referred to the rank

and file. This was confirmed by the perambulating title of the national committee, which was 'The National Administrative Council of the Shop Stewards and Workers' Committees'. Thus the first national committee was formed, but held theories which prevented it from giving the leadership which the movement needed.[6]

This attitude to leadership was not an aberration on the part of a few prominent stewards, but a function of the rejection of politics, the element which could fuse a *minority* of the class who held revolutionary ideals into a party capable of suggesting initiatives to guide the struggle of the masses. The stewards understood neither the leading political role of a revolutionary party, nor its ability to guide the immediate industrial struggle of a rank-and-file movement.

Thus one of the main weaknesses of the engineering shop stewards' movement was its opposition to *all* leaderships — whether from official or unofficial sources. Murphy wrote: 'It matters little to us whether leaders be official or unofficial, so long as they sway the mass, little thinking is done by the mass.'[7] The point was underlined by an article he wrote in **Solidarity**:

> . . . one of the first principles of the shop stewards' movement and workers' committees, they obey the instructions of the rank and file and not vice versa. This repudiates the charge of the press and those good clear-thinking people who refer to those wicked shop stewards who bring men out on strike. Shop stewards do not 'bring' men out on strike, the shop stewards' duties do not involve 'leadership'. As a matter of fact the whole movement is a repudiation of 'leadership'.[8]

Of course the wartime shop stewards were 'guilty' of leadership. However, the syndicalist blindness to politics in the grand sense also hid from the stewards the leading roles they themselves took in raising self-confidence among the rank and file. For it was leadership that they gave when they suggested initiatives which involved the broadest numbers or mobilised workshops in direct action. This was not comparable with bureaucratic authoritarianism or the pursuit of parliamentary careers, but it was a form of leadership nonetheless.

There was another unofficial movement at work at this time. It was centred in the mining valleys of South Wales and took the form of what we today call a 'broad left'. It too was influenced by syndicalism, but operated in very different conditions from those of the engineers. The contrast between the two movements is instructive.

Mining trade unionism was based on the unity of the workplace, the community and the collective organisation, since the colliery, the union lodge, and the pit village were all found in the same location. Thus the nature of the industry discouraged the division into skilled and unskilled trade unionism that was found in engineering. Most organised coalminers were members of one body, the Miners' Federation of Great Britain (MFGB). The engineering industry, by contrast, had more than 200 unions.[9] The unit of organisation of these numerous unions tended to be the geographical branch, not the workplace. This was because many members were in small workshops scattered over wide areas, and because each union organised just a section of the workforce in any one factory.

In mining, because there was no split between workplace and union branch, the grievances of the rank and file tended to be channelled directly into the official machinery, as were the efforts of militants. While this situation allowed for greater rank-and-file influence *within* the union, it inhibited rank-and-file action independent of it.

In engineering the union branch was poorly attended and bore little relation to the immediate concerns of the workplace. These were more effectively dealt with by shop stewards who, for much of the time, had to operate independently of the official structure in order to represent workers on day-to-day issues.

In engineering solidarity meant cutting across the sectional divides between skills and between factories. Miners were still organisationally separated from workers in other unions, but the MFGB was a very large section indeed, and solidarity in the pit was automatically translated into an effort to transform the lodge and district union. None were as skilful in this as the South Wales miners.

As early as 1911 the pit militants could claim a major success. By putting pressure on the machinery of the South Wales Miners' Federation (SWMF), they were able to dictate the manifesto by which the union campaigned for the fight for a national minimum wage. They could therefore claim some credit for the 1912 national miners' strike which followed.

The militant miners were organised in an Unofficial Reform Committee (URC) established in May 1911. Its title tells us it was committed to *reform* of the union. Certainly this reform was from below, with the maximum mass pressure of the rank and file, but it was still reform of the union machine, not an alternative to it.

The most important publication of the URC was the famous pamphlet, **The Miners' Next Step** (1912), which proposed rank-and-file action and control as a counter to bureaucracy.

The Miners' Next Step was subtitled 'A Suggested Scheme for the Reorganisation of the Federation' in South Wales. It stated that 'the cornerstone of the whole scheme' was 'real democratic organisation'. Traditional trade unionism was to be turned upside down, with the rank and file in total control of the official structure.

> I. *The lodges have supreme control* — All the initiative for new proposals, policies and tactics, remains with the lodge. Nothing becomes law in the organisation unless it receives the sanction of the lodges, or a ballot vote of the coalfield.
>
> II. *The executive becomes unofficial* — As has been shown before, democracy becomes impossible, when officials or leaders dominate. For this reason they are excluded from all power on the executive, which becomes a purely administrative body; comprised of men directly elected by the men for that purpose.
>
> III. *Agents or organisers* become the servants of the men, directly under the control of the executive, and indirectly under the control of the men.[10]

From the same ideological starting point — syndicalism — the authors of **The Miners' Next Step** had drawn different conclusions from those of the engineering militants.

Murphy's pamphlet, **The Workers' Committee**, was the clearest exposition of the engineering stewards' movement. It put forward a complete national structure *in competition* with the authority of the existing unions. Such a position was logical for stewards faced with the multiplicity of engineering unions and their craft jealousies, just as the URC's ideas were logical in terms of the mining industry and union.

Because **The Workers' Committee** proposed a separate structure to the official apparatus, it had to be concerned with its own special forms of organisation. This had to embody a mass rebellion against the full-time officials and against union constitutionalism, since both of these reinforced sectionalism in the industry and crippled the workers' fighting strength.

For the URC, on the other hand, the centre of their work was the miners' union constitution, and how it could be improved to

give full control from below. The strongest organising force was
held to be the union itself. Of course, to function as an agitational
current at all, the Unofficial Reform Committee had to hold meetings. The production and distribution of propaganda required
some sort of limited centralisation, but the level of organisation
could afford to be low, since the intention was not to substitute for
the union, but to improve the union's effectiveness. The internal
life of the lodge, regional and national conferences were the real
arena for URC militants.

A remarkably loose attitude to self-organisation ran right
through the history of the Unofficial Reform Committee until the
formation of the Miners' Minority Movement in the early 1920s.
Indeed to give a single name to the current of South Wales militancy
is a distortion of the truth. In his excellent history of the movement,
Mike Woodhouse has discovered a perplexing variety of titles
under which the militants could be found to operate.[11] What was
common to all of them was a belief in collective organisation as
represented by the mass membership of the miners' union, rather
than any belief in the value of a separate organisation of militants.

The initial network of contacts seems to have been formed
under the auspices of the Plebs League, a body that ran educational
classes and was strongly syndicalist in its ideas. The Plebs League
and its parent body, the Central Labour College, provided just the
sort of loose discussion group atmosphere in which the unofficial
movement could operate effectively and the URC returned to this
form of link-up many times when more solid organisations crumbled
away. The Unofficial Reform Committee itself followed in the
wake of a strike at the pits of the Cambrian Combine, and it was the
URC that published **The Miners' Next Step** in 1911. A year later
the militants were associated with the Rhondda Socialist Society,
again a broad-based group in which a variety of opinions could be
aired. Expansion in influence led to the South Wales Worker
League in 1913. At the end of the year, contact with Mann's
Industrial Syndicalist Education League encouraged the formation
of a Trade Union Reform League, soon renamed the Industrial
Democracy League.

Even the war could not put a stop to the breakneck turnover in
organisation and name. In 1915 a new body called the Pioneer
League emerged to provide the necessary links. Then there was a
gap until 1917 when a new revival took place, this time through
Central Labour College classes. Two years later came the South

Wales Socialist Society, and an expanded version of **The Miners' Next Step** was published by its 'Industrial Committee'.

This list is not advanced for pedantic reasons, but to show how little importance the URC militants attached to firm organisation outside the local union. It will be noted that most of the above names refer directly to South Wales. As long as the issues confronting mining trade unionism could be fought on regional lines (with occasional sorties on to the national stage, such as during the minimum wage campaign of 1911–12) there seemed little need for anything but a local network. The concept of a revolutionary party was ignored, as was the need for strong and independent rank-and-file organisation. URC supporters believed that what was needed was merely a link between militants, a propaganda outlet (most of these organisations produced their own newspapers — **The Rhondda Socialist, South Wales Worker, Pioneer**) and a room to meet. Anything as formal as membership cards or rigid constitutions simply did not seem worthy of consideration. As Woodhouse puts it:

> The organisation of the URC was consequently of the loosest form. W H Mainwaring kept a book of about 200 addresses of contacts in South Wales, and in the MFGB generally, and it was through these that **The Miners' Next Step** . . . was distributed and the particular policies of the URC on specific issues taken into the lodges.[12]

That was in 1911. But ten years later, despite a series of major victories in shaping local and national miners' union policies, nothing had changed. Hewlett, a current URC leader, had to explain the following to the Scottish engineers, with their tradition of strong self-organisation through Workers' Committees:

> I know there is an idea abroad that South Wales is covered by a network of Unofficial Committees. This is not so. In fact, there is no permanent unofficial organisation in the coalfield. What does happen when it is necessary, is that the advanced or rebel element does meet and discuss matters, arrive at decisions, then goes back to their respective pit committees and lodges, put their views forward, have them thoroughly discussed, and if their opinions are accepted the delegates to the councils and conferences are instructed accordingly.[13]

At the base URC militants were linked with the daily struggles of the rank-and-file miners, which they channelled into the union for action. It was this that kept the unofficial movement alive through an extraordinary succession of events stretching from the

Labour Unrest to the General Strike and right into the 1930s. This lifeblood flowed as long as these syndicalists maintained contact with each other and expressed the needs of the rank and file in struggle.

The URC was therefore deeply affected by the rhythm of unrest which, like human breathing, lifted the movement up and down ceaselessly.

Another factor reinforced this oscillation. The URC was not a one-way channel. It was influenced directly by the rank and file, but because of its orientation on reform of the South Wales Miners' Federation, it was also influenced from the top downwards. If the aim is to reform an organisation then concessions from above have to be applauded. If the aim is to cajole officials into adopting a certain course, then good behaviour must be rewarded by relief of pressure. This meant that unofficial agitation was switched on or off depending on the current posture of the local union bureaucrats.

A brief survey of URC agitation brings these influences out clearly. In 1912 distribution of **The Miners' Next Step**, and the union reform campaign that went with it, were halted for fear of disturbing negotiators during the minimum wage campaign. As the local press put it:

> someone seems to have thought that publication of the scheme at this moment of crisis and negotiation was inopportune and likely to prove embarrassing. They hold that the minimum wage must be made secure before the conspiracy can be developed.[14]

The settlement that followed and the boom conditions of 1913 led to a collapse in URC activity after its promising start. The **South Wales Worker** is quoted as complaining:

> The Rhondda during the past year has been a place of the dead . . . so far as any public activity is concerned. No indication has been evident in the Rhondda of the seething unrest in the outer world.[15]

Yet the Rhondda was the core of the URC influence. The same year official acceptance of much of the unofficial programme dealing with the unifying of wage rates led to further passivity among the organised militants. Why organise separately if the union is carrying out the reforms demanded?

Both engineering and mining activists rejected the idea of leadership. While this was mistaken insofar as it meant denial of a role for revolutionary political leadership, the blanket condemnation was prompted by a thoroughly healthy abhorrence of trade union bureaucrats and parliamentary politicians.

Nevertheless there was a big difference between the miners' aim of reforming officialdom and the engineers' attempts to by-pass it.

The Miners' Next Step implied a certain strategy. If the scheme was adopted it could hardly be left to its opponents to carry it out. Working to take over and reorganise the union meant inevitably taking official positions at some point. While the Socialist Labour Party had placed an absolute ban on accepting union positions, the URC was, despite its fear of 'leaders', quite ready to put its best elements forward. As early as 1911 Rees and Ablett of the URC won places on the South Wales executive. Many others with even more famous names were to follow the same path. Thus Frank Hodges — who, as leader of the miners, contributed to the infamous sell-out on Black Friday alone with Jimmy Thomas and Robert Williams — began his career identified with the URC.

The entire history of the URC was one of constant friction between the younger generation of militants fresh from the collieries and those who, pursuing the aim of reorganisation, had gone into the official apparatus. The first evidence of hostility between the new and old militants came in 1914, when Ablett and other URC nominees on the South Wales executive were attacked by one militant in these terms:

> They were pledged to abstain from supporting reactionary policies; they were not to take part in the administration of such policies; they were to keep revolutionary policies and militant programmes to the fore; they were to force the executive committee to take action along the lines laid down by the militant section of the coalfield. Have they done this? Unhesitatingly we answer 'No'. They have ceased to be revolutionary except in words.[16]

Four years later George Dolling and Nat Watkins, soon to be prominent in the Miners' Minority Movement, returned to the attack after a new attempt to revive the URC had failed. Their criticism laid bare one important reason for this failure:

> Today there are those in the socialist ranks who, having grown respectable and law-abiding, act the part of the puppy dogs of capitalism.

Addressing the old leaders of the URC, they went on:

from you we expect better things. Act and live up to it by writing a line
of encouragement so that this work may go on . . . We write believing
that amongst the number which comprised the URC there must be
quite a lot who, like ourselves, are dissatisfied with the present state of
affairs . . . we ought to be a 'Ginger Group' constantly attempting to
galvanise the executive committee into life, and focussing their efforts
in the direction of our programme.[17]

But the old 'ginger' method had never been fully effective. The
process of degeneration and rebirth was built into the method of the
URC. Rank-and-file agitation was bound to throw up new and vigorous forces, but exclusive emphasis on reforming the union creamed
off the best of them, and isolated them from their base.

A trade union official's origins in an unofficial movement
could not give a lifetime inoculation against the disease of bureaucracy. The falling away of direct links with the rank and file,
addressing them from platforms rather than working alongside
them and sharing the common experience, had its effect. The
URC's candidates inevitably were drawn into official ways of thinking after holding senior positions for some time.

The URC was a channel upwards for rank-and-file grievances,
but it was also an escalator which carried the best militants up the
structure of the union and dropped them into the bureaucratic
mire when they reached the top. In a situation of mass reformism
no other fate was possible for trade union officials out of reach of
the politics and discipline of a revolutionary party.

Although the Unofficial Reform Committee was in favour of
organisation and action separate from the official machine, unofficial strikes were never treated as an alternative to official ones. The
URC itself organised countless unofficial actions, large and small,
but apart from their immediate objective, the URC leaders saw
them primarily as a means of shifting the officials in the right
direction. They were not valued for themselves as evidence of
rank-and-file self-reliance.

The Unofficial Reform Committee's attitude meant that strike
committees never took on a permanent existence apart from the
lodge, in the way that engineering strike organisations had done.
Thus the miners never developed their own workers' committees.

Like the engineering shop stewards' movement, the Unofficial
Reform Committee was vague in its politics. It was felt that
maximum unity to win official action on immediate issues was

more important than the broader, more hotly disputed questions of the time. This attitude ran right through the various organisations which the Unofficial Reform Committee inhabited outside the official apparatus. It was well illustrated by **The Rhondda Socialist**, one of the URC's temporary mouthpieces. When the paper was accused of being a 'jumble of Syndicalism, Labourism and Socialism', its editor replied:

> Now there are various 'schools of thought' in the socialist movement
> . . . But we are, as socialists, all united for one objective — we all
> desire to abolish capitalism and establish the socialist state . . .
> Naturally we differ as to the best means of bringing it about.[18]

When the war broke out the political weakness of the Unofficial Reform Committee led to its complete paralysis. Not that there were no serious industrial disputes in the South Wales coalfields: in July 1915 and again in 1918 there was considerable unrest among miners, but in neither did the URC play a significant role.

The main cause of the paralysis that afflicted the Unofficial Reform Committee was the split in its ranks regarding its attitude to the war. Noah Rees, Frank Hodges and Will John, members of the South Wales miners' executive, supported the war and participated in the recruitment drive. George Barker and Tom Smith, two of the closest supporters of the URC, did likewise, only moving to a position more critical of the war towards its end. Even Ablett, known for his radical views, made no 'unambiguous statement of opposition to the war until 1917; indeed he advanced as a reason for accepting the Lloyd George terms [of July 1915] the need to assist the war effort.'[19]

However things changed when the miners' exemption from conscription was lifted in early 1917. The War Office began a 'comb-out' of unskilled men and in April the situation on the Western Front led it to step up its requirements. By early 1918 the miners were facing the same pressure for conscription as the engineers, with the government asking for 50,000 soldiers and 50,000 reserves.[20] But the revolutionary socialist current in South Wales was even weaker than in engineering, and when the Unofficial Reform Committee got around to raising the war issue it was most influenced by the policies of the Independent Labour Party.

The Independent Labour Party (ILP) was a thoroughly reformist party which rejected Marxist ideas of class war and preached a sort of 'ethical socialism'. It was led by Ramsay MacDonald, who

was a pacifist. But the tenor of his pacifism can be judged from the
following quotation. Though he disliked war, he feared even more
that strike action might disrupt its continuation:

> under the present circumstances and during a war, purely industrial
> strikes have no connection with ILP policy . . . They belong purely to
> the wage-earners' industrial policy, and appeal far more directly to the
> materialised sentiments to which the war party trusts for working-
> class acquiescence than to the political and spiritual outlook of the
> ILP.[21]

Despite its shortcomings, when rank-and-file miners felt dissatisfied or union officials buckled under pressure from the employers, the Unofficial Reform Committee proved itself a superb
fighting mechanism, because it was so deeply rooted in South
Wales miners' collective organisation. Like the shop stewards, this
movement showed the potential for self-activity and mass struggle
on the part of the rank and file.

The unofficial movements in engineering and mining were
children of syndicalism. The similarities between them were great
— industrial militancy, reliance on the rank and file, but also
weakness of politics, looseness of organisation, and an inability to
overcome the narrow horizon of their specific industry.

The shop stewards' movement and Unofficial Reform Committee co-existed in time, but they never blended. Each retained very
different approaches to trade unionism. Yet in spite of this they both
held important lessons for revolutionary work in *all* trade unions.

The stewards' *independent rank-and-file movement* fitted best
where there was a self-confident workplace organisation which
could be spurred into self-activity. The miners' URC was appropriate
when struggle was limited to official trade unionism. It embodied
the very best of what a 'broad left' had to offer. Though, like all
broad lefts, the Unofficial Reform Committee suffered from the
constant influence of the trade union machine, it often proved
invaluable in channelling rank-and-file initiatives.

The two movements were able to weaken the hold of bureaucracy by their intervention. Though different, together they offered
a manual for effective revolutionary activity in trade unions. But to
use these lessons to the full, a strong revolutionary party was
essential.

Left to themselves both movements were pregnant with
dangers. Without the guidance of a Marxist party with roots in a

number of industries and areas, the stewards' movement was easily isolated and smashed once the forces of the officials and government were freed from the constraints of war. The shop stewards' concept of workers' committees, when applied in unfavourable post-war conditions, led to a propagandist dead-end. In Scotland, for example, 'social soviets' were set up which pretended to be rank-and-file bodies when the real ones had disappeared. The URC's method, on the other hand, resulted in successive generations of workers' leaders being turned into bureaucrats, while the rank and file were all too often tied to official structures.

Only a revolutionary party could analyse the changing needs of each period, generalise from the different outlooks born of separate industries, and cure the blindness to politics. Industrial agitation had to be made part of a broader strategy for winning working-class power before it could achieve permanent results. The two unofficial movements could arouse mass action, but could not provide the necessary political leadership for it.

PART TWO:
BRITISH COMMUNISM AND THE ROAD TO THE
GENERAL STRIKE

Chapter Seven

THE MISSED OPPORTUNITY

THE FOUNDING Congress of the Communist Party of Great Britain
(CPGB) — the Communist Unity Convention — took place from 21
July to 1 August 1920.

A number of groups which stood on the platform of 'soviet
power' were involved in the discussions: the BSP, the SLP, the
Workers' Socialist Federation, the South Wales Socialist Society, a
number of left-ILP members and sections of the National Guilds
League. Of these the BSP, and after them the SLP, were by far the
most important. Over a period of many months' negotiation these
groups, raised in the British tradition of sectarian bickering,
managed to overcome their differences. However there were losses
on the way. A substantial proportion of the SLP preferred to stay
with de Leon's sectarian schemes and did not join the new party.
Neither did Sylvia Pankhurst's Workers' Socialist Federation.

The delay in establishing the party had a serious bearing on its
future. Had the CPGB been established at the time of the rising
militant struggles of 1918–19 it would have got off to a grand start.
Intervention in events would have trained and consolidated the
small and politically weak party. But this was not to be.

With the armistice of November 1918 trench warfare on the
battlefields of continental Europe gave way to class warfare at
home. In return for self-sacrifice the British people had been
promised 'a land fit for heroes'. Instead the 'victory' brought them
the same rotten housing, the same boss, the same or lower wages,
the same old system of exploitation. The workers' response was to
organise and to act on a scale never seen before. On average 4½
million working days had been lost in strikes during each of the war
years. In 1919 the figure was a massive 34,483,000.

Predictably, the first confrontation occurred in the armaments
industry. This was a crucial fight. For if the power of the shop

stewards' movement was to be maintained, the workers had to guarantee that the inevitable fall in demand for munitions would not result in mass sackings and the victimisation of militants. The issue on which the stewards chose to stand their ground was therefore shorter hours.

The way this battle was conducted showed both the strengths and weaknesses of the movement. Placing tremendous emphasis on the rank and file had the virtue of overcoming bureaucratic control; its vice was that unless there was a clear central leadership (in the *revolutionary* sense of that word) there was a tendency for the movement to fragment. Workers in one area would fight this week on one issue; next week another area might take up a different issue and so on. To fight a united battle the centrifugal tendency engendered by always looking to workshops and the rank and file had to be countered by a strong sense of politics and a conscious aim for centralisation. This was not to be.

When the war ended and engineering workers began to be laid off, Glasgow was once again in the vanguard. On 27 January 1919 the Clyde Workers' Committee, in conjunction with sympathetic local officials, called a strike for a 40-hour week. The shop stewards' leaders were fully aware that much more was at stake than hours or even employment. On 1 February Gallacher wrote: 'Choose ye this day . . . between workers and capitalist, between constitutional methods and working-class action. Shame on you if you fail now. Join the fight.'[1]

Some 100,000 workers did just that on Clydeside. The spirit of the strikers was magnificent. There were roving mass pickets of up to 5,000 workers; many women were involved; a daily news bulletin was published and sympathy action spread to other parts of Scotland and to Belfast. Yet the strike was still fairly localised. That was why the government was able, on 1 February, to send troops into Glasgow and break the spirit of the strikers. Once the Clyde had collapsed shop stewards all over the country fell victims to the sack and the dole.

Of course the presence of tanks and machine guns on the streets of one city was intimidating, but if there had been strikes in every city and in every industry, not just concentrated in one or two engineering centres, then the government would have been totally powerless. Why was the 40-hours strike so easily isolated and smashed? The answer lay not in the strength of the government but in the shop stewards' political ideas. Although they had a conception of the 'self-emancipation of the working class' being 'the act of the working class itself', they did not conceive of the role of a workers' political party in drawing all sections of the class into action.

Writing 15 years after the event, J T Murphy tells us that the 'greatest mistake' of the Clyde Workers' Committee

> lay in the fact that it had done nothing to prepare the movement beyond the Clyde. Although it was represented on the National Committee of the Shop Stewards, it had not even acquainted this committee of its plans.[2]

He was quite correct to point out this blunder, but as we have already noted the stewards nationally shared this haphazard attitude towards centralised organisation. At the very moment when the stewards' national administrative council was most urgently needed to spearhead resistance to unemployment, **Solidarity** published the following note:

> To the National Administrative Committee of the Shop Stewards and Workers' Committees. Your existence is being doubted. The war [is] finished. Are you?[3]

The council was clearly inactive at this time of crisis, and the initiative was left to the government and the trade union bureaucracy.

The union leaders were well aware that by abjectly surrendering to the bosses during the war they had alienated the membership. Accordingly they sought to redress the balance by a display of some very left-wing rhetoric. They managed, in conjunction with the government, to steer British capitalism safely through what John Maclean called the 'rapids of revolution'. A brief survey of Cabinet discussions shows how close Britain came to major civil disorder.

On 8 January 1919 the prime minister, David Lloyd-George, informed the Cabinet:

> '. . . some 1,500 soldiers (Army Service Corps at Park Royal) had arrived in Downing Street. Attempt to stop them marching to Whitehall, without success.'
>
> Chairman of Imperial Staff: 'The soldiers' delegation bore a dangerous resemblance to a Soviet'.[4]

On 22 January Lord Curzon said that:

> he was alarmed by the fact that no concerted action was being taken . . . combatting the spread of Bolshevism in this country.[5]

On 24 January the Cabinet was worried about a police strike that risked spreading. Six days later they discussed the use of troops in Glasgow. General Childs agreed that this had worked in the past but warned:

> at that time we had a well-disciplined and ignorant army, whereas now we had an army educated and ill-disciplined.[6]

Nevertheless the risk had to be taken, and as we have seen, it paid off for the government.

But from now on the Cabinet's main tactic would be much less direct than the large-scale deployment of troops. They had in the official trade union machine a more reliable ally. Winston Churchill explained this to his colleagues on 4 February 1919:

> the trade union organisation was very imperfect, and the more moderate its officials the less representative it was, but it was the only organisation with which the government could deal. The curse of trade unionism was that there was not enough of it, and it was not highly enough developed to make its branch secretaries fall into line with head office.

Bonar Law added that he

> thought that the trade union organisation was the only thing between us and anarchy, and if the trade union organisation was against us the position would be hopeless.[7]

The defeat of the Clyde engineers in January 1919 still could not turn back the flood-tide of working-class demands. Every day of that year an average of 100,000 workers were to be on strike. A vast range of industrial, social and political issues flared up together, fanned by war weariness and the profiteers' open enjoyment of their wartime gains, and ignited by the initial outburst of militancy in the first month of the new year. A new feature of the industrial militancy of 1919–1920 was the willingness of many sections of workers to engage in sympathetic action to back the demands of other workers.

The period from 1911 to 1919 had been an artificially prolonged boom for the economy, and this was to continue into the spring of 1920. Unemployment was low throughout the decade, while prices rose at a tremendous rate — with a particularly inflationary period after the war. Since trade union organisation was necessary if workers were to attempt to keep up with the runaway cost of living, and as labour was scarce, there was a rapid growth in union membership. In the pre-war period from 1910 to 1914 the total membership of all unions rose by roughly 65 per cent, and in the next six years the 1914 figure rose by more than 100 per cent to a peak of 8,334,000 in 1920.[8]

This represented a tremendous advance for the working class, and the uncontrolled and unofficial character of many of the strikes showed that the new members were not a passive tool in the hands of the bureaucrats. But there was no force capable of presenting a revolutionary direction to the turbulent masses. The working-class movement, like nature, abhors a vacuum, and this was quickly filled by the trade union leaders. The uncertain situation gave people like Robert Smillie of the miners and Jimmy Thomas of the railworkers a constant headache. Nevertheless they were the sole centralising force in this vast army, and therefore their decisions carried tremendous weight.

The officials felt both the need to rein in the masses and to mantain their credibility by a show of left-wing demagogery. The contradictory character of this new phase of trade unionism was represented by the Triple Alliance, recognised as the most powerful trade union body in the country until the debacle of Black Friday in April 1921. The Alliance of the MFGB, the National Union of Railwaymen (NUR) and the National Transport Workers Federation had its origins in the 'labour unrest' of pre-war days. Despite the widely-held conviction that the Triple Alliance was a victory for syndicalist ideas of industrial unity and general strikes, the trade union leaders adopted the strategy as a means of enhancing their bureaucratic control.

A historian of the Alliance has outlined its function quite clearly:

> [It] was not designed to make rapid responses to sudden crises. Nor was it primarily intended to undertake sympathetic strikes in support of the sectional claims of its constituents . . . To many of its founders, indeed, it was valued as a means of averting stoppages . . .
>
> . . . the Alliance was in no sense a 'victory for the syndicalist idea'. It was not, that is to say, a concession to rank and file militancy . . . it was designed specifically to control and discipline such militancy.[9]

In 1919 and 1920 the Triple Alliance was able to contain and destroy militancy because it also appeared poised to lead the class forward. This meant that the membership of all three constituents of the Triple Alliance felt constrained to wait for their leaders to move as one body. The government saw this and was able to buy off one section and thus paralyse the other two. Three unions for the price of one was a bargain indeed!

The strategy was unveiled on 1 February 1919 when the 48-hour week was conceded for railworkers. Unrest on the railways was by no means abated, as the implementation of the new hours by a number of employers provoked spontaneous strikes over cuts in meal times and tea breaks. The increasingly militant mood rang a warning bell for the Cabinet, but they found an ally in J H Thomas, who told a meeting of London tube workers:

> We as trade unionists have got to keep clearly in mind that we have to make our sectional claims consistent with and part of our duty as citizens of the state.[10]

At the same time the miners were spoiling for a fight. Even before the beginning of the 40-hours strike on the Clyde, the miners demonstrated their readiness to struggle. In a conference at Southport on 14 January the Miners' Federation resolved to demand a 30 per cent increase in wages, a six-hour working day, and nationalisation of the mines with a measure of workers' control. When these demands were rejected, the federation referred the issue to the members. A ballot returned an overwhelming majority in favour of strike action. (The voting was 615,164 to 105,082), and notices were duly tendered.

> Presented with this ultimatum in the latter days of February the government found itself in a hazardous position. All the advantages were on the side of the miners. Coal stocks were at famine level, London having only three days' supply. At the same time the other members of the Triple Alliance (railwaymen and transport workers) were in consultation with the miners, and had themselves tabled demands for which they were in negotiation. In short, Mr Lloyd George and his colleagues were confronted with the alarming prospect of a general strike fraught with revolutionary implications.[11]

Lloyd George adroitly nominated a Royal Commission presided over by Mr Justice Sankey to look into the miners' case. An Interim Report presented on 20 March considered a wage advance of two shillings per shift, a reduction of the working hours from eight to seven, with effect from 16 July 1919, a six-hour day with effect from 13 July 1921, and indicated that its final report would recommend the nationalisation of the mines.

The miners' leaders, Robert Smillie and Frank Hodges, accepted the inquiry. With great difficulty they persuaded their members to postpone action until the Interim Report was published on 20 March. Frank Hodges later wrote in his autobiography that he and Robert Smillie

> threw in the whole weight of our argument and influence to get the men and delegates to accept the Royal Commission. Hours, days, were spent in this tussle and in the end we won.[12]

The difficulties that the leaders faced were due to the hardened realism of many in the pits. Writing of the feeling in South Wales, Ness Edwards recalled:

> that it was generally felt by the active rank and file elements that this Sankey Commission was merely a tactic of the government to put off the evil day of the trial of strength . . . for had they pressed forward their nationalisation proposal considerable chance of success existed.[13]

However the militants were in a minority. The Sankey Commission was accepted by a massive majority of miners in a ballot in April 1919. The strike notices were withdrawn and the coal crisis ended for the time being.

The government sighed with relief. On 23 June the Sankey Commission presented its final report, recommending nationalisation of the mines and the granting of a share of control to the miners. After the impetus for the strike had passed Lloyd George knew that the announcement on whether or not the report would be implemented could be put off.

Hardly had the mining crisis subsided when in June 300,000 cotton workers struck for a 48-hour week and a 30 per cent wage increase. They won. In July the police went on strike against a government Bill prohibiting trade unions in the police force. The strike was only partial and centred on London and Liverpool. It was beaten and many policemen were sacked.

Now the railwaymen began pressing forward their claim for higher wages. The government procrastinated. Negotiations dragged on from February to August, by which time the mining crisis had passed. In August the government tried to bribe the locomotive men, who were in a separate union, ASLEF, by meeting their demands, hoping by this to isolate the NUR. In September, following the same line, the government presented the NUR with the provocative imposition of wage cuts. This time, however, it miscalculated: the locomen, spurning the August bribe, struck to a man with their comrades in other grades. Thomas and his executive committee felt the strike was inevitable, for anything less would have resulted in a series of local and sectional walk-outs. The strike lasted from 27 September to 6 October.

That the NUR executive failed to invoke the Triple Alliance in order to fight a united struggle was a significant turning point for the post-war movement. Two weeks previously Thomas had congratulated the miners for not taking action on their own, yet here were the railworkers doing just that. Despite the tremendous militancy throughout the country the possibility of united action by the leading unions was being systematically undermined from the top. In its place came bureaucratic negotiation. Even though the government was forced to improve its offer its major objective had been attained and a serious crisis avoided.

Rank-and-file confidence is not something that can be accumulated and stored like money in a bank vault. It is a perishable commodity which dissipates if unused for any length of time. The union bureaucracy, by methods of bargaining and procrastination, can all too easily set the agenda and timing of workers' struggle. It requires a strong counterweight to prevent this.

On 18 August Lloyd George announced in the House of Commons that the government rejected nationalisation of the mining industry, thus throwing overboard the Sankey Report. The miners' campaign had been dragging on for so long that there was no enthusiasm for immediate strike action in response. The spark had gone out of the miners' spirit.

Nevertheless the MFGB leaders were compelled to react. They put the issue before the Triple Alliance, which decided to suspend a ballot for action on the nationalisation issue until after the Trades Union Congress the following week. The crucial decisions were therefore firmly passed on to the TUC. Feeling was running high when it met on 8 September but in no part of the debates or motions was there any recommendation of a course of action to be taken. Smillie moved the miners' resolution on nationalisation, which rejected the government's position and in the event of it not changing its mind called for 'a special Congress to be convened for the purpose of deciding the form of action to be taken to compel the government.' Thomas seconded the resolution and congratulated the miners on the great service they had rendered to the trade union movement by the conduct of their case before the commission. In the course of his speech he made the significant statement that the miners had::

> shown themselves statesmen in coming to the congress, because had they attempted to take action on their own, I should have been the first to condemn them.[14]

Few would have imagined that this threat would be carried out seven years later to bring the General Strike to a close.

On 9–10 December 1919, the Special TUC met in London. It took two important decisions. Firstly action for nationalisation of the mines was to be replaced by an educational campaign on the theme of 'mines for the nation'. Secondly a resolution was passed creating a General Council which would be an executive body for the TUC with a greater role than the old Parliamentary Committee. Like so many things in this period of transition, the latter move bore a left and a right face. The left face implied that the General Council was to be a 'General Staff of Labour' and champion the fight of the workers in all their battles. The shrewd right face was represented by Ernest Bevin of the Transport Workers. He was bureaucracy incarnate, and saw in a reorganised TUC a body suited to those days of mass membership and large units of organisation which, directed by an executive, had the power to win negotiations and thus minimise strike action.

In March 1920 the TUC finally buried the idea of general strike action to win nationalisation of the mines.

Throughout 1919 the government had tried to isolate one section of the working class from another, and largely succeeded in doing so. Even if they were forced to make concessions, they managed to avoid the danger of a general, united, revolutionary working-class movement. The post-war boom made it possible for the employers to meet most of the unions' wage claims; and the policy of the trade union and labour leaders enabled government and employers to avoid a direct confrontation of classes.

In summer 1920 the first signs of the end of the post-war boom began to show. Wholesale prices stopped rising, sagged and began to fall steadily. By winter severe depression set in and unemployment started rising from month to month. In the autumn of 1920 there were 250,000 unemployed. By the end of the year the figure had risen to 700,000. By February 1921 the million mark was passed. By March it was 1.3 million, by June over 2 million (17.8 per cent of insured persons). The number fell a little at the end of 1921 and was 1.5 million in 1922, but it was to be many years before the unemployed total fell below one million.

The employers took advantage of this situation with a big offensive on workers' standards of living, clawing back all the gains of the war and post-war period.

On 31 March 1921 the miners were locked out, as they refused to agree to a wage cut and to the replacement of the uniform national wage agreement by district agreements. The miners appealed to their associates in the Triple Alliance, the railwaymen and transport workers, who declared a general railway and transport strike in their support. But on Friday 15 April — Black Friday — Jimmy Thomas of the NUR and Robert Williams and Ernest Bevin of the Transport Workers betrayed the miners and called the action off.

The miners, now completely on their own, struggled on for three months and then capitulated, accepting the owners' terms. After the 1921 lock-out the average wage per shift worked went down to less than half what it was in the winter months of 1920–21.[15]

Throughout industry the employers' attack was pressed home. Reductions were enforced on engineers, shipyard workers, builders, seamen (the ships' cooks and stewards unsuccessfully struck), cotton operatives (after a general lock-out). By the end of 1921 wage-cuts averaging no less than eight shillings a week had been suffered by 6,000,000 workers.[16]

Before the termination of the miners' strike on 4 July a great cotton lock-out took place . . . Five hundred thousand workers were locked out from 3 June until 27 June when they resumed on the basis of four shillings and five pence reduction in the pound [22 per cent] on current wages.

Then came the turn of the workers in the engineering industry, who were involved in a fourteen weeks' lock-out which began in March 1922. Hardly had this started when the shipbuilding workers were plunged into a defensive struggle against wage reductions. These were followed by the strike of the printing trades against a demand for 15 shillings a week reduction in wage rates. These defensive struggles continued in the various industries right through 1922.[17]

The downturn in the class struggle led to a weakening of the power of the rank and file in the face of the employers and increasing dependence on the trade union bureaucracy.

By far the strongest shop stewards' organisation during the war existed in the engineering industry. In 1919 the defeat of the 40-hours strike put an end to this power. As J T Murphy put it:

> independent activity of the trade unions and the re-transfer of workers from the engineering industry and the dismissal of active shop stewards readily reduced the shop stewards' committees to propaganda bodies within the unions. [18]

The 1922 lockout of engineers killed the shop stewards' movement stone dead. As Murphy explained to the Fourth Congress of the Comintern (November 1922):

> In England we have had a powerful shop stewards' movement. But it can and only does exist in given objective conditions. These necessary conditions at the moment in England do not exist . . . You cannot build factory organisations in empty and depleted workshops, while you have a great reservoir of unemployed workers. [19]

The massive retreat of the working class after 1919 affected the rank and file's independence from the trade union bureaucracy. Such independence is a function of the confidence of workers in the face of the employers.

Chapter Eight

THE FIRST FEW YEARS OF THE BRITISH COMMUNIST PARTY

LENIN EXPECTED that the newly-formed Communist Party of Great Britain would be characterised by the following features:

> Unbreakable ties with the mass of the workers, the ability to agitate unceasingly among them, to participate in every strike, to respond to every demand of the masses — this is the chief thing for a Communist Party, especially in such a country as Britain.[1]

But the Communist Unity Convention did not bode well for such an interventionist party. Alfred Purcell, shortly to be elected to the party's provisional executive, put the party's attitude to workers in struggle in these terms:

> it was our business to go to them and say: 'While you are prepared to revolt, we, at the same time, are prepared to show you the machine that must be used in order to take possession of the means of production' . . . It was useless continually prodding and pinpricking the working class; we were not going to get the best from the working class by doing that; we had to take them in hand and show them the way.[2]

On paper the party's industrial policy was 'that it shall be the duty of the branches to form Communist groups in trade union branches and to work inside the trade union movement'[3] but there was little more said on industrial work, apart from the interjection of a Birmingham shop steward who believed that 'the only party who could discuss these activities were the shop stewards . . . our activities were perfect through the shop steward movement.'[4] Evidently many of the old ideas about the separation of politics and economics, as well as a propagandist approach, still persisted. The best elements of the shop stewards, people like Arthur MacManus and J T Murphy, were not present at the Communist Unity Convention.

Things improved when a few months later at the Second 'Unity' Congress in Leeds, 29–30 January 1921, a section of the SLP — including MacManus, Murphy and Tom Bell — joined the party. Although the SLP element was in a small minority in the party they played a dominant role in the leadership in the first years of its existence. It was they who framed the first strategies for Communist industrial work, since most of the former BSP members were clearly unsuited for such a task. Their presentation of policy was an improvement on the past, but they still saw the role of the political party primarily as a sort of militant leaven to rank-and-file activity. The first issue of **The Communist**, the party's newspaper, carried an article by MacManus which said that the 'Task awaiting the Communist Party' was to

> take fullest advantage of every opportunity to acquaint the workers of Communism; explain it to them inside of the workshop and outside; assist and encourage the formation of shop steward committees in every workshop, plant or factory; develop the interest of the worker in that committee; explain the possibility which is latent in such organisation, and by insistent discussion and endeavour to wean away his faith from the false moral values of capitalism.[5]

Though this article showed an understanding that political work and industrial agitation were connected, the link was still put in an abstract and basically propagandist way. The Communist Party had not recognised that the decline of the engineering shop stewards' movement necessitated a change of tactics. The lesson of the wartime period, that the trade union officials could not be trusted, was still understood, but the party tended to wait on the spontaneous activity of the rank and file to deliver the action. Amidst retreat and rising unemployment, such activity was not forthcoming.

The party was not soft on the officials, calling the Triple Alliance 'the greatest fraud of modern times',[6] but the alternatives suggested were vague and general, however formally correct they might have appeared. This was illustrated by an open letter issued after the miners' 'Datum line' strike of October 1920, in which an advance in wages was won, but the pressing political issues of nationalisation and workers' control were not broached:

> The chief defect of the Triple Alliance . . . is the fact that [it] is in the main run by reformist leaders. A Triple Alliance strike means a general strike, and a general strike means probably a revolution . . .

So long as the Triple Alliance is not controlled by revolutionaries — or at any rate a militant rank and file, just so long will the leaders of it, when brought to the brink of a strike, shrink from the responsibility involved in a general stoppage . . . In order to win the next struggle, the intervening period must be spent in overhauling all the machinery of the federation, from the district to every pit. At every election of a lodge secretary the candidates should be tested by their fitness in, and capabilities for, a national strike . . .

Remember that reformist leaders will shrink back at the last minute.

Remember these things and select men who understanding that a strike may lead to revolution will not on that account shrink back.[7]

This was an excellent description of the likely behaviour of officials confronting large-scale struggle. It was far superior to the analysis given by the Communist Party just before 1926 and was a visionary forewarning of the events of Black Friday, then six months away. But the course of action proposed — the demand to 'overhaul' the federation, was an insufficient guide to action for party members and sympathisers on the ground.

As the danger of a national lock-out of miners drew nearer in April 1921, **The Communist** warned its readers to 'Watch your leaders'.[8] Practically every issue for the next few months contained the same call. The 30 April edition had a variation on the theme when it said:

We repeat, watch your leaders! Watch even the left-wingers for their own sakes as well as your own. Being a 'leader' is very unhealthy work. One is cut off from the influence of the rank and file, and is plunged into the artificial life of hotel, conference and the political maelstrom. The most vigorous left-winger is apt to wilt and fade under these circumstances. *Watch them!*

But apart from passively 'watching', the concrete activity proposed for the Communist Party and its supporters was totally unrealistic:

See there is a workers' committee in every workshop, mill and factory. Link these committees up in every industrial area with a general workers' committee, which shall act as the potential strike committee for your area. Get this local area committee in touch with the National Workers' Committee Movement . . . Then the general strike which we foreshadow means revolution. Certainly.[9]

Throughout the period before Black Friday **The Communist** carried practically no detailed discussion of how the membership should intervene in particular struggles or what strategy should be pursued.

This weakness was discovered by Radek who, as secretary of the Communist International, reported on the state of the British Communist Party. He wrote:

> To my question, what do you tell the masses, what is your attitude to nationalisation? What is your attitude to the present concrete claims of the workers? one of the [British] comrades replied: 'When I ascend the rostrum at a meeting I know as little about what I am going to say as the man in the moon; but being a Communist, I find my way along when I speak.'

Radek retorted:

> We consider it our duty to say the following, even to the smallest Communist Parties; you will never have any large mass parties if you limit yourselves to the mere propaganda of Communist theory. [10]

Radek's criticism and the shock of Black Friday showed the British Communists that their approach to industrial work was unsatisfactory. The party was traumatised and was forced to reconsider its whole approach, and in particular to think about building a leadership inside the trade union movement. For the British unions were foundering. As reports arrived of trade unionists ripping up their membership cards in disgust, Tom Bell called on every Communist to bail the movement out. Denunciations were not enough.

> Let the treachery of the leaders by all means be placed on record and exposed, but we must go further. We must win the confidence and support of the masses by hard persevering work, helpful criticism and personal sacrifice on behalf of the masses themselves. Beginning in a small way, and encroaching on the leadership of the organisations, capturing post by post, and all the time rendering useful service to the workers, that is the most effective way to shift the reactionary leaders and gain the leadership for Communism. [11]

Bell had laid to rest the syndicalist notion that all leadership was evil and corrupting. But to jump from a feeling that action could come only from rank-and-file movements independent of the officials, to a position of seizing every union post and thus overcoming the restraints of bureaucracy, was indeed an enormous leap. However, it is important to understand the conditions in which this leap was made before considering its political implications. In 1921 the situation was viewed with alarm. By April 1922, with hundreds of thousands of engineers locked out, the tone was one of desperation. **The Communist**'s headline was: 'Fight, damn it! Fight!', and it went on to say:

> It is scandalous that [the unemployed] should have to take the lead in everything.* Has all the spirit passed out of the employed trade unionist? Fight! Damn it! Fight![12]

Tom Bell's argument, that opportunities for a rank-and-file movement had passed, and that the Communist Party should now offer 'hard persevering work, helpful criticism and personal sacrifice' was a good starting point for a discussion of union activity. But there were dangers if the significance of Black Friday was not understood. Two different lessons could be drawn. One was that no trade union leader, neither left-talking Robert Williams, nor out-and-out right-winger Jimmy Thomas, could be trusted. They had to be challenged from below, not just by propaganda but by consistent work related to the level of the movement. The alternative conclusion could be that Black Friday had occurred because the Triple Alliance chiefs were 'bad' leaders who should be replaced by 'good' ones. At a time when rank-and-file workes were losing confidence and self-organisation was in decay, the latter seemed an easier option.

But there was quite a resistance in the party to any move to the right — to the orientation on trade union electoralism. To give an example, here is an extract from an excellent article in the **Communist Review**. It posed all the problems and began elaborating some of the solutions. It started by criticising the pure syndicalist approach which Tom Mann had put forward in a recent **Herald** article. First it quoted Mann's article:

> 'Refuse to allow executives to shape the policy for the rank and file. The membership must decide upon the objective and the policy by which it shall be achieved, and executive committees and officials must carry out the desires of their members'. This is echoed and

---

*The backbone of the unemployed workers' movement of the time came from the large number of victimised engineering militants and veterans of the shop stewards' movement. They played an important role in organising the fight of the locked-out engineers in 1922.

re-echoed throughout the land, both in the Red Trade Union International and the Workers' Committee movement.

This form of protest will not do . . . Leaders we need and must have. The democracy which the revolutionaries should aim at is the democracy which will enable the workers to do more than merely examine a ballot paper . . . It must enable the workers to quickly remove leaders who will not lead. [But] the cry of 'Elect new leaders' sounds very much like an echo of the old socialist parties . . . Elect new leaders by all means, but will anyone kindly calculate the number of years necessary for a formal ballot box removal of the reactionary trade union bureaucracy? . . . The reactionary leaders will have to go. But they will have to be removed by a fight directly against them rather than through formal removal via the ballot box.

This does not mean that we should relax for one moment the attack through the union ballot box . . . Indeed the ballot box method stands in the same category in relation to unionism, as parliament does in relation to the conquest of the state. Both are weapons to be used . . . [But] in neither case have we control of the elected person. One of the elementary measures we should popularise . . . is the right of having the power to recall the elected person.

Then we should consider greater measures of organised action whereby the masses will thrust aside the reactionaries as the struggle widens and deepens . . . One section cries out for the One Union for One Industry, another for One Big Union, and some for workers' committees . . . They sidetrack the masses on to a formal, debate concerning *forms* of organisation . . . The swiftly changing phases of the struggle have swept away the condition which made the shop stewards and workers' committees the natural mass expression of the requirements of the moment . . . We need much more than propaganda for industrial unionism. We need *plans* of immediate organised action, definitely related to the existing organisational forces of the proletariat, the application of which will force them into action. For it is by action that situations are produced which offer the opportunities necessary for the revolutionary changing of leadership . . .

We gave vigorous criticism of the leaders of the union movement in the crisis leading to Black Friday. We exposed them. We warned the masses to 'Watch their leaders'. We fostered the idea that the Triple Alliance would fail. But when it did fail the revolutionary movement was nearly as demoralised as the union movement in general. We had not, to any large extent, considered or advised the masses what they could do in such an eventuality. Yet everything cried out for the preparation of a new centre of leadership in the organisations involved, to which the masses could gravitate as the leaders moved towards failure. The lesson is obvious and exceedingly important. Immediately there is the least sign of action developing in any organisation the revolutionary movement, and especially the Communist Party, ought to immediately take the measure of all the forces operating, the potentials of the situation, the limits of the organisations involved, and how the organisations can be used to drive the leaders along the revolutionary path or out of the way.[13]

This article shows that effective Communist work in the trade unions requires attention to detail, the ability to work inside the unions but carry the struggle beyond them when it becomes possible, an awareness of the value of resolutions, election campaigns and so on but also the aim of building a rank-and-file leadership to fight the bureaucracy rather than pursue purely organisational reforms to remove them.

However there were other reactions in the Communist Party to Black Friday and its aftermath. One was to call for the TUC to fight workers' battles. This call for 'a General Staff of Labour' had been a favourite slogan of the BSP. In 1920 Murphy, writing in the shop stewards' newspaper, had poured scorn on this idea:

> The General Staff of officialdom is to be a dam to the surging tide of independent working-class aspiration and not a directing agency towards the overthrow of capitalism.[14]

But two years later his tone had changed. Analysing what would be the development of trade unions in a crisis he still refers to the rank and file, but they play second fiddle to the bureaucrats:

> To get the everyday results from wage negotiations etc. in an era of expanding capitalism (the era in which the trade unions made their greatest progress) became an art in which Mr Thomas excelled. It was in this era that practically all the trade union leaders of today came to power at the head of powerful organisations with strong vested interests binding the membership.
> Revolutionary leadership under these conditions could only be the exception andnot the rule. Only when the general economic situation changes and forces the masses of leaders into revolutionary situations and policy can there be a general revolutionary change in leadership. Such change is rapidly taking place today and producing all the forces making for a change of leadership. The capitalists can no longer make

the old concessions and the fate of the unions and the masses is now at stake. Under these circumstances it is useless and wrong to relate to trade union leadership as a static unchangeable monument. It is subject to changed circumstances as is everything else. Nor can we assert that the change will come along a single track. This will operate in many ways. *In some cases the union leaders will feel their fate bound up with the fate of their union and will fight even in a revolutionary fight. In others, new elections will throw up new leaders through the normal operation of the union apparatus, and still again, changes may be made through the organised pressure and activity of minority movements.*[15]

There were reasons why Murphy shifted his ground so far from his earlier position. Although the Bolsheviks' achievements in the Russian revolution led him to abandon a generalised hatred of all leadership, the implications for revolutionary leadership in trade union struggle had still to be thought through. Murphy had not recognised the fundamental difference between *revolutionary* leadership — the art of encouraging rank-and-file self-reliance, and *reformist* leadership — which consists of spurring bureaucrats to act on behalf of the rank and file.

In the June 1922 edition of **All Power**, Tom Quelch also took up the question of leadership. His answer was to return to the theme he had popularised in his BSP days. In an article prophetically entitled: 'Under the Banner of the General Council' he wrote:

> The struggle must be waged under the banner of the General Council of the Trades Union Congress. We want no Black Fridays, no Triple Alliance debacles, no puny blowing-off of individual trade union pop-guns against the mighty cannon of capitalism. We want an intelligent understanding of the strength and purposes of the enemy and the rallying of all working-class forces to meet it on something like equal terms.
>
> All trade unionists must insist on the General Council, which has been informed of all the succeeding stages of the negotiations, taking charge of the struggle.[16]

Harry Pollitt, a rising star in the Communist Party, followed Tom Quelch in his proposal:

> Get your branch to demand the *General Council of Trade Unions* to issue a definite ultimatum to the employers *that no further reductions will be tolerated.* A special trades congress should be convened so that the whole union movement can agree on a plan of campaign and

action, not only to resist reductions, but to *immediately challenge the employers' right to run industry.*[17]

In another article Pollitt suggested that it would be possible *first* to give the General Council the necessary power and *then* improve its composition:

> We support the aim of the present General Council [for more power] not because we have such great faith in it, but because the principle is right, but once the principle of centralised leadership is established the next step is to change the personnel of the General Council. This can be done by steady persistent work inside the unions. Take a long view of things. The more revolutionary delegates we get elected the sooner do we break down the present system whereby the general secretaries determine who goes on the General Council . . . and sheer necessity will throw up a General Council that responds to the needs of the times.[18]

The idea of 'sheer necessity' transforming the unions was to become a favourite of the Communist Party. What mechanical determinism!

A completely opposite position was put forward by Pollitt's close ally in the Communist Party, the talented but highly erratic Rajani Palme Dutt. In the **Labour Monthly**, which he edited, Palme Dutt gave a brilliant refutation of the growing trend in the party. He believed that:

> . . . the cry for the General Council as the solution for the labour movement is as foolish as the cry for the League of Nations in the international field . . . And the parallel is so exact because the error at bottom is essentially the same: the belief that a combination of the existing forces will achieve a solution, when it is the existing forces themselves that are at fault.

His conclusion: class unity cannot be achieved on a purely trade union basis. What is needed is unity under political party leadership.

> only the political struggle of the working class as a class can unite the workers; the only uniting force of the working-class movement can be a political party of the working class. The trade unions are by their nature separatist: only a political party can be the combining force . . . Unless that party develops the working-class movement will continue to drift in sectionalism and confusion. Only when a political party of the working class can unite the workers around the common demands of the political struggle and so rally around those demands

the manifold organisations of the working class, only then and by those means will the unity of the working class be achieved.[19]

Palme Dutt's counter-position of revolutionary party to trade union officialdom, and his understanding that the one precludes the other, was an important warning. We shall see that it was not heeded, for Palme Dutt was out of step with the rest of the Communist Party leadership.

By the end of 1922 the battle of ideas was over, and the theory of the General Council as 'General Staff' (with a modified leadership, hopefully) was enthroned in the Communist Party. By suggesting that the bureaucrats might be prepared to face up to the needs of class struggle when the crisis of capitalism became critical, this theory fostered the most dangerous illusions.

Of course revolutionaries cannot be abstentionist towards the right and left in the trade union bureaucracy. Whatever resolutions, organisational changes or actions the left bureaucrats take should be applauded, *but only insofar as they provide opportunities for rank-and-file action.*

As a revolutionary party, the CPGB held out the only possibility of conducting a revolutionary strategy in the unions. However there was no guarantee that it would do so, unless it was theoretically clear. Unfortunately this was not the case.

The party's early industrial policy reflected one wing of the factions that formed the party in 1920 — the SLP/shop steward grouping which made propagandist calls for workers' committees. These were inappropriate for the 1920 period, not just because of the local contraction in engineering, but because post-war only a minority of any particular workforce — pit, factory or rail depot — saw the need for independent rank-and-file organisation. A pure rank-and-file strategy, basing itself on the self-activity of the majority in any section, was bound to fall flat.

In the crisis following Black Friday 1921 the policy of working within unions to campaign on the most basic of issues, from local grievances to national pay campaigns, would have been far more fruitful than calling for workers' committees which were not viable at that time. But the new strategy that the Communist Party adopted went much further than that. It was largely derived from the BSP. It aimed at conquering the unions or, if that proved impossible, finding left bureaucrats to cooperate with. This grouping in the party put forward slogans about making the TUC a

'General Staff of Labour' and giving 'More Power to the General Council'. This led them to strive for more left-wing officials as their chief aim. These ideas were totally misguided. Their starting point was the false premise that the basic problem was the organisational machinery of the trade unions, rather than the self-confidence and fighting power of the rank and file.

Chapter Nine

THE MINORITY MOVEMENT

IN JANUARY 1921 a British Bureau of the Red International of Labour Unions was established. To carry its propaganda the Bureau took over from the Glasgow Shop Stewards' Movement the journal **The Worker**, then from the beginning of 1922 published a monthly magazine titled **All Power**.

In the summer of 1922 the British Bureau of RILU, which worked as the chief industrial arm of the Communist Party at that time, organised a number of regional conferences around the theme 'Back to the Unions' and 'Stop the Retreat'. They could not have been more timely. The haemorrhaging of union membership continued unabated, and in 1922 alone one-fifth of all union members quit.

The London conference, held on 23 September 1922, was attended by 300 delegates, who represented 176 trades councils and trade union branches. Resolutions were adopted on the fight to defend wages, to resist the lengthening of working hours, and on workshop rights and conditions. Similar conferences were held at Birmingham, Sheffield and Cardiff. These conferences had an aggregate attendance of 905 delegates, those from trade union branches representing 166,800 workers, and those from trades councils and district committees representing a membership of 851,840. Thus the Communist Party claimed 1,018,645 workers were represented at these rallies around the militant slogans of the British Bureau of RILU.[1] RILU's peculiar method of accounting ignored the difference between revolutionary political organisations (where numbers represent an accurate assessment of committed activists) and elections of delegates through trade union channels (where bloc votes must be measured against the level of rank-and-file involvement).

Clearly it was an achievement to gather an important section of union stalwarts together to discuss stopping the retreat, but to be realistic in taking the campaign forward a proper estimate of forces had to be made. The Communist Party came to hold a distorted view of its own influence because it accepted bureaucratic methods of calculating strength in the class.

Under the initiative of the Bureau, a number of new organisations began to develop in particular industries. The most important was the Miners' Minority Movement which started in South Wales. Even before the Minority Movement initiative, RILU had drawn its only mass support from the miners. Thus at the Blackpool conference of the MFGB in 1922 more than 118,000 votes were cast for affiliating to RILU in the name of the South Wales miners.[2]

The Miners' Minority Movement established in South Wales *was not* a rank-and-file organisation. As Murphy explained:

> It is not a question here, be it noted, of setting up a rival organisation. It is one of calling to officials and the rank and file alike to present a United Front against the capitalist offensive.[3]

This was an accurate description of the way the MMM took shape in South Wales. Its first public pronouncement was signed by a number of leading officials including Noah Ablett and Arthur (A J) Cook. It is quite likely that the gathering of such prestigious signatures was the only means of getting an unofficial revival off the ground in the tough conditions of the time. One correspondent in Scotland explained the problem:

> In several of the collieries extreme difficulty is being experienced in finding men who are prepared to accept responsibility of local branch offices or to act on pit committees . . . A deliberate line of policy . . . is also badly required.[4]

In such a situation it was correct to assume, as the sponsors of the MMM did, that:

> the rank and file at the pits dare not, for fear of victimisation, express themselves . . . [but] conditions have forced men to think, and in every district an MM is being formed, this time with the help of full-time officials, who cannot be victimised by the powerful coal magnates.[5]

Soon after the miners came the Metalworkers' Minority Movement, which was announced in the October 1922 **All Power**. It presented a programme of demands including:

£4 for 44 hours — abolition of overtime.

General opposition to payment by results.

Workshop Committees to be formed under the terms of the shop stewards and Workshop Committee agreement . . .

Elimination of non-unionism.

Under the heading 'Union Reorganisation', the programme called for

joint committees [to] be formed with district committees and branches of other unions in the industry, in conjunction with the RILU to initiate an amalgamation campaign to secure *'One union for the industry'*.[6]

Such programmes were to be drawn up for each of the various Minority Movements which emerged in industries ranging from engineering and shipbuilding to transport, building, the railways and vehicle-building.

A fundamental weakness of the Minority Movement was the fact that the shop stewards' organisation was now a shadow of its past self. This is evident if we look at the working of a local Minority Movement organisation such as the Coventry branch.[7] Its detailed minutes show that the branch was based on groups in the following organisations: Amalgamated Engineering Union, Workers' Union, National Union of Vehicle Builders, United Patternmakers Association, Building Trades, Miscellaneous Engineering, Stoke Heath Women's Guild, and the trades council. It seems that these were informal caucuses which met mainly to prepare for intervention at the branch meetings of these various bodies. Interestingly, there were no specific issues that were taken up for campaigning by the entire Coventry Minority Movement in the mid-1920s.

Aggregate meetings of the Coventry Minority Movement branch were held approximately monthly with roughly 20 to 40 people in attendance, and district committees occurred every other fortnight with some 12 to 20 attending. In the first three months of its existence there were two references to strikes or mass meetings. The minutes of the first meeting, on 25 November 1925, mention a report of a mass meeting of corporation workers protesting against the 'attitude of municipal authorities in relation to superannuation scheme', but no action was recommended for Minority Movement members. Then on 24 February 1926 we find a reference to a dispute involving the Musicians' Union and that 12 comrades volunteered from the meeting to attend the picket. There is then a gap for three years and two months without a single mention of a strike — except for the General Strike and miners' struggle which followed.

It is important to note that the secretary, a comrade Stokes, appears to have been a careful and prolific minute-taker (1,000 words per meeting on average) so the failure of the minutes to mention strikes carries some weight — it is not simply an omission.

So if the Coventry Minority Movement largely ignored strikes, what then did its members do? Partly they involved themselves in propaganda work. At various times they laid special emphasis on sale of **The Worker**. A certain amount of effort went into single-issue campaigns such as a 'Free Speech Committee' and a Back to the Unions Campaign Committee. An important area of work — indeed the very basis of the National Minority Movement — was in gaining official trade union support through winning affiliations from union branches. During the years that strikes were ignored, the Coventry Minority Movement members still found time to discuss the Co-op elections, in October 1926 announcing that three of their members were standing in the local elections on a trades council ticket.

What the activity of the Coventry branch and the rest of the National Minority Movement showed was that although it had been modelled on the successful efforts of South Wales miners, it lacked the same rank-and-file input but retained its orientation on the official union apparatus. This does not mean that the National Minority Movement had nothing to say about shopfloor organisation and the like: it always referred to the need for factory committees, but its chief policies militated against such work since they looked to officials to provide leadership on behalf of the rank and file. Without a clear understanding of the relative worth of official or unofficial activity it was not surprising that the hard, thankless grind of daily shopfloor agitation should be discarded in favour of the easier task of winning resolutions and affiliations.

Apart from in the mining industry there is little indication that the Minority Movement was particularly close to the rank and file. In the pages of **The Worker** only the builders' section seems to have had shop steward support and that only in the London area.

Another sign of serious weakness in this area of trade union strategy was that when it came to questions of internal union democracy the National Minority Movement had very little to say. In the early days, Communists had proposed a number of safeguards against bureaucracy — the right to recall officials, that their wages should be dependent on wages in the relevant industry, regular elections and the like. But these were noticeably absent from the programmes of the various Minority Movements.

One measure of the movement's official influence can be guessed from the number of union branches that supported the Communist Party in its attempt to affiliate to the Labour Party. In June 1923 support came from 17 AEU branches, 16 MFGB branches and four NUR branches — with the furniture trades union NAFTA and the shop workers' union NUDAW both supporting nationally.[8] However, since the AEU branch was geographical the 17 branches meant far less in practical terms of rank-and-file influence than did the miners' lodges. Experience showed that mining, and South Wales in particular, remained the bedrock of the National Minority Movement right up to the General Strike.

The industrial scene in 1923 and 1924 was not all darkness. There was a significant improvement in the economy. French occupation of the Ruhr and the protest strike by German workers increased the demand for British coal, so that in 1924 some wage increases were achieved by British miners. The percentage of unemployment for all industries fell from 13.6 in January 1923 to 7.0 in May 1924. The improvement encouraged workers' struggle.

Soon, although struggles were being regularly defeated, they were bubbling to the surface more and more frequently. It took the personal intervention of Labour Party leader Ramsay MacDonald to resolve the builders' lock-out in the spring of 1923. Naturally he forced a decision extremely favourable to the employers. But no sooner had the builders returned than boilermakers came out over the issue of overtime. The same week a dispute flared up involving vehicle builders who were demanding the recognition of their shop stewards' committee, and the same union even dared respond to yet another employers' call for wage cuts with their own campaign for a wage *rise*.[9]

At the end of April 1923 Tom Bell summed up the position when he said that 'already signs are abroad of a recovery from the savage and brutal offensive of the employers . . . The workers are gaining in confidence'.[10] The revival was sustained right through 1924, as this entry in **The Worker** which reviews the first seven months of 1924 showed:

January–March   Strike of locomotive engineer drivers and firemen
                which brought out into the open tremendous cleav-
                age of sectionalism.
February   Strike of dockers.
March   London tramwaymen — all buses out in sympathy.
April   Unofficial shipyard strike in Southampton for nine
                weeks. Failure of strike at Wembley exhibition.
June   Unofficial railway shopmen strike.
July   National builders' lockout for six weeks.[11]

Two strikes that were particularly important for the Communist Party took place in the docks. The first unofficial strike in April
1923 was a precursor of a much larger explosion in July. A spontaneous walk-out against wage cuts led to the following editorial
comment in **Workers' Weekly**:

> The officials of the Transport and General Workers' Union (including
> members of our own party and supporters of the RILU) we regret to
> say, have, during the last ten days been using the whole apparatus of
> the union to drive men back to work who wanted to fight. Party,
> revolutionary pledges, responsibility of leadership have all been for-
> gotten or given second place . . . This is no new phemonena.[12]

This passage is very reminiscent of the repeated complaints by
rank-and-file members of the miners' Unofficial Reform Committee about their erstwhile comrades who had gone on to better and
more bureaucratic things.

An article in the August edition of **All Power** gave a full history
of the big unofficial docks strike of July 1923 which spread from
Hull to London, Cardiff, Liverpool and beyond:

> The strike has had all the characteristics of a widespread revolt. It has
> been completely unofficial. At one time there were over 100,000 men
> out on strike.

The article described the obstacles facing the strikers, among the
greatest being the union officials:

> From the beginning all the forces of the capitalist enemy have been
> consciously mobilised against the striking workers. The power of
> their union has been withdrawn from them. Their union officials have
> solidly lined up with the enemies against them.

But this hitherto excellent article drew the following 'vital lessons':

> 1) That unofficial strikes begin wrong because they start off with a division of the workers' forces — many workers who are good and loyal members of their trade union remaining at work out of very loyalty to the organisation.

The fact that many workers will passively accept union rulings on which strikes deserve support does not mean that the fight of 100,000 dockers was wrong. The willingness of so many to act in the face of tremendous odds should not have been condemned but welcomed.

Worse was to come:

> 2) That unofficial strikes begin wrong because they leave the machinery of organisation in the hands of those who oppose the strike.
>
> 3) That unofficial strikes begin wrong because from their very nature careful plans of campaign cannot be elaborated and clear objectives aimed at.

What did **All Power** think was needed instead?

> a great clearing-out of disloyal and non-dependable leaders and officials in the trade union movement is necessary, and . . . immediate steps should be taken in all unions to so circumscribe their officials with regulations as to ensure them faithfully carrying out the wishes of their members.[13]

Obviously revolutionaries do not always prefer unofficial strikes to official ones in whatever circumstances. There might well have been good reasons for arguing that the dockers' strike could be more successful if it was official. But to line up in the middle of the dispute *against* unofficial strikes was wrong, and not simply because it showed a lack of solidarity. The argument for official action could have been put in this way: unofficial strikes in one industry, at a time when general rank-and-file confidence is still low, mean that there is no choice but to fight for maximum official backing, both in order to win strike pay and also to elicit solidarity from other sections too afraid to act without official sanction.

Given the balance of class forces in the summer of 1923 such a tactical judgement might have been justified. However, as it stood, the article must have been received as a condemnation of unofficial action. The author shows some remorse for the tone of his article when he says that despite his criticisms of unofficial action

the fight is on. The dockers are fighting for bread now. They are on
the streets now. And it is the duty of all workers to aid them in their
fight.[14]

The Communist Party indeed threw itself into the fight with all
vigour and even produced a daily strike paper to assist.

The party's attitude to unofficial strikes was not uniform. It
was torn between its theoretical weakness and dependence on
official leadership and its gut reaction as a revolutionary workers'
organisation. Thus, a year later a **Workers' Weekly** editorial drew
these lessons:

> The unofficial strike of the railway shopmen stands out as an event of
> profound importance. Taking it in its bare facts — an 'unofficial'
> revolt . . . This alone is a reminder salutary to all, of the fact that
> however completely the workers may seem to be crushed, the instinct
> to revolt against oppression remains an indestructible feature of human
> consciousness.
>
> With all its organisational weakness an 'unofficial' strike, because of
> its sheer hopeless desperation, has a moral effect upon the whole
> working mass that official strikes frequently fail to convey . . . [and
> defeat] adds to it since the prime agent of the defeat is not so much the
> boss as the official trade union machine against which a mass of
> impatient and imperative resistance is piling up every day.
>
> Official trade unionism grew up, developed its policy, and solidified
> its conceptions in a period of expanding capitalism and latent working-
> class consciousness . . . It therefore developed its officials for the special
> task of diplomatic wangling, from a boss fearful of losing his share of a
> boom period, the utmost possible in the way of concessions . . . Now
> that capitalism has ceased to expand . . . official trade unionism is in a
> cleft stick. They built up their power in demanding a share of the . . .
> gains. What case have they against accepting a share of the 'losses'?
>
> The unofficial strike cuts right across the facile and treacherous philo-
> sophy of class-peace and class collaboration. The unofficial strike takes
> trade unionism itself back to the practical facts out of which it was born
> and reveals in a flash the ghastly contradiction between trade unionism
> as a living fact of the workers' class struggle and the obsolete and
> cowardly doctrine which official trade unionism has sought to substi-
> tute for the genuine article.[15]

The fact that the same party could produce the dismal analysis
in **All Power** and this magnificent piece of work was a sign of the

inner contradiction developing in its trade union work — between serious revolutionary agitation among the rank and file, and the tendency to channel this towards officialdom.

The test of an approach to trade union work is its attitude to unofficial strikes. The aim of the National Minority Movement was to bring these into the official fold, not with the idea of giving the rank and file a chance to develop under the protective umbrella of official support so much as preventing what union leaders saw as dissipation of trade union resources. The intention was to make strike action bigger and more effective, but the party mistakenly looked to the officials to do this. Writing on behalf of the Metalworkers' Minority Movement, Wal Hannington argued:

> We aim not at unofficial but official strikes, in which the whole membership of the trade unions shall be pressed into the struggle against the organisation of the employing class. But when conditions force an unofficial strike, then we aim at broadening and continuing the struggle to make it an official one.[16]

Another **Workers' Weekly** article which was published just before the founding conference of the National Minority Movement showed how the Communist Party wanted the rank and file to regard the movement:

> . . . it is regrettable that the workers, though dissatisfied with the official leadership of the trade union movement, have so far been unable to unite their forces under a National Minority Movement that can bring unity of action . . . The first organisational attempt to bring the active workers together under a common leadership will enable them to work inside their existing organisation . . . This [Minority Movement campaign] would express itself in a more influential character upon the official leadership of the trade unions and would compel them by reason of its force to definitely take a move forward.[17]

No doubt the majority of Minority Movement members gave support to unofficial strikes, whatever their rights or wrongs. But the organisation to which they belonged did not look upon these actions in the light of their effect on the rank and file, whether positive or negative. Its attitude was that strikes should always be official. Today revolutionaries would argue that there are times when it is better that a strike if official, and times when it is best left free to develop unofficially. The deciding factor is always the confidence and success of the rank and file, not the needs of the trade union machine.

Towards the bureaucracy or the rank and file?

As we have said, by far the most important section of the Minority Movement was that of the miners. The Miners' Minority Movement was closely tied in with the structure of the Miners' Federation of Great Britain. This was particularly true in South Wales, where, according to Woodhouse:

> A J Cook was publicly giving his blessing and that of other left-wing officials to the movement with the ingenious argument that the Miners' Minority Movement was a necessary part of the South Wales Miners' Federation in so far as the latter was officially too involved in day-to-day routine to devise effective policies to meet the needs of the rank and file . . . This was a view [of] relevance to the South Wales situation where there was so well-established a tradition of 'ginger group' activity within the South Wales Miners' Federation that movements of this type could well be considered an integral part of the union itself, a phenomenon whose existence was tolerated, even expected by the executive committee and rank and file alike.[18]

It was not just that perhaps as many as half the South Wales executive supported the Miners' Minority Movement and looked at it in this light. Arthur Horner, who was the most prominent Communist Party miner, also saw the role of the Miners' Minority Movement as being a means of helping to keep officials in touch with feelings at the base of the union:

> At present, no lodge can have access to the executive committee of the South Wales Miners' Federation, except through the district officials, whilst for, say, the general secretary of the MFGB to hear or do anything except through the stages previously mentioned would be considered guilty of such a breach of etiquette as to almost amount to sacrilege.[19]

At that time the Miners' Minority Movement's close relationship with officials was probably the only means of getting a mass movement off the ground in the face of bitter employer opposition. But what direction would this movement take once it could stand on its own two feet?

The Miners' Minority Movement was pulled in two opposite directions: towards strengthening the rank and file for future struggles, or subordinating them to the official machine. The second was reflected in an article in the newly-established fortnightly, **The Mineworker**, by Tom Quelch who drew the following familiar lesson:

> This time the lessons of 1921 must not be lost . . . This time the miners must go into battle with the full and complete backing of the whole trade union movement . . . When it is definitely known that a fight is inevitable, then the executive of the MFGB must enter into negotiations with the General Council of the Trades Union Congress and with the aid and lead of the General Council every vital section of the trade union movement must be rallied.[20]

Yet soon after this appeared, another article put the rank-and-file case excellently, pointing out the fundamental weakness of the bureaucracy and the fact that the real fight must come from those at the point of production whose power depended on their *own* self-confidence and organisation:

> When are our generals and other officials going to prepare the rank and file of the miners for the coming onslaught? . . . Are we going like lambs to the slaughter again? . . . If not, then it is up to the rank and file to get busy themselves . . . When is the British rank and file going to wake up and appoint men hot from the coalface to do battle for them. Men who will have a stake in the game and whose bread and butter depends on the settlement they get and who, whenever they win or lose, have to come straight back to the coalface and work daily under the agreement they themselves have made . . . It is my contention that it is the rank and file who will eventually work out their own salvation . . . *The self-consciousness of the miners is now a vital part of the dynamism of social progress.*
> This is at once an explanation and the justification of the tactic of class struggle.[21]

The healthy instincts of many MMM members were again revealed when **The Mineworker** came to discuss the formation of workers' unity through an Industrial Alliance of miners, railwaymen, transport workers and engineers. This body was a revamped Triple Alliance on an even bigger scale:

> All we do know is that a committee has been established to look into the matter . . . We do not suppose there is a single reflecting trade unionist in this country who is not certain in his own mind that this committee was appointed very much as Royal Commissions are appointed by parliament, *to shelve the whole matter*. The actual truth as

far as those attending this particular conference is concerned is that while on platforms up and down the country, they mouth specious phrases about working-class unity, when it comes to actively establishing it they play the game of wreckers and saboteurs . . . The class solidarity of the workers cannot be imposed from above. It has to be developed from below, amongst the rank and file.[22]

Several articles have been quoted here because they stand in marked contrast to the rest of the National Minority Movement. The other sections lacked the miners' close relationship with struggle at the point of production and were more preoccupied with the official channels. Even this piece from **The Mineworker**, which accepted the now orthodox Communist Party line on centralised leadership, conceived of the process in far more active terms than usual:

The whole of the trade union movement must actively participate in the fight led by the General Council of the TUC . . . The rank and file must speed up this coming together. Joint committees of all sections of workers who are now faced with struggles must be established in every locality. Deputations from the miners' lodges should visit the local branches of the National Union of Railwaymen and the Amalgamated Engineering Union to discuss with the members of those branches how best the struggle can be waged and what steps can be taken to ensure the greatest cooperation and solidarity. Similarly, deputations from the NUR and AEU should visit miners' lodges.[23]

This greater rank-and-file orientation was notwithstanding the deep penetration of the MMM into the structures of the official apparatus. A high proportion of articles in **The Mineworker** were written by full-time officials, who were known as 'miners' agents'. The election of A J Cook as MFGB secretary in 1924 was hailed as a victory of the MMM and his speeches and articles always figured prominently in **The Mineworker**. But this does not mean that it slavishly followed his every move, for remarkably little campaigning was actually done in its pages for his election, and it certainly was not turned into an electioneering sheet for him.

The close overlap of industry/union and community in mining provided the ideal conditions for this kind of grassroots agitation within the union machine. The combination of hard-won militancy and attention to detail in union matters made the Miners' Minority Movement the healthiest section of the National Minority Movement. It therefore provided the model which other Minority Movement sections tried to emulate. But because they mostly lacked the network of rank-and-file activists, the fighting tradition and special conditions of the mining industry, none was nearly as successful.

A better understanding of the South Wales movement and the environment in which it functioned might have been a useful corrective to the politics of the National Minority Movement. It would have been a warning against reading too grandiose a design into movements in other unions which consisted of little more than a programme and campaign for branch affiliations or executive positions. Just as the criterion for establishing an independent rank-and-file movement was a high level of shopfloor militancy, so even a much lower level 'broad left' type operation required some activity at the base, if it was not to be a paper organisation.

Despite the mythology that has grown up around it, the National Minority Movement established in 1924 was *not* a rank-and-file movement, and it explicitly rejected that description. This contradicts a commonly accepted view on the left. However, the historical evidence for the period up to 1926 definitely refutes the idea that independent rank-and-file organisation was the aim.

Writing in 1923, Gallacher, a man who had been at the very centre of the Clyde Workers' Committee, and who therefore knew just what a rank-and-file movement looked like, stated:

> The movement that is springing up all over the country . . . is not a rank-and-file movement, but rather it is one that reaches through every strata of the trade unions. The driving force must necessarily come from the rank and file, but we should never forget that local officials, district officials, and national officials (a few of them at any rate) have never been led away by the desire to settle the troubles of capitalism.[24]

A rank-and-file movement is not based on damning all officials, but on supporting them 'just so long as they rightly represent the workers', and '[acting] independently immediately they misrepresent them', as the Clyde Workers' Committee leaflet put it.[25] However the engineering stewards during the war had not seen their role as gingering up trade union leaders either. They fully expected the officials to fail in the struggle. They based this belief on an analysis of trade union bureaucracy that showed that official betrayal was inevitably built into the structure of unions. Neither had the workers' committees been anti-union. They were, after all, based on the union dues collectors — the stewards. The Sheffield Workers' Committee had, like others, included members of the local district committees, and the Clyde Stewards had cooperated with official.elements in a joint committee during the 40-hours strike.

A refusal to have anything to do with trade union leaders did not make a rank-and-file movement, but the expectation of official betrayal and the independent organisation needed to counter this did.

We do not argue here that such a rank-and-file movement was possible in 1924. The lack of shopfloor organisation in many industries would strongly suggest that such amovement just could not have been built then. But this did not mean that what fighting spirit did exist should be marshalled behind left-talking officials. And this *was* the intention of the founders of the National Minority Movement. The following confused article from **The Worker** shows how the spirit of a rank-and-file revolt was present, but how it weighed less in the scales than what was seen as the membership's duty to provide a crutch for overburdened 'enlightened' officials. This was the united front tactic turned upside down:

> We do not mean to assert that all the officials are sabotaging progress, and all the rank and file are brave and progressive spirits. Such a picture is simply a caricature of the actual situation. *What exists is a situation in which a small minority of the rank and file are struggling against the passivity and ignorance of the mass of the workers.* Unless the broad popular masses can be reached and quickened through the activity of the left-wing, the enlightened officials are weighted down and cannot move. That being the case the struggle of the left-wing for leadership is not merely an anti-official struggle. It is much more than this. It is a struggle to reach the ordinary worker, to convince him of the need for new policies and new methods of struggle. *The business of the Minority Movement is not merely to wangle positions for those who support its policy, it is the more fundamental task to capture the rank and file, of recreating the will to fight. Only by those who go into positions of authority in the union movement having behind them a solid basis of rank-and-file support will we be able to make progress.*[26]

The Minority Movement approach, like that of the Unofficial Reform Committee, was a two-way bridge between the official structure of the union and the rank and file. Only with a clear understanding of the relative importance of the rank and file and officialdom (something which is patently missing from the article quoted above), could there be a guarantee that it would not be a bridge leading the rank and file into the arms of the officials.

It was all very well to accuse the majority of the rank and file of passivity and ignorance, but they alone had the potential to mount a real fight for working-class interests. If that was lost sight of, all sorts of dangers could ensue. If independent rank-and-file organisation had been the long-term goal, then the National Minority Movement could have been invaluable. It would have provided the opportunity for using the 'enlightened' officials to help relieve pressure on the rank and file. It is the latter who are 'weighted down' by the foreman and the boss and 'cannot move', not the officials!

Towards the machine

When Arthur Horner came to discuss how the National Minority Movement would achieve its programme his main proposal was that:

> The National Minority conference . . . pledges the NMM and all its supporters throughout the country to unceasingly work in the respective trade unions for the concentration of trade union power in the General Council of the TUC, and the alteration of the constitution of the General Council to admit the best, wisest and most aggressive fighters on behalf of the working class as members.[27]

Elsewhere Harry Pollitt explained what steps were necessary to make the TUC the centre of Communist Party industrial activity:

> First, every member inside a trade union must pay particular attention to the date of nomination for delegates to the Congress . . . [Then] *12 weeks before the Congress assembles* [we must decide] the resolutions which we must aim at:
> Increased power for the General Council
> Immediate campaign for the six-hour day
> Affiliation of the Unemployed Organisations
> Foreign policy
> United resistance to wage reductions
> Direct rank-and-file representation on the General Council.
> . . . We must learn too how to wangle and beat them at their own game. The 'diehards' and reactionaries will never be shifted by calling them names; *it is elections and how to use them* that matter.[28]

This was a classic example of what today is known as 'Broad Left' strategy.

Obviously the TUC lefts would not just fall into the arms of the Communist Party, so a two-pronged strategy was pursued: on the one hand appeals for a united front, on the other direct efforts by Communist Party members to win positions. There is nothing wrong with efficiency or attention to detail in trade union affairs. In bureaucratic organisations a knowledge of how they work, when and how to put resolutions, is valuable if one's voice is not to be strangled by red tape. But there is a world of difference between on the one hand using such occasions as a platform, as a means of either verbally attacking the bureaucracy or using divisions within it to create opportunities for rank-and-file activity, and on the other believing that revolutionary change can be brought about by worthy TUC resolutions or the right men in the top posts.

Harry Pollitt converted the membership of the Communist Party, and that of the National Minority Movement, into a resolution-moving machine, whose chief aim was to give 'increased power to the General Council'. The timing of the annual National Minority Movement conferences was highly significant. They were held a week before the TUC Congress and their main subject matter was resolutions for the TUC. Electioneering also became an important part of the work. The firm grip this had taken at party headquarters is demonstrated by the industrial activities listed by MacFarlane in his appendix on 'The Communist Party and the Trade Unions, 1924/5'. Half the activities mentioned are solely concerned with elections or TUC resolutions. These are as follows:

22 November 1924   Industrial department issued bulletins regarding the election of an additional organising secretary in the ASLEF.

26 November 1924   Industrial department circularised all party members in the Amalgamated Society of Woodworkers re the nomination of members as delegates to the TUC.

1 December 1924   Industrial department prepared a resolution on Workers' Control of Industry for the TUC. . .

6 December 1924   Industrial department issued special bulletin re . . election for the Final Court of Appeal in the AEU.

6 January 1925	Industrial department issued bulletin re elections to executive committee of the British Iron, Steel and Kindred Trades Association and the election of delegates to the Labour Party Conference, TUC and the annual general meeting of the NUR.
14 January 1925	Industrial department issued bulletin to party members in the AEU instructing them which candidates to support.
22 January 1925	Industrial department issued bulletin re forthcoming elections in the Boilermakers' Society and the annual conference of the Shop Assistants' Union.[29]

The reader should not take from this the impression that rank-and-file Communists were totally absorbed in electoral work. The party had created, in **Workers' Weekly**, a lively interventionist newspaper whose quality and agitational style easily outclassed the socialist press of the past. Through hard work its circulation had been built up to a regular 50,000 copies or so. In addition an impressive effort was put into overcoming the loose propagandist methods of pre-war socialism. The CPGB made itself into a disciplined, centralised party capable of taking its initiatives into the working class.

The turn towards Communist Party factory branches was evidence of this. In the summer of 1925 there were 68 such groups. Each produced factory bulletins which dealt with issues ranging from the workplace to national and international politics. These branches had from three members upwards, and by the time of the General Strike one-sixth of the party's 6,000 members were involved.

However the following article, which urged the building of a serious revolutionary party with rank-and-file roots, was at variance with the main thrust of the leadership's policies — which were orientated on the bureaucracy:

If we are going to create, not only a change of organisation, but a change of outlook amongst the rank and file, then we must get contacts with the rank and file in the workshop . . . Only by this continual workshop contact and propaganda amongst the rank and file, only by gathering the rank and file around the active men in the party and the Minority Movement can we create that level of consciousness in the trade union membership that will prevent the large organisations from becoming merely the plaything of bureaucracy, a bulwark of reaction . . . Without this, the various proposals for concentration of power in the trade union movement may conceivably mean not a concentration of leadership for class struggle purposes, but a Gompers* dictatorship in the trade union movement of this country.[30]

This argument was in direct contradiction to the general strategy of the party and in the end one side had to give way. The benefits of such things as the factory branches or the **Workers' Weekly** were swamped by the false strategy of the party leadership. This ultimately prevented the party from playing the leading role that the exertions of the members had earned it.

---

*Gompers was the extreme conservative leader of the 'business union' American Federation of Labor.

Chapter Ten

TAILING THE LEFT LEADERS

AT THE TUC Congress in Plymouth in September 1923 a whole number of left speeches were made by union leaders. Such militant words had been heard before and proved worthless. But now the Communist Party was only too ready to accept them at face value. George Hicks, a member of the TUC General Council, was quoted approvingly in the party's newspaper:

> What is needed is for about half-a-dozen trusted men to draw up a programme clear and direct, which can be the acknowledged trade union platform, and then a properly organised campaign to preach it.

Harry Pollitt of the Communist Party echoed this sentiment:

> A few leading men, if they would only see the opportunity before them, could at this moment achieve anything by coming together on a clear definite programme and rally all the active elements in the trade unions.

The **Workers' Weekly** gave the following explanation for the emergence of a vocal left current in the bureaucracy at this time:

> . . . inexorable facts. The pressure of the economic situation, and the refusal to struggle on the part of the old leadership, is compelling all the elements which stand for even the bare minimum of the working-class struggle to come out into the open, in co-operation with the Communists in heralding a revolt . . . It does not matter how limited may be the immediate aims of the movement, or how open to qustion the associations or previous record of some particular leader within it. These tendencies none the less represent a real movement within the working class . . . they represent the breaking of the ice; they are the heralding of the Spring.
> Into such a movement for the rallying of the working class the

Communists will throw themselves wholeheartedly, without fear
for the future, for they know that the struggle itself must bring
clearness.[1]

The insistent reference to the 'old' leadership and the 'inexorable facts' driving the unions leftwards suggest that there must
have been a 'new' leadership in the making. The 'old' lot were a
'reactionary set', while the new leadership's main fault was its lack
of clarity, which would be sorted out in the struggle. We will deal
later with the underlying theory behind this emphasis on 'left'
versus 'right' or 'new leaders' versus the 'old'. But it is worth
noting how short the memory of the Communist Party was. The
new leaders made no speeches as remotely revolutionary as those of
Robert Williams, nor was there a syndicalist-sounding Triple Alliance bestriding the land. Yet such an editorial could be written
when the disaster of Black Friday was just two years past.

Of course the rallying call of some TUC lefts could prove
extremely useful in promoting a revival of militancy on the ground,
but to develop that further one could not dupe oneself, and the
workers, that such 'left' tendencies could be embraced 'without
fear for the future'. To do so was to disarm criticism of the
inevitable sell-outs that would occur once a serious revival got
going.

Pollitt's campaign for unity consisted of promising the
leaders indemnity from having their left credentials questioned as
long as they made the correct noises. The 'rancour' of the workers
would be quelled and the 'associations or previous record' would
be wiped from the slate. In other words the rank and file would be
told to forget that these men played the role of trade union
bureaucrats.

Purcell, who had now broken with the Communist Party,
clearly wanted the memory of his renegacy obliterated — and
demanded that as his price for supporting a party initiative:

> I would readily associate with it for this purpose [rallying the unions]
> but if it is merely to be used as a vehicle for personal attacks upon
> certain individuals, then I must continue to await the 'petering out' of
> this absurd and puerile method of agitation.[2]

A week later his indemnity was granted.

But the memory of some rank-and-file party members was
not quite as short as those of the party leaders. The edition of

Workers' Weekly that carried Purcell's letter included these brief comments, the second of which came from a Staffordshire miner:

> It is no earthly use looking for help from above — this will come from below.
> It is the militant element from amongst the rank and file that will save the trade union movement.

In the eyes of the leaders of the CPGB, who had now lost the point of production and the rank and file as their central means of reference, the comings and goings of the bureaucracy and the details of official policy acquired an inordinate importance.

By 1925 the party was tied to the coat-tails of left trade union leaders such as Purcell, George Hicks and Alonzo Swales, who spoke patronisingly of the Minority Movement. Thus in January 1925 Swales, then president of the TUC, stated:

> Like all countries we in England have our militant section, our extremists . . . We have met abuse sometimes and discipline was upset. But only good comes from this new blood. Most of my colleagues were young firebrands, but responsibility has sobered them down. I hope to remain a rebel against present-day society.
> Instead of expelling these young people, we allow them to come in and take their share in the movement.[3]

Throughout 1924 **Labour Monthly**, under the editorship of Palme Dutt, encouraged practically all of the 'lefts' to contribute their thoughts on 'new policy' for the trade union movement. The results were an appalling testimony to what the best of the bureaucracy had to offer, and give a rare insight into the workings of the bureaucratic mind.

> A A Purcell (TUC Chairman):
> Now all these programmes, platforms, policies and manifestos have their place. I have been in at the drafting and distribution of millions of them, but never once did I believe they would do the thing the enthusiasts desired.[4]
> Will Lawther (Durham Miners leader):
> Every few years . . . new movements spring up, manifestos are scattered broadcast, all urging the same object . . . and yet after the new movement has had its vogue, something further has been discovered, and that is that no progress has been made.[5]

Some even dragged out the corpse of Karl Marx for their justification:

> George Hicks:
> It is impossible under capitalism to get away from the Marxian law of wages. I do not apologise for studying commercial practicability. As a trade union official I am forced to live in a real world.[6]

Month after month the same dross was churned out, and eventually Palme Dutt was forced to draw a veil over the whole business. His 'Postscript' tells us that:

> The series of articles . . . has constituted a serious and important experiment in working-class discussion . . . from representative and responsible leaders. [But] it is impossible to read this series of articles and to consider all that they imply without a sense of tragedy.[7]

Palme Dutt actually went further than most Communist Party members in questioning the current strategy of wooing such people. For these bureaucrats offered

> nothing but an endless succession of vague generalities, about 'old policies', 'new policies', 'programmes', 'solidarity', 'unity', 'ever-improving standards of life', etc., etc.[8]

And tucked away in the footnotes, Palme Dutt gives this gem about Robert Williams, former Communist and as transport workers' leader a co-architect of Black Friday. Williams explained the value of left phraseology to the union bureaucrats in this way:

> Only recently a wealthy shipowner asked a colleague of mine: 'Why is it your friend Williams will make those wild-cat speeches on the platform when he is so able in conducting negotiations at the conference table?' I replied by saying: 'Convey my compliments to the gentlemen, and say that perhaps a few more wild-cat speeches would bring a little more success at the conference table.'[9]

The Anglo-Russian Trade Union Unity Committee

The decisive shift of the Communist Party to the right was spurred on by the establishment of the Anglo-Russian Trade Union

Unity Committee.* This was all part of the policy of the new ruling group in Russia, around Stalin, which was searching for bureaucratic allies abroad.

A delegation of Russian trade unionists attended the Hull Congress of the TUC in September 1924, following which six delegates of the TUC went to Russia. On their arrival dicussion took place with Soviet trade union leaders, and it was agreed, subject to endorsement, to set up an Anglo-Russian Committee to work for international trade union unity. Responding to the Russian policy, the CPGB enthusiastically campaigned to secure the General Council's endorsement of this proposal. On 26 January 1925 the Minority Movement organised a conference on International Trade Union Unity, which was attended by 617 delegates representing 600,000 workers. [10]

---

*In their book **Trade Unions and Revolution: The Industrial Politics of the early British Communist Party** (London 1975), James Hinton and Richard Hyman argue two main points.

Firstly, they deny Trotsky's thesis that the British Communist Party was 'misled and corrupted by the Stalinist bloc within the Comintern'. Indeed, they say, 'almost always the CPGB itself stood to the right of the majority in the International' (page 72). This argument is wrong. While the Comintern made many left pronouncements, the logic of its search for reformist allies on the TUC inevitably distorted the trade union policy of the British Communists. Of course there were opportunist tendencies in the CPGB before the rise of Stalin. Already in previous chapters we have documented false ideas dating from the British Socialist Party. But there was an equally powerful tradition of hatred towards the union bureaucracy and an understanding of the need for rank-and-file independence. The success of opportunism in the British Communist Party was guaranteed by the Russian leaders' promotion of the Anglo-Russian Trade Union Unity Committee and the smothering of debate inside the International.

The second argument put forward by Hinton and Hyman is that during the early 1920s 'a cadre party placing primary emphasis on the *quality* rather than the quantity of its membership could alone have succeeded in sustaining the British revolutionary tradition in such unfavourable circumstances (page 73).

Duncan Hallas has refuted this point: ' "Quality of membership" for what? The "high quality" members of a revolutionary organisation are those with high ability to *lead their fellow workers in the class struggle*. They can in no case be developed *apart* from the struggle for mass influence. Give up that, and you revert to the status of a propagandist sect . . . It was the historic achievement of the CPGB to *overcome* this tradition of abstract propagandism.' (Duncan Hallas, 'The Communist Party and the General Strike', in **International Socialism**, first series, number 88 (May 1976).)

Palme Dutt waxed eloquent at the prospect of unity between
RILU and Amsterdam:

> A new force has appeared upon the horizon of the British working-
> class movement to raise a note of challenge. The inscription that it
> bears upon its banner is International Trade Union Unity . . . To
> oppose it is to oppose the workers' common struggle, and therefore to
> oppose the victory of the workers.[11]

The words of the TUC bureaucrats were now no longer to be
regarded as hollow phrase-mongering. They must represent a mass
movement among the workers. Pollitt wrote in **Workers' Weekly**:

> The suggestion of the formation of an Anglo-Russian Unity Commit-
> tee is not the result of a happy inspiration of certain left-wing trade
> union leaders but is the outward manifestation of . . . the simple fact
> that experience in the class struggle has more and more convinced the
> workers that only by united action nationally and internationally can
> their struggle be successful.[12]

The idea that the bureaucracy might have its own reasons for
making such moves does not appear to have crossed the minds of
leading Communist Party members. They had completely lost
touch with reality, thinking that when the bureaucrats talked left
the masses were pulling their strings. In fact, it was the other way
round, and they had only to look at the size of the revolutionary
movement in Britain, a few thousands only, to see this.

Now the task had changed: from achieving a 'general staff of
labour' by replacing the General Council with avowed revolutionaries (a doubtful tactic in the first place), it was now to push the
current General Council forward, giving it the confidence to uphold the international unity campaign — confidence that they
would not be criticised by the Communists. In an article ironically
entitled 'Our Principles', George Hardy, organising secretary of
the National Minority Movement, answered the question whether
the fight against reactionary leaders such as J H Thomas was more
important than a TUC/Russian union deal. For Hardy criticism of
the likes of Thomas was secondary:

> we do not make the above a condition of international unity. If we
> did, we would probably preclude many a trade union official who is
> now supporting us. We would be erecting an obstacle against unity
> itself.[13]

Every great crisis in the labour movement forces the unions to readjust, and in the process argument and splits may occur. At the outbreak of the First World War the sharp rightward pressure of imperialism not only smashed the political parties of the Second International, it paralysed the international trade union movement. Within individual states unions were rent by open divisions, often between bureaucrats and organised rank-and-file movements. The leftward impact of the Russian revolution and post-war crisis also caused splits, witness the division between RILU and the Amsterdam International, or in France between the right and left-wing union confederations.

Trade union unity is always an important question. The working class is only strong because it is a collective class which creates the wealth of the world through social production. Trade unions are based on collective action such as strikes. Obviously, anything which increases the numbers involved in collective action is to be welcomed. The old adage 'united we stand, divided we fall' is the fruit of long and bitter experience. However unity of the class is not the same as an Anglo-Russian union committee, nor a more powerful TUC General Council. And it can only appear to be so if one is blind to the existence of the bureaucracy.

The first priority in every question always has to be the *unity and fighting capacity* of the rank and file. All other aspects of trade unionism have to be subordinated to this and judged in its light.

The attitude of revolutionaries to trade union unity at the official level can be complex. There are occasions when bureaucrats use the threat of a right-wing breakaway as an excuse to blackmail the left into abandoning principles and accommodating to reactionary pressures. Here the price of unity is a paralysis worse than the disease it was meant to cure. At other times different conditions apply. A split in a union or friction between unions may lead to division where it counts, among the membership, who are thus weakened at the point of production.

The effect of establishing the Anglo-Russian Trade Union Unity Committee was not to strengthen the rank-and-file trade unionists of Russia or Britain. The rising Stalinist bureaucracy in Russia were in favour of this move for reasons of political expediency. It hoped that the committee would 'play an enormous role in the struggle against all possible interventions directed against the USSR.'[14] As Trotsky was to point out, the only realistic defence of a workers' state is to spread revolution internationally.

The committee did not do this. In fact its tendency was to weaken the truly revolutionary forces in Britain by granting the lefts on the TUC General Council a false radical credibility at very little cost. The Anglo-Russian Committee demanded nothing of them except a few worthy statements in the press. The credibility the TUC lefts gained was used to discourage independent rank-and-file initiatives during the 1926 General Strike.

Tragically the highest sentiment of revolutionaries — the feeling of international solidarity — was being perverted. The Communist Party and Minority Movement became cheer-leaders for left bureaucrats. The prestige the Bolsheviks had rightly won by their revolution was being used to enhance the reputation of reformist bureaucrats in Britain, and assist the manoeuvres of Stalinist bureaucrats in Russia.

Chapter Eleven

THE WRITING ON THE WALL:
THE COMMUNIST PARTY AND 'RED FRIDAY'

THE PERIOD from early 1925 to December 1926 was dominated by the battle of miners and coalowners. On 29 July 1925 Prime Minister Stanley Baldwin told the miners' leaders 'that the government would not grant any subsidy to the industry, and that it must stand on its own economic foundations.'[1]

Next day the **Daily Herald** reported a conversation between Baldwin and representatives of the MFGB in which the prime minister twice insisted that 'all the workers of this country have got to take reductions in wages to help put industry on its feet.'[2]

Baldwin's statement about the necessity for universal wage cuts was a catalyst for trade union leaders' resistance. They all knew that these were not empty words. The government's decision to return to the gold standard in April 1925 increased the probability of an employers' attack on workers' wages. A return to the gold standard meant effectively a major revaluation of sterling, and this put particular pressure on export industries, including coalmining.

Some signs of this capitalist offensive were visible in the summer of 1925. In June the AEU informed the General Council that it had received demands for longer working hours and a lowering of wages in the engineering industry. Shortly afterwards the woolen textile unions were confronted by a call for a 10 per cent wage cut. Almost simultaneously craftsmen in the railway workshops were asked for a reduction of 5 per cent.[3]

On 23 July the Special Industrial Committee of the General Council of the TUC decided to call sympathetic action on behalf of the miners should it be necessary.

'Their duty was clear,' said A G Walkden, of the Railway Clerks' Association. 'The General Council was brought into being to deal with that sort of situation. They did not want to see the miners let down.

They realised that after 1921 when the miners were defeated, everyone else was attacked. There had been four years of disaster since. The railway magnates were waiting their chance to get this union down. That would happen in every industry.'

And Walter Citrine, acting secretary of the TUC, made the same point:

If the industries fought singly they would be broken singly. Only if they could get trade unions to rally to the support of the miners now had they any chance of settlement in other industries threatened by attacks.[4]

The decision was timely. On 30 July the mine-owners announced that they would end the 1924 agreement, cut wages, abolish the national minimum, revise wage determination from national to district agreements, and maintain standard profits, no matter how low wages fell. That same day the Special Industrial Committee, having met the transport unions, resolved that the movement should refuse to handle coal. The decision was immediately and unanimously ratified by a Special Conference of Trade Union Executives.

Next day Baldwin met the miners' executive and the special committee of the TUC jointly. He explained that the coalowners had agreed to suspend lock-out notices, that a Royal Commission into the coal industry would be appointed, and that the government would, in the meantime, guarantee financial subsidies until 30 April 1926. Such were the events surrounding 'Red Friday'.

The capitalist press greeted the government's announcement of 31 July with fury. The **Daily Express** raged, in an editorial entitled 'Danegeld', about extortion by the use of force, and the **Daily Mail** in another headed 'A Victory for Violence', expressed the feelings of the great majority of Tories.* But Baldwin had no choice but to back off. As he told his biographer, G M Young, several years later: 'We were not ready'.[5] The government had been caught off balance by the unity of the trade unions in support of the miners.

---

*Not everyone on the Labour side was enthusiastic about Red Friday either. For example, J H Thomas thought that there was 'nothing more dangerous for the future of the country than that employers and government were compelled to concede through force what they refused to concede through reason.' (**New York Times**, 19 August 1925, quoted in W M Crook, **The General Strike** (Chapel Hill 1931), pages 295–6.)

How did the Communist Party prepare for 'Red Friday'? Its whole method was summed up in the title of an article by Harry Pollitt: 'Make the leaders lead'.[6] The ten-point programme recommended in the Minority Movement's paper confirmed the general direction:

Items for immediate attention

1) Send name and address of TU branches you know have voted for affiliation.

2) Get your branch to affiliate to the Minority Movement.

3) Have your branch apply for a speaker from the Minority Movement.

4) Have our literature on sale at branch meetings.

5) Get your branch to affiliate to the trades council if not already affiliated.

6) Have your branch pass a resolution on international unity.

7) Form a minority group in your area.

9) Order literature from this national office at once.

10) Subscribe to 'The Worker'.[7]

The essence of these proposals was that militant efforts must be directed through official channels.

In many ways the result of Red Friday, though hailed as a success by the left, weakened the possibility of successful mass struggle. If battle had broken out in July 1925, for a start the government would have been less fully prepared. A miners' strike in the approach to winter was far more of a threat than one which began in spring. But more important, if the general strike had not been officially planned and dominated, but had broken out spontaneously in August 1925 it would have had a better chance of success. Class unity would have been built from the bottom up, the self-reliance of mass pickets, the solidarity won by rank-and-file miners' pickets reasoning with rail and transport workers, would have been to the fore. The studied sectionalism of May 1926, which allowed millions of workers to be held in reserve as passive spectators, might have been overcome.

If the Communist Party had had a proper understanding of trade unionism it would have recognised that Red Friday and Black Friday were not poles apart — they were but two different examples of what the trade union bureaucracy was capable of. In neither case had the rank and file been involved in real struggle on their own behalf. Both times bureaucratic calculation had determined the decisions that were taken. On Black Friday a full Triple

Alliance strike in the atmosphere of post-war turmoil was judged
too risky an enterprise, since it would inevitably mean a serious
clash with the state. On Red Friday, with the loss of membership
and tremendous financial damage since 1921 still fresh in their
minds, the bureaucracy felt it had to make a defensive stand. As the
rank and file were still pitifully weak the TUC felt confident that it
could control and limit the action.

However the Communist Party drew the wrong conclusion
from both Black and Red Friday. In 1921 the recognition of a crisis
in the leadership of the working class led the party to propose the
idea of 'more power to the General Council'. Yet it was precisely
the dangers of such a bureaucratic combination that Black Friday
had demonstrated. Red Friday now reinforced the impression that
the current labour organisations were capable of leading the working class to victory.

Whatever secret doubts the main Communist Party leadership
had harboured about the left trade union leaders were swept away
by Red Friday. Gallacher's reaction may appear rather extreme,
but he was merely expressing what was inherent in the policy of the
party and the Minority Movement — the idea that the main
purpose of revolutionary activity in the unions was to 'make the
leaders lead':

> Comes a real working-class crisis, and what happens? . . . The leader-
> ship passed into the hands of good proletarians like Swales, Hicks,
> Cook and Purcell. And this proletarian leadership and the proletarian
> solidarity it was capable of organising and demonstrating *was the real
> big thing that came out of the struggle*.
>
> These comrades must be encouraged and strengthened, the united
> movement they represented must be developed and stimulated so that
> it may be possible to pass from defensive to offensive action.

Gallacher then describd the encounter between the prime minister
and the TUC leaders before Red Friday:

> Swales and his colleagues were not timid, cowardly, middle-class place-
> hunters. Strong in their working-class courage, with a united working
> class behind them, they slammed back straight at Baldwin. 'All right,'
> said Swales, 'I also am a pacifist *just as you are*, and if it comes to a fight
> we'll use every available force to smash you and the employers you
> represent.' *And there spoke the working-class dictatorship*.
>
> There we had what Marx calls 'the confrontation of classes'. The

Capitalist Class and the Working Class, face to face, sizing each other up and prepared for the conflict that can only be ended by the Dictatorship of the Working Class overcoming and suppressing those who put privilege and profit before the welfare of the workers.[8]

While praising the behaviour of the left trade union leaders, the Communist Party consistently argued that the stand of Red Friday had won only a temporary truce. The **Workers' Weekly** carried regular warnings, counting out the weeks to the expiry of the subsidy. The idea of impending struggle set the tenor of the Second National Minority Movement Conference on 29 and 30 August 1925.

The conference was attended by 683 delegates. Apart from 145 Minority Movement branches, these included representatives from 41 trades councils, 126 metalworkers' organisations, 103 building workers' organisations, 75 transport workers' bodies, 33 miners' lodges and a few others. All this added up to a claimed representation of 750,000 workers. It was noticeable that two important recent disputes, an unofficial strike of seamen and the violent struggle of anthracite miners in South Wales, while noted, evoked only messages of sympathy, rather than a detailed discussion. The idea of a rank-and-file restructuring of the trade unions by the election of all officials, the right of instant recall and so on was not even mentioned.

The main thrust of the conference inevitably centred on the coming national conflict over the miners. Tom Mann's chairman's address could hardly have laboured the point more heavily:

> *Are we prepared to meet the opposing forces when the next round begins? . . . We ought really to prepare and that without delay. I feel confident, I may say without a moment's hesitancy,* that all present at this Conference are fully determined *to be prepared.*[9]

There are two forms of preparation for a war. The first is technical, the second is political. In a class war, where the main weapon is the ideological readiness of the combatants, technical factors come a poor second. Indeed, it is impossible to prepare the technical side effectively unless the political needs of the class are fully understood. And most important of all if the 'general staff' of your army can be expected to stab you in the back right in the middle of the crucial battle, then the troops must be prepared to form their own independent leadership. This was certainly not the impression given at the Minority Movement Conference.

No attempt was made to counter the chief weakness in the workers' camp, the domination of the movement by a treacherous trade union bureaucracy.

The only way to form effective plans of battle was to assess the rank-and-file mood and thus the true strength of the class. But the conference showed that no one in the Minority Movement leadership was looking in this direction. Since Red Friday the Communist Party was under the illusion that Swales and the General Council sitting at a table with Baldwin represented class facing class, just as the 683 delegates embodied the support of 750,000 workers. How else are we to interpret the estimate of the Minority Movement's influence given by the Communist MP Saklatvala to the conference:

> the actions of the Minority Movement for the last two years have cemented and closely knitted up the workers in every trade union movement so that we have saved one million miners, with five million souls dependent upon their earnings to be kept from starvation.[10]

This was no isolated boast. It was repeated to the Comintern by British delegates a few months later:

> I think that it is not an exaggerated claim, and I think that anyone who cares even to casually study the British labour movement would agree that it was the Communist Party and the Minority Movement, more than anybody else or any other organisation, who were responsible for preparing the ground which made possible and inevitable what is now known in British labour history as 'Red Friday'.[11]

The proof of this claim was not the action of the rank and file or even the Communist Party itself, but:

> If you had seen the press, the newspaper placards, that were got out all over the country, talking about the Communist victory, the Communist policy, the Communist gains, and bemoaning the fact that the Minority Movement had gained the ascendancy in the trade union movement, and that something had got to be done about it![12]

Of course, if one's reference point is not the rank and file but the union bureaucracy or the 'red scare' tactics of the press, such an exaggeration is fully explicable. A hint of realism might have entered the proceedings if the circulation of **The Worker**, the National Minority Movement paper, had been considered as a partial measure of the movement's real influence. In the spring of 1926, when the movement's 'Conference of Action' claimed to represent one million workers, **The Worker** announced that it was aiming at, but had not yet reached, a fortnightly circulation of 25,000 copies![13]

The Communist Party's self-image in the trade union movement was indeed an accurate index of how it generally understood revolutionary work in the trade unions at this time:

> Take, for example, London, where for the purpose of conducting the party work its apparatus and organisation are divided into 29 local organisations under the supervision of the London Committee. In this area there are at least 500,000 trade unionists, organised within more than 4,000 local trade union branches . . . The party is handicapped, however, having only 1,400 members in London, of whom not more than 1,000 are members of trade unions, the rest being housewives and unemployed.
>
> . . . in the central industrial body of London, on the London Trades Council, with its various 125 councils sending delegates, there are 47 Communists, the fact that we have managed to get not only into 125 local Trades Councils but have also managed to get out of their 125 delegates 47 Communists, you will agree that our work is well directed and effective. I want you to take this as proof of the effective, well co-ordinated, well-organised fraction work in London.[14]

The problem with the party's interpretation of its work was not only that it mistook delegates on trades councils (positions far removed from the rank and file at the point of production) as evidence of major industrial strength. It also tended to equate its periphery of trade union support with political influence for the party, and see events such as Red Friday as an example of its political power.

Around every interventionist Marxist party there are those workers who, though not full members, sympathise with revolutionary ideas and would agree with nine out of ten points in a political programme ranging from Marxist theory to international and domestic policies. These are a party's immediate source of recruitment and growth. There are others, often greater in number, who — as workers facing the boss — are ready to fight. They may well *disagree* with nine out of ten points in the party programme but are willing to *act* on party industrial initiatives. An even more diffuse source of support may come from some who attend union branches and are only prepared to vote for left-wing resolutions or delegates rather than acting themselves.

These peripheries do not remain static. In periods of struggle many passive trade unionists will become militants; many militants may move towards a more generalised understanding of society, and so on. At other times the party's emphasis may have to be limited to the direct periphery of political sympathisers. While the situation may shift, the important distinction between these groups should not be forgotten. This is essential, for it is on the basis of the different political weights of each of these layers that an assessment of appropriate tactics is made — how to build the party, what forward industrial initiatives can be taken.

In 1926 the CPGB combined a blindness to the distinction between these peripheries with a confusion between bureaucratic positions and real rank-and-file influence. The result was a complete inability to make the fine tactical judgements that were required.

The party's attitude to its own trade union officials also revealed problems, as is shown in this testimony from George Hardy, leading Communist Party member and acting secretary of the National Minority Movement in 1926:

> We must work with our comrades to seek and obtain influential positions in the trade union movement. But there is a tendency, on the part of some of the other comrades, that when our comrades obtain these positions . . . they commence fault-finding with party members who are trade union leaders. We have two perspectives arising on this question.
>
> On the one hand [we] try to bring non-Communist left-wing union officials closer to the Communist point of view, by being very lenient with them, by being very persuasive, by long discussions, by trying to influence them in every way. Yet, on the other hand, when our party members become trade union officials, there is a tendency sometimes to say: 'Now that you are a Communist trade union official, you must do as we lay down, and every part of our policy must be put into operation.'
> Comrades, this is an impossibilist attitude towards trade union officials who are Communists. We must not put the comrades in an impossible position. The attitude will lose influence for the party . . . A Communist trade union official, loaded up with details, who even drifts away from the party line, should not be regarded because of this alone as a hopeless right-winger.[15]

The Scarborough Congress of the TUC, following closely on from Red Friday and the Second Minority Movement Conference, reinforced every one of the illusions. The militant speeches of Swales and company, the resolutions in favour of factory committees, against imperialism and interference in Germany, seemed to confirm everything that the Communist Party said about its own influence and the sincerity of the lefts on the General Council. Murphy, for example, wrote:

> When Swales delivered his opening speech the real temper of the Congress began to manifest itself. The more militant he became the more the delegates responded to his fighting challenge.

As the Congress proceeded not everything went exactly the way of the lefts but:

> Then came a welcome change. Young comrade Josephs of the Garment Workers moved that the trade unions should aim at the overthrow of capitalism and set to work to create factory committees as the unifying machinery for the workers in their struggles. Pollitt seconded. I heard that Thomas could not go against the resolution because he had instructions from his delegation to vote for it.
> A compositor supported the resolution, and then a miner, Sexton, amidst laughter from the Congress, tried to scotch the resolution by describing it as a Communist plot. Congress on a card vote declared for the ending of capitalism.[16]

That the Communist Party could believe the union bureaucrats would seriously attempt to build a powerful factory committee movement, let alone abolish capitalism, showed how far they had drifted since the founding of the party. Even the Second Congress of the Comintern, which underestimated the importance of rank-and-file organisation as an independent force in workers' struggle, had still visualised factory committees as a base from which the bureaucracy could be fought within the unions. But it had never suggested that trade union leaders could be induced to build such organisations, for obvious reasons. Bureaucrats might find it convenient to pass worthy resolutions, they might even be induced to tolerate tame stewards' organisations as long as they served as channels for official instructions, helped recruitment and the collection of subscriptions. But they were not in the business of undermining their own authority by restructuring the union movement from the bottom upwards! The factory committee resolution remained a dead letter.

The true test of bureaucratic conferences has always been their willingness to act on concrete and immediate issues, but the Communist Party did not see any significance in the fact that the recent unofficial strike of seamen was almost totally ignored at Scarborough. This was a particularly scandalous episode, with the seamen's leader, Havelock Wilson, pleading with the employers to *cut* the wages of his members. This is what he said to the employers:

> It is better for us to suggest a reduction (and when I say that is what we suggest, I want you to understand that this is our offer) and we advise you strongly to accept it. Well, that is the position. So we offer you the £1.[17]

Only the Minority Movement had put any effort into aiding the striking seamen, but the Scarborough conference preferred to show solidarity with its own kind, and passed over Havelock Wilson's behaviour in silence.

Red Friday and Scarborough did have the appearance of left triumphs. But the same could not be said of the Labour Party's Liverpool Conference at the end of September 1925. This was a scene of vicious anti-Communist witch-hunting at which the 'good proletarians' of the General Council remained enigmatically silent, and watched their 'comrades' get hammered.

The government was quick to take its cue from the evident lack of support for the Communist Party among Labour movement leaders and arrested twelve of its leading members, including Gallacher, Pollitt, Campbell, Bell, Murphy and MacManus. Despite, or perhaps because of, their spirited political defence and exposure of the political bias of the judiciary, several of them were given sentences that ensured they were behind bars when the coal subsidy ran out.

The bitter anti-Red attacks made at the Labour conference had been seen before, and similarly the 'lefts' had stayed silent before. There had been, for example, fewer official messages of support to the Second National Minority Movement Conference than to the first. This had been explained away not by the fact that the radicalism of the lefts was merely skin-deep, but that they were so serious in their revolutionary ardour that anything (such as association with a vocal minority) which might impede their mission of mass struggle had to be avoided:

Some prominent trade union leaders who sent telegrams of support to the Minority Movement conference last year refrained from doing so this year.

We can understand the reasons. Firstly, the fact that the press set up a howl after Red Friday has frightened the trade union right wing, who have communicated their fear to some of the lefts. Secondly, some of the lefts, recognising that a struggle is bound to come with the employers, believe that they will mobilise the workers for the struggle more easily if they are not openly identified with the Reds of the Minority Movement.

The Communist Party's answer to them was:

So follow the Minority lead and be not afraid.[18]

Ridiculous though this argument was, it was dredged up as an explanation of events at Liverpool:

Was all that has been written and spoken about the leftward trend of the working class simply a delusion? . . . The big trade union leaders were scared stiff by the anti-Red clamour of the press. They believe that they are on the eve of heavy struggle and that the less association that they have with the 'Reds' the more public sympathy they will get and the better able they will be to rally their forces.[19]

Harry Pollitt's explanation was even more ingenious:

He said the left-wing were silent at Liverpool because it was obvious to them that they had only two alternatives: Liberalism of the [Labour Party] executive committee, or Communism. They were not ready to accept Communism fully. We must redouble our work.[20]

Nonsensical though this logic was, it was rigorously applied to the 'lefts' to explain every failing or omission right from the summer of 1925 to the General Strike and even beyond.

The events of late 1925 did however elicit a serious and important political debate within the Communist Party, during which it sought to rationalise its current approach to the working-class movement and the turn-round in policy that had been made since the founding of the party. The theory of the 'general staff of labour' had moved from the margins of party thinking in the early 1920s to occupy an ever more important place. Although always false, its origins lay in a recognition of the need for centralised working-class leadership, as opposed to the shop stewards' total reliance on spontaneity.

In the early days of the theory it had at least been understood that the party itself would have to fill the leading posts with its own members, or very close sympathisers, if a genuine leadership was to be created. But in 1925 the sense of urgent struggle, the founding of the Anglo-Russian trade union committee, Red Friday and Scarborough had finally dispelled even this qualification to the slogan of 'More Power to the General Council!' '*All* power' to the likes of Swales and Hicks *as well as* right-wingers Thomas and Pugh (for were they not on the General Council too?) was only a step away now.

Chapter Twelve

THE LEFT-WING MOVEMENT

A COUNTERPART to the Minority Movement in the unions was the
Left-Wing Movement established in the Labour Party at the end of
1925. Before discussing this movement, let us sketch the attitude
of the CPGB to the Labour Party.

Lenin had argued, at the Second Congress of the Communist
International, that the Labour Party was a *bourgeois* party:

> Of course, most of the Labour Party's members are working men.
> However, whether or not a party is really a political party of the
> workers does not depend solely upon a membership of workers but
> also upon the men that lead it, and the content of its action and its
> political tactics. Only that determines whether we really have before
> us a political party of the proletariat. Regarded from this, the only
> correct point of view, the Labour Party is a thoroughly bourgeois
> party, because, although made up of workers, it is led by reactionaries,
> and the worst kind of reactionaries at that, who act quite in the spirit
> of the bourgeoisie. It is an organisation of the bourgeoisie, which
> exists to systematically dupe the workers.[1]

Lenin believed that the Communist Party should try to affiliate to the Labour Party on a short-term basis. He was rightly trying
to counter the ultra-left tendency of some Communists who saw no
point in relating to reformist organisations. He ended his speech
with the following words:

> If the British Communist Party starts by acting in a revolutionary
> manner in the Labour Party, and if the Hendersons* are obliged to
> expel this party, that will be a great victory for the communist and
> revolutionary working-class movement in Britain.[2]

---

*Arthur Henderson was leader of the Labour Party during the First World
War.

When the Communist Party accepted Lenin's suggestion that they apply for Labour Party membership (by 100 votes to 85 at its founding congress) there was a risk that at least some of the members would see in this a means to accommodation with Labour, not the way of an open offensive against it. This was especially true of the ex-BSP group who made up the majority of the membership of the CPGB. After all, the BSP had been affiliated to the Labour Party from its inception. And as BSP activity had been largely limited to parliamentary and municipal propaganda, the danger was severe. The affiliation of the Communist Party could be the slippery slope to opportunism.

Much depended on the clarity of the membership in undertaking the manoeuvre. Unfortunately, those who argued for affiliation at the Communist Unity Convention do not seem to have understood Lenin's position at all. One recurring argument ran like this:

> Let us see that we unceasingly carried out our task, until such time as the Labour Party became a Labour Party with a Communist mind — and this could be done, for what we said today our Labour leaders would have to say to-morrow — and inscribed on the Labour Party banner were the sickle and the hammer.[3]

Lenin, in his speech at the Comintern Second Congress, explicitly rejected the BSP view of the Labour Party, and argued against William MacLaine, the BSP delegate who

> called the Labour Party the political organisation of the trade union movement, and later repeated the statement when he said that the Labour Party is 'the political expression of the workers organised in trade unions'. I have met the same view several times in the paper of the British Socialist Party. It is erroneous.[4]

Future developments would show that Lenin's worry that the ex-BSP members would accommodate to the Labour Party was not without foundation. After 1920 Communist Party attempts to affiliate had been rebuffed regularly at every Labour Party Conference. But the ability of the Communists to work within local branches and through the unions at national conference meant that they could not be driven out so easily. Despite lack of success the focus had gradually shifted from a short sharp tactic of exposing the reformist leaders to one where the Labour Party was seen as open to conquest in the same way as the unions were supposed to be. It could be won not solely by earning the support of the rank and file, but actually gaining control of the machine.

Perhaps the seeds of this degeneration had been present from the first. Even when the Communist Party adopted Lenin's affiliation strategy it is doubtful if it had the clarity and firmness to lead its disparate membership into this difficult struggle for revolutionary ideas within a deeply reformist party. The danger was that it would lose more to the influence of this reformist milieu than it gained in recruits for the revolution.

The campaign for affiliation soon ceased to be a temporary manoeuvre and became accepted as valid in itself. Already in 1922 **The Communist** carried an article which said:

> The Communist Party wants to be able to advocate the working-class programme on an equal footing with any other party, before the whole proletariat . . . and it cannot do this effectively outside the all-embracing working-class organisation — the Labour Party. Naturally it is willing, once inside, to accept the decisions and abide by the rules of that organisation.[5]

The introduction of the united front slogan was wrongly interpreted by many as a justification for such an approach. At the Fourth Comintern Congress the British party 'came in for a little rough handling' on this account, and Murphy, who as an ex-SLP member had always had a much harder attitude towards the Labour Party than the ex-BSP members, agreed:

> Running throughout the party appears to be the notion that the party exists only to become a left wing of the Labour Party, that we ought not to criticise its leaders, that everything should be submerged to the idea of getting the Labour Party into power via parliament. In addition there are many pursuing a policy of hiding the fact that it is the Communist Party which is giving a lead; they object to programmes for the unions or other labour organisations going forward in the name of the party . . . I have looked through the election material of members of the party, and in many cases it would be difficult to discover from the printed matter issued that they were members of the party.[6]

The election of the first Labour government threw Palme Dutt, as editor of **Workers' Weekly**, off balance. Thus on 8 February 1924 he wrote: 'We are not fighting against the Labour government, which it is our concern to uphold and sustain against the attacks of the bourgeoisie.'[7] A week later he had to carry this stinging reply from Murphy:

> . . . if the voice of working-class criticism is silenced because Labour is in office while in a minority in parliament, and pursuing a Liberal policy, how are we to develop the class-consciousness of the workers and free them from the snares of capitalist Liberalism? It seems to me that this would be a surrender of the revolutionary movement to MacDonald on a par with Macdonald's surrender of the Labour Party to Nationalism.[8]

Most of the party needed very little persuasion to accept this when they saw the Labour government in operation, at one time threatening to use troops against a dockers' strike. Murphy's argument is as valid today as it was in 1924.

Although Palme Dutt's uncritical support for the MacDonald government was ridiculed, the fact that a leading member of the CPGB could suggest such a policy at all illustrated the party's weaknesses.

By 1925 the party had drifted rightwards once more. As with the trade union movement, so now in the Labour Party 'good proletarians' (the Labour Party equivalent of the General Council 'lefts') could do the job of leading the working class politically. The role of the Communist Party in all of this was seen as providing the energy and organising thrust behind developments. In other words the Communist Party was, as with the unions, adopting a 'ginger group' approach, seeking to use the revolutionary political pressure of its supporters to force the left leaders to lead inside the Labour Party.

Hence it was becoming increasingly difficult to separate the Communist Party's approach to the Labour Party from that to the unions. The party no longer saw the class struggle in the workplace as being the most important guideline for its work, but differences between left and right official leaders. The gap between the bureaucracy and the rank and file, and the fact that the former were functionally locked into the perpetuation of the capitalist system, was overlooked. Exactly the same method of analysis could be applied to the Labour Party, but in this organisation it had even more bizarre consequences since the Communist Party also claimed to be a political party in direct competition with Labour.

There was, however, a *qualitative* difference between the trade unions and the Labour Party. It was not so much a matter of ideology. The vast majority of the members and leaders in both organisations were reformists of one sort or another. But the trade unions, whatever the ideas of the membership or the leaders, are organisations linked to collective struggle. Their ultimate source of strength lies in the creative capacity of workers at the point of production. Trade unions therefore have a relationship with the class struggle.

The Labour Party's function then, as now, was quite different. This was notwithstanding the fact that its base consisted of practically the same people as the trade unions (with the addition of some middle-class elements not eligible for union membership, but these did not make a decisive difference at the time). In the leadership of the party were many prominent union leaders who doubled as members of parliament. Thomas and Purcell were examples. But the Labour Party existed to win elections and hoped by doing so to push reforms through parliament. True, the 1924 experience of Labour in government was an unmitigated disaster, but still hope sprang eternal that next time would be better.

Despite the fact that Labour's principal financial support was its affiliated trade union membership, the party had no direct relationship with the point of production. The bureaucracy signed the cheques and cast the block votes at conference, not the rank and file. Further, the ordinary union member's connection with the party was either totally passive (a few minutes spent putting a cross on a ballot form every few years) or at best consisted in canvassing during election campaigns with the idea of attracting as many voters as possible.

Thus despite the overlap of membership and leaders the unions and Labour Party were functionally separate and subject to very different influences. The workplace and the polling booth confront people in different ways, the one as members of the working class in a collective unit, the other as individual citizens of the national state. For these reasons revolutionaries cannot have the same approach to trade unions and the Labour Party. One is the mass organisation *of* the working class, the other claims to be a mass organisation *acting on behalf of* the working class.

The Communist Party did not see things in this light by 1925. In the unions the National Minority Movement pushed the Purcells and others forwards. In the Labour Party this job was to be done by a 'Left-Wing Movement'. Just as the Communist Party abdicated leadership to the General Council lefts, so by putting all its efforts into a party tied to bourgeois parliament it was giving way in political terms to left reformism.

The distance the party had travelled on this road was clarified by Palme Dutt in an article of May 1925, though he still wrote in very radical terms:

> The new revolutionary tasks, the revolutionary approach to the fundamental conceptions of State, Democracy, Empire, War, the need of a revolutionary mass party — these are not yet understood. And until they begin to be understood the Left Wing beats against the wall of its own limits.
>
> *These limits must be broken down* . . . To raise the Left Wing to revolutionary consciousness — this is the supreme task.

He concluded:

> *The development of the Left Wing is not only the key to the development of the Communist Party; the development of the Communist Party is also the key to the development of the Left Wing.*[9]

The successful overthrow of capitalism in Britain will need the mass of left-wing Labour supporters to be won to revolutionary ideas. But this cannot be done by seeking to become a permanent faction in an organisation dedicated irrevocably to winning power through parliament. A programme of raising revolutionary consciousness among a mass of reformists is only possible through real class struggle. Thus the centre of the fight has to be the collective struggle of the workers, not their votes in a ballot box.

Just as the TUC 'lefts' had never intended their wild-cat speeches to be anything more than useful bargaining counters and spurned direct association with the as yet irresponsible 'firebrands' in the Minority Movement, so the prominent Labour Party lefts steered clear of involvement in the Communists' Left-Wing Movement. The campaign for its formation was launched through a new paper, **The Sunday Worker**. This included several leading party members, such as William Paul and Tommy Jackson, on its editorial staff. In circulation terms, the paper was an astounding success, selling a regular 85,000 copies.

The paper at once got down to the business of organising the Left-Wing Movement. In the run-up to the Liverpool Labour Party Conference of 1925, it carried an article by Purcell which said the conference must be the unification of our movement. Every element of the Left-Wing and Communist section that can give the Labour Party an additional ounce of strength must be enrolled at once.[10]

Nothing daunted by the fact that Purcell and company did not use an ounce of strength to defend the revolutionary left at Liverpool, the paper went on to organise a meeting of 'well known trade union leaders, Labour MPs, members of the Plebs League, the Communist Party and ILP.' There William Paul moved a resolution which began:

> While warning the workers against any attempt whatsoever to form a new party, it thought that no barrier should prevent united action.

It then enunciated the principles behind the Left-Wing Movement:

1) World trade union unity.
2) National trade union unity from the factory to the General Council.
3) Solidarity between British labour and the oppressed peoples of the Empire.
4) A policy for the next Labour government aiming at overthrow of the capitalist class.
5) Self-defence against fascism.[11]

Hicks nervously seconded the motion, explaining that he did so purely on the grounds that he thought it worthy of debate. But the ensuing row, which featured former Communist Party members such as Raymond Postgate, Frank Horrabin and Alf Purcell, meant that it had to be adjourned:

> Postgate said he thought it very unwise to try and pass the resolution and argued that only a general discussion should take place. He was supported by J F Horrabin and two Members of Parliament who argued that a Left Wing that included the Communists would not be very successful. A A Purcell was afraid that the resolution would lead to the formation of a separate organisation within the Labour movement.[12]

In 1923 Purcell had demanded his pound of flesh from the Communist Party in return for a little radical rhetoric on the trade union front. But now the Labour lefts were even more avaricious. When, as a result of the Liverpool Conference, the Labour Party moved towards expelling its troublesome Communist supporters, Frank Horrabin demanded that since the Communist Party consisted of people wanting to build inside the Labour Party they should 'face the existing situation, resign that membership and remain in the Labour Party as left-wingers.'

He was evidently incensed by the idea that *he* might be called upon to defend Communists from expulsion. These victims of a right-wing witch-hunt, he said,

> have no right to throw the onus of taking action with regard to the expulsion decision on the Left-Wing comrades inside the Labour Party.[13]

This tells us something of the calibre of such 'Left-Wing comrades'. But Pollitt's reply to Horrabin's spineless attitude was hardly more forthright:

> No, Frank, we are not going either to resign from, or to liquidate the Communist Party . . . I tell Comrade Horrabin straight away that without the Communist Party there cannot be any organised Left-Wing inside the Labour Party . . .
> But what I do accept that what is wanted now is for all those of us who are dissatisfied with Liverpool, and who are anxious for a real genuine organised Left-Wing Movement to get together.[14]

And so the campaign for the Left-Wing Movement rolled on, and with it the identity of the Communist Party became weaker and weaker. Saklatvala, a Communist Party member who was elected MP on a Labour Party ticket, wrote that the chief danger was that the Labour Party might be contaminated by the sort of attitudes held by the Liberal Party. Therefore:

> Any new separate party of Left-Wingers would be a convenient surrender to the right-wing leaders and a splendid weapon to place in the hands of the reactionaries . . . despite the Liberalising agencies at work in the Labour Party there are, thank goodness, more powerful agencies determined that the Labour Party shall become a Workers' Party.[15]

If a 'separate party of Left-Wingers' was a weapon in the hands of the reactionaries then how did Saklatvala see the Communist Party? Obviously more as a wing of the Labour Party than as a revolutionary organisation with a goal all of its own.

In February 1926, in a series of articles on 'What is this Left Wing?', Willie Paul outlined how, when Labour came to power on a socialist programme (such as anti-imperialism, nationalisation, workers' control and a levy on capital), the government would be bound to its promises:

> We know that it may be almost impossible to get the present right-wing leaders of the Labour Party to carry out the socialist policy we have outlined . . . [So we must pass resolutions that] clearly state that any future Labour premier and Cabinet should be elected at a specially summoned joint conference of the Labour Party and Trade Unions.[16]

Any resemblance to political organisations of the mid-1980s and their programmes is by no means accidental.

It was tragic that the Communist Party should lose faith in itself as a revolutionary party in outright opposition to reformist politics. But there were powerful forces pushing it in this mistaken direction.

Chapter Thirteen

VIEWS FROM OUTSIDE: TROTSKY AND THE COMINTERN

THE DRIFT of the CPGB towards tailing the left bureaucracy of the unions and Labour Party can be seen partly as a result of the Comintern's confused policies, as well as the mistakes of the British Communists themselves. The orientation of the International compounded the political weaknesses of the CPGB instead of correcting its course, and this was particularly marked after ill-health forced the departure of Lenin from the scene.

Pressure from the Comintern came in two ways. On the trade union front the promotion of an unprincipled international unity, at any cost, led to the Anglo-Russian Trade Union Unity Committee. This deal gagged criticism of the trade union bureaucracy as a whole. For as Losovsky made clear, to ask anything of the officials might jeopardise the cordial relations the Russian state bureaucracy wished to foster:

> To go to the reformists and say: 'Refuse to go into coalition with the bourgeoisie', means that we demand from them the impossible, and we should know beforehand that the reformists cannot accept such a proposal . . . we know what an abyss divides the reformists from us Communists . . . but nevertheless, we propose the calling of an international congress.[1]

There was no common ground yet the Communists wanted an agreement. Obviously this could be bought only by abandoning the revolutionary principles that made the reformists hostile.

This thoroughly opportunist position was disguised by a lot of left rhetoric about the right-wing union leaders being 'social fascists'. At RILU's Third Congress in 1924 Losovsky announced that 'three-quarters of the reformist trade union leaders have become fascist'.[2] This nonsense was used as a smokescreen to excuse the alliance with the left bureaucrats which, because it committed the latter to nothing, was worthless.*

The second area in which the Comintern spread confusion was concerning the role and significance of the revolutionary party. At the Fifth Congress of the Comintern in June/July 1924 Zinoviev, referring to the CPGB and its leaders, such as Bob Stewart and Arthur MacManus, made this cryptic comment:

> In England, we are now going through the beginning of a new chapter in the labour movement. We do not know whether the Communist Mass Party of England will come, whether only through the Stewart-MacManus door — or through some other door. And it is entirely possible, comrades, that the Communist Mass Party may still appear through still another door — we cannot lose sight of that fact.[3]

Zinoviev was looking for a short cut. By talking of this mysterious 'other door', he implied that a mass revolutionary party could be built by the current around the Labour and TUC lefts. This ludicrous notion, that left reformist bureaucrats would somehow play a role with which they did not agree and which meant their own dethronement, led away from the construction of a conscious revolutionary organisation.

This tendency was, however, well disguised. Zinoviev talked a lot about the 'Bolshevisation' of the various Communist Parties, which in actual fact meant subordination to the dictates of Moscow. The truth was that in regard to Britain he was abandoning the Bolshevik tradition of the revolutionary party.

In the whole of the international Communist movement the only major figure to stand out against the drift towards Stalinism, and maintain a Marxist analysis of the British situation, was Leon Trotsky. He was able to do this notwithstanding his poor sources of information. Indeed, he was in many ways misinformed since, as we have seen, the British Communist Party had no more understanding of major political events such as Red Friday or the Scarborough TUC than they did of their own role and influence.

This meant that some of Trotsky's formulations were wrong or telescoped events. He especially exaggerated the subjective preparedness of the Communist forces, thus thinking revolution far closer than it was. Marxism does not claim to be infallible; what it does is use a scientific theory of society, coupled with an ability to

---

*The theory of social fascism had not been developed at this time, but was to become the cornerstone of the ultra-left turn made by the Comintern in 1928.

learn from the class war, to correct mistakes and enhance the
intervention of revolutionaries in the struggle for socialism. This
correct use of the Marxist method shines out of Trotsky's writings
on Britain in the mid-1920s.

His first concern was to reassert the central importance of
building a party of revolutionaries committed to the overthrow of
capitalism. This ran directly contrary to Zinoviev's hints that there
might be some easier and less painful path to workers' power
through alliances with reformist leaders:

> The Communist Party will . . . be able to take the lead of the working
> class only insofar as it enters into an implacable conflict with the
> conservative bureaucracy and the Labour Party. The Communist
> Party can prepare itself for the leading role only by a ruthless criticism
> of all the leading staff of the British labour movement.[4]

Trotsky ended his important book **Where is Britain Going?**
(1925) with these words which must be read as a polemic against
Zinoviev:

> The whole world situation and the role of the British proletariat in
> production and in society will guarantee its victory — on condition
> that there is a correct and resolute revolutionary leadership. The
> Communist Party must develop and come to power as the party of
> proletarian dictatorship. There are no ways round this. Whoever
> believes there are, and propounds them, can only deceive British
> workers. This is the main conclusion of our analysis.[5]

Trotsky insisted again and again on the dangers of tailing the
left bureaucrats or minimising the importance of building a revolutionary party. Thus in January 1926 he wrote:

> The ideological and organisational formation of a genuinely revolu-
> tionary, that is of a communist, party . . . is conceivable only under
> the condition of a perpetual, systematic, inflexible, untiring and
> irreconcilable unmasking of the quasi-left leaders of every hue, of
> their compromises and of their reticence. It would be the crudest
> blunder to think . . . that the task of the struggle for a united front
> consists in obtaining a victory for Purcell, Lansbury, Wheatley and
> Kirkwood* over Snowden, Webb and MacDonald.[6]

---

*Lansbury, Wheatley and Kirkwood were the current heroes of the left in
the Labour Party.

Trotsky made absolutely no concession to any of the left bureaucrats, not even to Cook, who was the most radical of them. He always mentioned Cook in the same breath as Hicks, Purcell and the other lefts. For example on 5 March 1926 he wrote:

> Both the rights and the lefts, including of course both Purcell and Cook, fear to the utmost the beginning of the *dénouement*. Even when they in words admit the inevitability of struggle and revolution, they are hoping in their hearts for some miracle that will release them from these perspectives. And in any event they themselves will stall, evade, temporise, shift responsibility and effectively assist Thomas over any really major question of the *British* labour movement.[7]

Trotsky saw straight through the tinsel and glitter of the Scarborough TUC that had so mesmerised Murphy:

> The resolutions of the congress were the more to the left the further removed they were from immediate practical tasks . . . to think that the leading figures at Scarborough might become the leaders of a revolutionary overthrow of power would be to lull oneself with illusions . . . It must be clearly understood: this sort of leftism remains only as long as it does not impose any practical obligations. As soon as a question of action arises the lefts respectfully surrender the leadership to the rights.[8]

This was written months before the betrayal of the General Strike on 13 May 1926 which so astounded British socialists!

Trotsky's analysis did not mean that the Communist Party should merely criticise from the sidelines, however. It had to intervene, but in a principled and clear way:

> The trade unions are the main mass organisations in Britain. But the struggle for influence with the masses organised in these unions should in no case lead to bowing down before the conservative forms of trade unions in the spirit of completely opportunistic tail-ending formations. The more rapid the revolutionary development in Britain and the more sharply new organisational forms (shop stewards, action committees) are counterposed to the old ones, not in circumvention of the trade unions but based on them — the more attention the British Communists should pay to the formation and development of new organisational forms based on the mass movement.[9]

A strategy for the Minority Movement which led *away* from dependence on the official union machine is evidently suggested here.

There might, on the other hand, be a case for creating a united front with left bureaucrats as long as the purpose and limitations of this are understood. For this argument Trotsky used Lenin as his authority:

> Lenin allowed the possibility of a temporary bloc even with opportunist leaders under the condition that there would be a sharp and audacious turn and a break based on the actions of the masses when these leaders began to pull back, oppose or betray.[10]

But as Trotsky went on to stress, at no time are the needs of the working class or the revolutionary party to be subordinated to maintaining such a bloc.

We can see how Trotsky understood the united front in his treatment of the Anglo-Russian Trade Union Unity Committee. The quality of his analysis stands out even though he ultimately changed his mind about the value of establishing the committee in the first place. In July 1926 he wrote the following:

> We were absolutely correct to conclude this alliance when we did, but in order to turn it against the opportunists; in order to push vacillating leaders forward as far as possible; and in order to expose them and break with them in the event of their betrayal.[11]*

Yet even at this time Trotsky was insistent that the committee could only be strictly temporary and a means to expose the bureaucrats through their failure to honour their radical promises. He was therefore appalled when the Russian leaders decided to keep the committee going even after the betrayal of the General Strike.

By 1928, if not before, it was clear to Trotsky that the strategy of the joint committee had been false all along, not so much for formal reasons, but because the intention of its Russian creators had *never* been to use the committee as a united front to *enhance* the revolutionary struggle in Britain:

> The point of departure of the Anglo-Russian Committee, as we have already seen, was the impatient urge to leap over the young and too

---

*This resolution was also signed by Zinoviev, Kamenev, Pyatakov and Krupskaya, and it is possible that Trotsky's argument was tailored to fit these people. However, Trotsky argued the same thing — that it was correct to establish the Anglo-Russian Trade Union Unity Committee — elsewhere at this time, and it seems likely therefore that this was his considered opinion.

slowly developing communist party. This invested the entire experience with a false character even prior to the general strike.[12]

On every major question in British politics preceding the General Strike, Trotsky offered by far the best approach available. His brilliant characterisation of the intellectual shallowness, religiosity and vacillating nature of the MacDonalds and Thomases is as fresh today as it ever was. Furthermore, it is just as appropriate to their modern equivalents as it was in 1925 and 1926. Trotsky saw straight through the seeming differences between these right-wing reformists and the more left-sounding George Lansbury in the Labour Party, or union leaders such as Cook, Purcell and Hicks. Beneath the appearance he divined the common reformist and bureaucratic ties.

Though incorrect in some details, Trotsky's penetrating analysis overcame the great geographical distance and paucity of information which cut him off from Britain. His skill came from the depth of his Marxism. Unlike so many who were caught up in the degeneration of the Russian revolution, Trotsky kept a firm grasp of the two fundamental lessons of Bolshevism — that a victorious struggle depended on the leadership which only a revolutionary party could offer, and that the emancipation of the working class could not come through bureaucrats, however radical they might sound, but only through the activity of the working class itself. There was no other way, however much the Communist Party leaders in London and Moscow would have preferred it.

In the faction fight that was fought in the Russian Communist Party and the International, the British sided with the majority Stalinist faction and so Trotsky's advice was not taken. The result was tragic. The period from the foundation of the British Communist Party to 1926 was filled with many events — Black Friday 1921, the engineers' lockout of 1922, the founding of the Minority Movement, Red Friday among others. At each point there were tactical choices to be made. These could have been decided in a Marxist direction, but unfortunately they were all too often influenced by the weak leadership of Zinoviev and later by Stalin. This was to be a determining factor in the development of the CPGB. If Trotsky and the Bolshevik tradition he represented had led the Comintern there is no doubt that many mistaken judgements would not have been made. The opportunities for building a healthy Marxist party in Britain certainly existed, but they were simply not taken as a result.

Chapter Fourteen

TIME RUNS OUT FOR THE COMMUNIST PARTY

SINCE ITS foundation in 1920 a curious process had taken a grip of the CPGB. In political theory the party had been in retreat. The leading role of the revolutionary party in its policies had given way on the industrial front to the TUC General Council, while the political break with reformism had been glossed over. Now the party was in the position which sections of the British left have been in ever since (and with no more likelihood of success): it was attempting to give the thoroughly reformist and parliamentary Labour Party a radical face. The class struggle, while still the party's central concern, was coming to be seen more and more as the casting of block votes by bureaucrats at conferences.

The odd thing about this theoretical retreat was that the Communist leaders actually felt they had made considerable progress. The discovery of centralised organisation and disciplined common action, the use of the party newspaper as an agitational weapon, the establishment of factory branches and a day-to-day contact with the industrial rank and file — all these things were indeed tremendous practical advances considering the history of the revolutionary left in Britain. But the Communist Party leaders did not derive their satisfaction from these achievements. It was the big numbers and big events that most impressed them — the considerable circulation for the paper that promoted the Left-Wing Movement, the one million represented at the National Minority Movement Conference, the combined power of the General Council and the Russian union leaders, and 'their' Red Friday.

That they saw these things as the chief and most meaningful advances for the British working class showed how far the party had slipped into the bureaucratic and reformist way of analysing events. In 1925 party theory had to be reworked to give a coherent justification for such attitudes. The centrist theory that emerged is still very much with us in the British labour movement today. It was a theory which explained why the avowed reformists of the left of the TUC and Labour Party were going to lead the working class to revolution in spite of themselves. The analysis also had to locate a function for the Communist Party, as a strongly organised body of people who saw themselves as revolutionaries, within this overall process.

J T Murphy once more showed his aptitude for theory, but now, in 1925, it was dedicated to a political outlook very different from that of wartime or the early years of the party. Murphy analysed the general trends in the British labour movement as follows:

> The working class is awakening and the fierce discussions raging throughout the Labour Party are . . . the manifestations of life and vitality, a class thinking over the ways and means to reach the goal it has set before it. It is out of this process in the Labour Party and the trade unions, which are the basic material of the Labour Party, that our party, the majority of whose members are inseparable from the Labour Party by virtue of their union membership, will grow to a mass Communist Party.[1]

This process of advance the bureaucratic leaders were powerless to oppose:

> It is one of the greatest ironies of history that the very people who are fiercest in the denunciation of the Communist Party, which contains the politics of the October Revolution, are repeatedly pushed into circumstances which compel them, time and again, to say and do the things which the Communist Party says are necessary.
>
> For example, Mr Bevin was exceptionally loud-mouthed in his denunciation of the Communist Party . . . We are not worried about Mr Bevin's personal feelings for us. More important than Mr Bevin is the fact that the unions, in order to defend their interests, got together and in the process proved the soundness of our revolutionary theories [on Red Friday].[2]

And according to Palme Dutt, in the inexorable march of history trade union officials will be made

> to recognise the necessity of class unity against the capitalist attack, and in addition are forced more and more to recognise the necessity of winning into their hands the organisation and control of industry.[3]

Of course if you see no distinction between bureaucrats and the rank and file, then if the workers are forced by crisis to move left, so too must the bureaucrats in equal measure. The General Strike was soon to confound this idea absolutely.

A little problem remained. The new theory did not seem able to explain the vicious attack made on the left at the Liverpool Labour Conference. However, it proved quite adaptable. The Labour right might resist the onward advance of the workers but they would soon have to yield to the left. Palme Dutt explained:

> . . . as soon as a change of conditions brings a real emergence and intensification of class struggle in Britain, it is natural that the class struggle, revealing itself first in its primitive economic forms without relation to political consciousness, should meet with heavy opposition and obstruction within the Labour Party . . . but must eventually win its way forward, within the ranks of the Labour Party.[4]

A mechanical faith in progress is a necessary assumption for those who tail left bureaucrats in unions or reformist parties. If they made a concrete analysis of events or remembered past betrayals too well they would be forced to recognise the weakness of their position.

Although this much was common ground for the Communist Party leadership, the precise manner in which the inevitable force of circumstances would translate into reality was interpreted differently by Murphy and Dutt. At one point in early 1925, Palme Dutt, erratic as ever, appears to have had a brainstorm. During it he did show an insight into the need for Communists to win influence not by fawning on the bureaucratic 'lefts' but by sharply challenging them and asserting the need for revolutionary leadership. In some respects his arguments were most effective and in startling contrast to everything else that the Communist Party said at this time:

> It is necessary to show that it is not sufficent to attack certain leaders, to call for a 'more energetic' policy etc., but that the supreme task is to forge in struggle an actual new leadership and a solid fighting force which can alone hew out a way for the workers. It is necessary to show that the Labour Party and the trade unions are by their nature *incapable* of leading the struggle of the working class in the present period, and in relation to the actual forces of the bourgeoisie and that such an effective struggle can only be waged by a solid phalanx of

workers fighting under a united revolutionary lead such as can only be realised in a mass Communist Party. It is necessary to conduct such a criticism of every individual 'left' leader, and of every halting uncertain semi-revolutionary advance, at the same time as pressing forward action to the utmost, as to compel the realisation of this conclusion, alike by every measure of success and still more by every successive failure.

The role of the Communist Party becomes of special importance in relation to the 'left' leaders.

His analysis of the 'lefts' was excellent:

> . . . so far as ideology and expression go, none of these left elements have so far shown any difference in principle from MacDonald and the right-wing.
>
> . . . at this point arises an extreme danger — the greatest danger of the coming period. It inevitably follows from the character of the left that they have not the necessary clearness or cohesion to lead, to form a united force or to carry out serious planning or preparatory work. At the same time they are easily able, owing to the weakness of revolutionary development in England, and to the authority and prestige of their positions, to win the ear of the masses with a handful of phrases and promises, and so to gather the rising movement of the masses to themselves and then to dissipate it in a comic opera fiasco.

Thus accurately predicting the events of the General Strike, he went on to pose the alternative:

> Against this danger the only safeguard of the workers is the Communist Party . . . The Communist Party must conduct an unceasing ideological warfare with the left, exposing from the outset every expression that betrays confusion, ambiguity, vain bravado, frivolousness, opposition to actual struggle and practical subjection to the right-wing. The Communist Party must press forward every direct expression of struggle to the practical tests of immediate action or preparation.[5]

Unfortunately Palme Dutt dropped his stance as quickly as he had adopted it, and it never became party policy.

The fact that after 1924 the British Communist Party lost its sense of direction — towards the building of a revolutionary party — was very much due to the influence of the Russian state bureaucracy in the Comintern. Through inexperience, the early Congresses of the Communist International had had difficulty in finding a correct policy towards trade unionism. But the importance of a party of the Bolshevik type in achieving socialist revolution was never lost sight of. After 1924, however, the Russian leadership, now a Stalinist clique, had become absorbed in bureaucratic ways of thinking. It lost the Marxist perspective of *class* struggle and sought progress not by serious revolutionary work, but through diplomatic manoeuvres and bureaucratic combinations. This new tendency communicated itself to the constituent parties of the Communist International.

This is obvious from the stance of the British Communist Party after 1924. The theoretical edifice which it built to justify its support for the left union bureaucrats and Labour lefts bore no relation whatsoever to the sort of class analysis essential to meet the needs of the working-class movement. The starting point for this must, of necessity, be the working class itself.

Although the Communist movement in the mid-1920s may have forgotten the experience of the Russian revolution, the prime lessons of that revolution are still clear.

The mass of workers *would change their consciousness only in the course of struggle, and the majority would only do so when the struggle reached revolutionary proportions.* A revolutionary party is the first and absolute essential if this process is to take place, since the overthrow of capitalism must be consciously proposed and fought for. But this is not the whole equation. Until the last minute the party is inevitably a minority of the class, since reformist ideas hold sway until the outbreak of revolution.

So as the struggle develops another body is required, an un-official organisation in which the party can argue its position among wide layers of the working class and through which the masses can transform themselves. In a crisis the class faces the immediate need to go beyond the constraints set by the bureau-cracy, which always attempts to keep struggle within the bounds of capitalism. Furthermore, since the change in ideas occurs during the heat of battle, the alternative unofficial movement must be democratic — for it must both centralise the workers' struggle and reflect their changing consciousness. It must be in constant contact with the rank and file and able to channel every change of mood instantly.

This cannot be done through official channels. Even if the best socialists could somehow win control of the top bureaucratic positions in the unions, without being corrupted along the way, the distance of the General Council from the rank and file at the point of production would make them incapable of giving the necessary leadership — leadership that reflects the highest point reached by workers' consciousness at any moment and takes it that one realistic step further. And the obstacles in the way of a reformist road to socialism through union officialdom are doubly as great when it comes to trying to change society through parliament.

The new unofficial body has to draw its delegates directly from the rank and file, organised through collective units in factories, pits and offices. Its members have to be subject to instant recall so as to reflect majority opinion as soon as it changes. Furthermore, it has to be capable of acting for itself. It cannot depend on pressurising others to act *for* the working class. It has to challenge the inevitable barrier posed by the trade union and reformist bureaucracies.

In other words, there has to be a rank-and-file movement with the potential for becoming a workers' self-governing organ — a *soviet* or workers' council. Successful leadership for the rank-and-file movement, and indeed the building of such a movement, depends on both favourable conditions and the intervention of a revolutionary party, conscious of the character of reformist leaders and the means required to overcome their influence.

Despite its numerically small membership the best service the British Communist Party could have rendered would have been to direct the attention of the vanguard of workers to the dangers of reliance on the bureaucracy and towards realistically exploring whatever independent rank-and-file initiatives were possible.

The alternative, which the party actually followed, was to lead the best fighters of the working class into a situation where the treachery of the leaders resulted not only in the general defeat of the class, but also the complete disorientation of the vanguard. No one could have asked a party of 6,000 to save the British working class single-handed. But given the party's pre-eminent position among the advanced and thinking workers, measures which built their confidence and self-reliance, combined with a Marxist understanding of the difficult period ahead, could and should have been offered.

This does not mean to say that the Communist Party were passive bystanders as the end of the coal subsidy drew near. The **Workers' Weekly** had been counting off the weeks as they slipped by; the Second National Minority Movement Conference had called for preparation, and indeed every ounce of energy was put into what the party judged as effective preparation for battle. In January 1926 the central committee laid out what was at stake:

> The miners, after the breathing space bought for the owners by the means of a subsidy, and the sham impartiality of the Coal Commission, are now threatened with an open attack on the seven-hour day, on the Miners' Federation and on wages. The owners have thrown disguise to the winds . . .
>
> These facts, taken together with the steady, if unobtrusive organisation of the OMS [the Organisation for the Maintenance of Supplies] point to a definite determination on the part of the British capitalists to prevent a repetition of Red Friday, to challenge the organised Labour movement and smash it.

The party was not about to run away. It had confidence in the potential of the working class:

> The workers can meet the capitalist attack and smash it, as on Red Friday. More: we believe that the British workers can turn their defensive into an offensive, and present a common demand for better conditions which will be the prelude to a complete victory over the capitalists.[6]

Yet the urgent measures the central committee proposed all went in the direction of the bureaucracy. Here is the complete list:

> 1. Summoning by the General Council of a *Conference of Trade Union Executives* in accordance with Scarborough decisions, to give wider powers to the General Council to lead the whole workers' industrial army.
>
> 2. In addition to the campaign for granting full executive powers to the General Council, the completion of the *Workers' Industrial Alliance*, to reinforce the workers' defensive preparations against the coming crisis, and in particular the inclusion of the NUR, AEU, Boilermakers and General Workers, etc.
>
> 3. A working agreement between the *General Council and the Co-operative Wholesale Society*, to ensure provisioning the workers, and a policy of mutual support between the two national centres of the trade union and Co-operative movements, the TUC and the Co-operative Union.
>
> 4. Formation of *Factory Committees* elected by all workers irrespective of craft or sex, in accordance with the Scarborough resolution, to

ensure unity of the workers from the bottom, and the calling by the trades councils and district committees, of conference to ensure union support for these committees.

5. A national campaign for *100 per cent trade unionism*, including a National Show Cards week . . .

6. Organisation of *Workers' Defence Corps*, composed of trade unionists, and controlled by trades councils to protect trade union liberties against the *Fascisti*, and calling upon the General Council to take steps to place the workers' case before the workers in the army, navy and air forces.

7. Formulation of a *Common Programme*, for the whole movement (£4 a week for 44 hours) supplementary to the special demands of each industry . . .

8. The strengthening of relations between the General Council and National Unemployed Workers Committee Movement in order to secure the realisation of the *unemployed* demands.[7]

Five of these eight proposals were demands for the union leaders to act. Only points 4, 5 and 6 — referring to factory committees, 100 per cent trade unionism and Workers' Defence Corps — gave any scope for rank-and-file self-activity, but as we shall see even these were not conceived of in such a way.

It was soon obvious to everyone that despite the fine words at Scarborough, the General Council was doing nothing seriously to prepare the movement. But still on 12 March 1926 the **Workers' Weekly** editorial was headed 'Let the leaders — lead' and its tone was one of pleading:

> Surely now, if ever, the Leaders of Labour must rise to the responsibilities? . . . Now or never is the time for the General Council to prove its worth and to show that it has learned, as it should have done, that in such emergencies as these the highest wisdom is the 'scorn of consequences'.

The final sentence was a threat without any teeth since the entire effort of the Communist Party was directed towards a successful official lead:

> If the leaders will not lead, the rank and file must replace them by those who will.[8]

On 21 March the Communist Party had its last opportunity to state its position at a major conference — the National Minority

Movement's special Conference of Action. The 883 delegates were claimed to represent one million workers, even though no direct shop stewards' representation was recorded. With the exception of 52 trades councils, 38 Minority Movement groups and 35 un-employed organisations, the rest of the 547 bodies spoken for were either union branches or district committees.

Far from denouncing the scandalous inactivity of the General Council, which was becoming daily more apparent, the **Workers' Weekly** opened its report of the conference in this way:

> The most unexpected event at the Minority Movement's Conference of Action on Sunday last was the presence as a platform visitor of W H Hutchison of the General Council . . . It is hoped that his guarded (but obviously sincere) approval of the conference decisions . . . is an indication that the General Council is contemplating further action in line with the Scarborough decisions.

Tom Mann's chairman's address left no room for doubt as to the dedication of the Minority Movement to the workers' cause in the coming battle:

> Let no man mistake us. We are out for militancy. We are out to fight the capitalists. And we know there is no hope unless we fight them and beat them . . . We are out for militancy; we are out for the workers, and if the hour comes we will die with them without asking anyone's help.[9]

The conference put especial emphasis on the formation of Councils of Action by the trades councils and Workers' Defence Corps; but neither of these was thought of as providing an alterna-tive to the officials. George Hardy, acting general secretary of the National Minority Movement, answered press stories about the Workers' Defence Corps:

> they imply that we are immediately going to arm the workers for a violent attack on capitalism. Nothing could be more laughably wrong . . . the Workers' Defence Corps is designed to protect trade union property, to steward meetings, defend Labour speakers at outdoor meetings, protect pickets and strike headquarters, and other such necessary activities. Most of these things have already long been done, but we want them done in an organised way. Hence Workers' Defence Corps.[10]

The Councils of Action were expected to be hardly more

challenging and were clearly seen as bodies that carried out official orders:

> The normal work of the trades council ought to be suspended or handed over to a small sub-committee of the executive. On the Council of Action should be brought representatives of every section of the movement at present outside it: trade union branches not affiliated, co-operative societies (including women's guilds), the organised unemployed, and Communist Party locals . . .
>
> Last year the General Council issued orders that coal should not be handled. Immediately they receive such instructions the council of action must see to it that pickets are out at every coal dump and railway siding.[11]

As the hour approached when the coal subsidy would end — and the coal lock-out be re-imposed, the Communist Party took comfort in its illusory faith in the General Council. Its final pre-strike editorial in **Workers' Weekly** admitted the possibility of a sell-out, but declared that: 'The TUC simply dare not do this thing.'[12]

The reasoning behind this had been explained by George Hardy some months earlier. After referring to the slogan 'All power to the General Council', he explains:

> Should they use that power wrongly, it only means that we have got another additional task before us of forcing them in the right direction, which direction they will ultimately have to take.[13]

Last-minute messages from RILU reinforced these mistaken views:

> We are confident the British trade unions and the General Council, having taken the initiative in trying to establish world trade union unity, will view with disapproval the rejection of united action in a case of such importance to the working class.[14]

Chapter Fifteen

THE TUC BLUFF IS CALLED

THERE WAS an enormous amount at stake in 1926. British capitalism was no longer the envied 'workshop of the world' as it had been fifty years previously. Despite its scramble for colonies, many rivals had grown up to challenge Britain's monopoly. A bloody world war had been fought to crush Germany, its most dangerous opponent. The British state thought it had won a great victory in 1918, but in reality the USA gained most by the mutual impoverishment of Europe's capitalisms.

Thus it was that by the mid-1920s the British ruling class *as a whole* wanted a readjustment of the economy. As in every capitalist crisis, the working class was expected to pay the price. So in some ways the battle of 1926 was no unusual event — the system has always and will always try to make the workers solve its problems. But the very depth of the crisis and scale of the struggle made 1926 exceptional. This was to be a battle of titans, with the ruling class ready to pit its combined economic, political and ideological battalions against the workers and their chief defensive organisations, the trade unions.

As we have seen, in July 1925 Baldwin had made it clear that *all* British workers had to become poorer so that he and his class could amass even more wealth. Meticulous government preparations for class war showed how the ruling class did not suffer from the blinkered sectionalism of the union leaders. It knew that if the confidence of one million miners organised in the MFGB, one-fifth of all trade unionists, remained intact, the entire offensive would fail. All their preparations were shaped by this broad class-conscious approach.

Much of the groundwork for facing an industrial emergency had been done a long time previously. The first permanent emergency machinery for maintaining services and supplies during national strikes was set up by the post-war Lloyd George government almost as soon as it took office. This was overhauled and improved in response to the national railway strike of October 1919, when a Supply and Transport Committee was formed within the Cabinet. The following year an Emergency Powers Act was enacted which gave the government wide powers in the event of a crisis. The plans were put into effect during the 1921 miners' lockout. In May 1923 J C C Davidson, who had been parliamentary private secretary to Baldwin during 1921 and 1922, was appointed Chancellor of the Duchy of Lancaster and immediately adopted the newly-created role of Chief Civil Commissioner, charged with designing 'in strict secrecy', an organisation to supply essential services in time of a general strike.[1]

When the first Labour government was formed in January 1924, Davidson was asked by another civil servant, Lancelot Storr, not to hand over the papers of the Supply and Transport Committee Organisation to the new Labour Minister, the Chancellor of the Duchy of Lancaster, Josiah Wedgwood. But his advice was ignored. However Davidson now urged Wedgwood to hold back the plans from his colleagues:

> I told him that, whoever was in power, it was his duty to protect the Constitution against a Bolshevik-inspired General Strike . . . I begged him not to destroy all I had done and not to inform his Cabinet of it. This did not concern party but was a national matter.[2]

When the Labour government went out of office and Wedgwood handed over again to Davidson, he said: 'I haven't destroyed any of your plans. In fact, I haven't done a bloody thing about them.'[3]

In fact the Labour government had used the strike-breaking machinery twice: during the dock and tram strikes called by the Transport and General Workers Union.

Red Friday made the government quickly overhaul and streamline the emergency machinery. On 6 August 1925 the Home Secretary, Sir William Joynson-Hicks, submitted a report to the Cabinet for the next national industrial dispute. The government effort would have one sole direction to prevent overlap of effort or internal confusion:

1. Supply and Transport Committee of Cabinet —
General direction of government arrangements for dealing with

> emergencies entrusted to Supply and Transport Committee of the
> Cabinet, to which all questions of policy are submitted for decision.[4]

While the general direction was determined centrally, individual
government departments were given enough flexibility to take
appropriate action. Strike-breaking was to be organised by a 'Food,
Fuel and Transport Sub-Committee' which would be closely backed
by physical force if necessary. Thus the 'Protection Sub-Committee'
included

> representatives of the Home Office, Scottish Office, Admiralty, War
> Office and Civil Commissioners' Department, and is responsible for
> supervising and co-ordinating any resources which need to be taken
> by the central authorities for protecting persons at work, transport,
> vulnerable points, etc. and for checking disorder.[5]

New arrangements were made to recruit 'volunteers' — strikebreakers — and especially detailed attention was devoted to road
transport:

> The Road Commissioners were all appointed and each Commissioner
> had prepared a list of Road Officers for the various centres in his
> Division. On receipt of a telegram each Road Commissioner was
> ready to proceed to his Emergency HQ and to appoint his Road
> Officers — the majority of whom had had experience in previous
> Emergencies.
> Chairmen of Haulage Committees had been approached to act at 82
> sub-centres and were prepared to set up their Committees on receipt
> of a telegram.
> Detailed instructions had been prepared and were ready for immedi-
> ate use . . . Within the limits of the instructions the arrangements for
> the organisation of road transport by the Ministry had been fully
> developed.[6]

The next day a decision was taken to:

> set up in each district a permanent headquarters where the emergency
> arrangements could be worked out in greater detail by the Emergency
> Staff.[7]

The country was divided into ten districts, each under the
control of a Civil Commissioner. For the purpose of recruiting
labour for the emergency, the country was divided into 80 areas,
each under the chairmanship of an influential local person. Each

division had its own Civil and Road Commissioner, plus Coal, Finance and Food Officers, appointed by the Ministry of Transport. Beneath the ten Divisional Road Commissioners were 150 Road Officers. The Food Officer had 102 Divisional Food Officers awaiting his orders. All this was done just one week after Red Friday and with eight and three-quarter months of the coal subsidy still to run! What a contrast this would be to the TUC's preparations.

As W M Crook, a historian of the strike, sums up:

> the government had prepared its weapons against possible industrial warfare; the railroads and the large industrial firms had laid in vast stocks of coal; and the output at the mines had been immense.[8]

The government's formal and secret plan for dealing with a future industrial emergency was supplemented by the informal but more public activities of the Organisation for the Maintenance of Supplies (OMS). The OMS was an unofficial body and was supposed to employ nobody in government service. In fact it was headed by men of the Establishment: its president was Lord Hardinge of Penshurst. On its council were Lord Ranfurly, Lord Jellicoe, Lord Falkland, Sir Rennell Rodd, Sir Alexander Duff, Sir Francis Lloyd, and other men who had at one time given notable service to the governmnent but had now retired from official participation in public affairs.

The OMS was defined as:

> an association of loyal citizens organised in the public interest to provide the government in times of emergency with classified lists of those who will assist in maintaining essential public services . . . food, water, light, power and transport, and who, when called upon by the constitutional authority, will cooperate in upholding law and order.[9]

In short, its purpose was to organise scabbing. OMS Committees were formed in 22 of the 28 Metropolitan boroughs, and efforts were made to spread this to the provinces. Volunteers in five categories were called for: Special Constables (under 45 years of age); workers to maintain public services; transport drivers; messengers and cyclists; and an unclassified group who would do clerical work or anything else not requiring technical skill.

Between Red Friday and the start of the General Strike, the OMS registered 100,000 volunteers, most of them in South East England.[10] So well advanced were government activities that the Home Secretary reported to the Cabinet on 22 February 1926 that 'little remained to be done before the actual occurrence of an emergency.'[11]

Yet in spite of everything the government did, the unions had the potential advantage. Workers vastly outnumbered capitalists. They alone had the skill and capacity to produce and transport the necessities of life for any length of time. Even the bulk of the army was recruited from the working class and in a major confrontation could well be expected to refuse to shoot its own class. The upper class was composed of parasites and so, despite its preparations, had to depend on the feebleness and treachery of leaders in the opposing camp to succeed. Only the TUC could snatch defeat from the jaws of victory.

The trade unions do nothing

The government was not alone in regarding Red Friday as no more than a temporary truce. Herbert Smith, president of the Miners' Federation, told its delegate conference in August 1925: 'We have no need to glorify about a victory. It is only an armistice.'[12]

What preparations did the leadership of the TUC make in the months before 1 May 1926, when the government subsidy to the mining industry came to an end? The answer is None. Thus the historian Alan Bullock, in his biography of Ernest Bevin, writes:

> In the seven months between [October 1925] and the crisis at the end of April 1926 which led straight into the General Strike, the full General Council did not once discuss what was to happen when the government subsidy came to an end on 30 April nor concern itself with preparations for the support of the miners — apart, of course, from receiving the reports of the Special Industrial Committee in the normal course of its monthly meetings . . .
>
> . . . the Industrial Committee took no more active steps than the General Council itself. It met twice between 1 October 1925 and 1 January 1926, resolving on the first occasion (25 October) to watch the course of events and meet again in 1926 'if circumstances warrant it', and on the second occasion (18 December) *not* to seek additional powers as suggested at Scarborough.[13]

The question of what measures were necessary in the event of a general dispute was first discussed on 27 April 1926 — three days before the day of reckoning. Bevin confirmed this at a Conference of Trade Union Executives in January 1927:

With regard to the preparations for the strike, there were no preparations until 27 April [1926] and I do not want anyone to go away from this conference under the impression that the General Council had any particular plan to run this movement. In fact, the General Council did not sit down to draft the plans until they were called together on 27 April.[14]

Before this the only preparations had been in building bureaucratic structures to deal with the mining crisis. In 1925 the Industrial Alliance was established between organisations representing workers in all forms of transport (railways, docks, waterways, road, sea, air), engineering, shipbuilding, iron and steel production, mining, and all forms of power production and distribution. This was the body that the Communist Party pushed for so vociferously, but it too did nothing.

Why did the trade union leaders not prepare for the showdown? First, being shortsighted, the General Council did not regard a further struggle as inevitable, unlike the mine-owners and the government, who obviously did. The trade union leadership, encouraged by the government, also preferred to wait for the outcome of the Royal Commission inquiry into the coal industry. They were induced to believe that somehow a solution would emerge. Some of the union leaders drew the wrong conclusion from Red Friday: they hoped that their dealing with the government would be like a poker game, that by bluffing they could avoid a real struggle.

The Samuel Commission

On 5 September 1925 Baldwin appointed a Royal Commission into the Coal Industry, chaired by Sir Herbert Samuel. Baldwin decided not to repeat the mistake committed in the composition of the Sankey Commission of 1919. The Sankey Commission had consisted of a chairman and twelve members, six of whom were miners or acceptable to the miners, and six mine-owners or acceptable to them. In the new Royal Commission working-class representation was completely excluded. Its chairman was Sir Herbert Samuel and its three other members were Sir William Beveridge, General Sir Herbert Lawrence, and Kenneth Lee.

Samuel himself had extensive family connections in the financial world, and considerable experience in government, having been Secretary of Sate for Home Affairs in the Liberal government after 1905 and British High Commissioner in Palestine 1920–25. Lawrence was managing partner of the bankers Glyn, Mills and Company, and on the board of several other companies. Kenneth Lee was chairman of the big cotton manufacturers Tootal, Broad-hurst, Lee and Company and chairman of the District Bank. Beveridge was a well-known economist and a Liberal.

Sheer kowtowing to men of substance must have led the General Council to pin their hopes on the Samuel Commission, that it would deliver them from the threatening struggle.

On 10 March 1926 the commission issued its report. This recommended the reorganisation of the mining industry: national-isation of royalties, amalgamation of existing mines, closer co-ordination of mining with electricity and gas production, improved research into the use of coal through new processes such as smoke-less fuel, and organisation of the cooperative selling of coal. To bring all these changes 'into full operation must need years', it said.

What about government subsidies to the coal industry? The answer of the report is clear:

> We express no opinion whether the grant of a subsidy last July was unavoidable or not, but we think its continuance indefensible. The subsidy should stop at the end of its authorised term, and should never be repeated [otherwise it] would constitute in many cases a door to the inefficient to the disadvantage of the efficient.[15]

The immediate needs of the industry, said the report, demand wage cuts:

> If the present hours are to be retained, we think a revision of the 'minimum percentage addition to standard rates of wages', fixed in 1924 at a time of temporary prosperity, is indispensable. A disaster is impending over the industry, and the immediate reduction of work-ing costs that can be effected in this way, and in this way alone, is essential to save it.

Yet while the verdict that rates of pay should be reduced was clear enough, the nature and conditions of the reduction were inadequately answered. How large were the cuts proposed? In an Annexe to the Report, the commission suggested that a 10 per cent decrease in the total national wage bill would 'nearly, though not quite, bring about a balance of costs and proceeds.' But because of the varying fortunes of the different coalfields, they concluded that 'greater reductions are almost certainly needed to give any chance of equilibrium in the exporting districts, and smaller ones would still leave a profit elsewhere.'[16]

Roughly speaking, the report can be summed up as proposing a reorganisation of the mining industry to be put into effect some time in the future, together with a reduction in wages to take effect immediately. While vague in its suggestions concerning state intervention, the report was precise in asserting that the miners should accept wage reductions or longer hours.

The commission admirably achieved its main purpose — that of giving an excuse to the Labour leaders to distance themselves from the miners. While the miners' leaders showed complete opposition to the report's findings, Labour leader Ramsay MacDonald rushed to declare that the report was 'a conspicuous landmark in the history of political thought . . . the stars in their courses are fighting for us.'[17] Using less flowery language, Ernest Bevin also recommended the report:

> I must confess that the report had a distinct fascination for me; I felt that if minds were applied with the right determination to give effect to it, what with reconstruction, regrouping and the introduction of a new element in the management of the industry, there would in the end be produced a *higher* wage standard. It may have meant some adjustments in varying forms, but this is nothing new; everyone of us has had to face these problems in other industries across the table and met and overcome similar conditions over and over again.[18]

Alan Bullock, quoting this, comments:

> To put it more plainly than anyone cared to at the time, the mining industry would never be able to pay a proper wage until it had been reorganised — and reorganisation meant closing uneconomic pits and drastically reducing the number of miners employed. To those outside the industry this was obvious, and if a thorough reorganisation could be secured, Bevin and other trade union leaders felt that a temporary reduction in wages was a price worth paying for it.[19]

Another recommendation for the Samuel Report came from Arthur Pugh, chairman of the TUC:

> It appeared to me that sound tactics implied an acceptance by the miners of the report in substance, subject to subsequent negotiations

on any point of reasonable modification, thus throwing upon the mine-owners the responsibility for the rejection of the report.[20]

To understand the impact of the Samuel Report on the General Council, let us compare the General Council's position towards the miners' demands before and after its publication. On 19 February 1926 a joint meeting of the Industrial Committee, representing the General Council and the Miners' Federation, had issued a clear statement of support for the miners' opposition to any cut in wages or extension of the working day:

> The attitude of the trade union movement was made perfectly clear last July, namely, that it would stand firmly and unitedly against any attempt further to degrade the standard of life in the coal fields. There was to be no reduction in wages, no increase in working hours, and no interference with the principle of National Agreements. *This is the position of the Trade Union Movement to-day.*[21]

However, in the days and weeks following the publication of the report, speeches by trade union leaders were published in which they distanced themselves from the position of the miners. The miners approached the Industrial Committee and asked them whether the General Council would continue to stand by the three fundamental points to which they were already committed. A letter from Walter Citrine, acting secretary of the TUC, to Miners' Federation secretary A J Cook was not reassuring:

> The committee fully realise the seriousness of the present position, but they are of the opinion that matters have not yet reached the stage when any final declarations of the General Council's policy can be made.
> It appears to them that negotiations are yet in a very early stage, and that efforts should be made to explore to the fullest extent the possibility of reducing the points of difference between your federation and the coalowners, and for that purpose they advise the immediate continuance of negotiations.[22]

At a meeting of the Industrial Committee on 21 April, both Arthur Pugh, its chairman, and J H Thomas gave their opinion that some sacrifices by the miners were unavoidable. 'On wages,' said Pugh, 'as a committee they could not see the miners getting out of that without some adjustment . . . The miners' slogans would get them nowhere.' Of their colleagues only Alonzo Swales objected to the assumption that such wage cuts must be faced.[23]

The TUC leaders showed themselves to be very reluctant allies of the miners. The miners' leaders nonetheless insisted on their three principles: no reduction to wages, no increase in working hours, and no interference in the principle of national agreement between union and employers. The miners' leaders alone showed angry defiance of mine-owners, government and TUC.

Behind the scenes leaders of the General Council, above all J H Thomas, were telling members of the government that they were ready to give way. Thus Tom Jones, the deputy-secretary to the Cabinet, wrote in his diary on 14 April 1926 that Baldwin

> had had a long talk with J H Thomas after dinner. JHT had described how for four hours he had fought with beasts at Ephesus upstairs, how he had taken the precaution to have a shorthand-writer, and everything had gone down on the notes. If that is true, it will be racy reading. JHT wants the PM to bring the two parties together, and to preside over their discussions. [24]

On 15 April Jones noted that Sir Alfred Cope, a coal-owner and managing director of Mond Industries,

> rang up and told me that Ramsay MacDonald and Clynes were passing the word along that the Miners were [to be] reasonable and conciliatory; otherwise public opinion would be alienated and in the event of a strike the prospects of the Labour Party severely damaged. [25]

Thomas was publicly doing his damnedest to dampen down the expectation of a general strike. Thus, on 18 April, speaking in Monmouthshire, he referred contemptuously to the current talk of industrial war:

> To talk at this stage as if in a few days all the workers of the country were to be called out was not only letting loose passions that might be difficult to control, but it was not rendering the best service either to the miners or anyone else . . . instead of organising, mobilising, and encouraging the feeling that war was inevitable, let them concentrate on finding a solution honourable and satisfactory to all sides. [26]

The right wing of the General Council were not the only ones who feared a confrontation. The most verbally radical of the lefts, A J Cook, a man who appeared on Minority Movement platforms and partly owed his position as MFGB secretary to its canvassing, was not exempt. From public platforms he inspired audiences with his vigorous championship of the slogan 'Not a penny off the pay, not a second on the day!'. In private his behaviour was rather less praiseworthy. Behind the backs of his own union's executive he was manoeuvring for a compromise.

Thus Jones wrote in an entry to his diary dated 14 April 1926 that he was wandering in the House of Commons:

> when I ran into Cook. Cook turned aside and whispered to me 'I'd like to see you tonight.' I whispered back my Hampstead telephone number.[27]

Next day, 15 April, Cook told Jones:

> We are economically in the weakest position we have ever been, and while a lot of our chaps won't agree with me, we shall have to have a national minimum not only with plusses above it, but minuses below it. I asked him what was the most helpful thing I could do in the interests of peace. He said, to get the owners to meet the PM as early as possible, next week, then to bring the miners to meet them, a joint conference with the PM presiding, and to keep them together while they thrashed out the wages issue.[28]

Despite all these manoeuvres the government and the coalowners left little space for compromise. On 16 April the coalowners declared a total lockout to start on 1 May. The General Council was crushed between its fear of a repeat of Black Friday, and nervous forebodings of the coming struggle. In the end it was pushed into the General Strike by government intransigence.

On Thursday 29 April a Special Conference of Executives of all trade unions affiliated to the TUC met in the Memorial Hall, Farringdon Street, and did not disperse until the afternoon of Saturday 1 May. This conference declared the general strike to start at midnight on 3/4 May in support of the miners. The decision was carried by 3,653,527 to 49,911. (Trade union executives representing 319,000 members did not vote as they did not have the opportunity to consult their organisations.) Only the Seamen rejected the strike call. In addition the National Union of Journalists, the Firemen's Union, and the Electrical Power Engineers Association did not join the strike.

The conference heard many fiery speeches. Ernest Bevin emphasised the historic importance of the occasion in his opening remarks:

We look upon your 'yes' as meaning that you have placed your all upon the altar for this great movement, and, having placed it there, even if every penny goes, if every asset goes, history will ultimately write up that it was a magnificent generation that was prepared to do it rather than see the miners driven down like slaves.

I rely, in the name of the General Council, on every man and every woman in that grade to fight for the soul of Labour and the salvation of the miners.

John Bromley, secretary of ASLEF, roused cheers when he said:

As far as my own people are concerned, every member of our union, without exception, will be thrown into the battle at once. That is rather a proud position to hold, that we shall at least be part of the shock troops . . . How proud I am to be a part of this great movement and to see this splendid response. We have comrades not only worthy of the name, but worth fighting for.[30]

There were, however, less sure voices. J H Thomas said:

My friends, when the verbatim reports are written, I suppose my usual critics will say that Thomas was almost grovelling, and it is true. In all my long experience — and I have conducted many negotiations — I say to you, and all my colleagues will bear testimony to it, I never begged and pleaded like I begged and pleaded all day to-day, and I pleaded not alone because I believed in the case of the miners, but because in my bones I believed that my duty to the country involved it. Therefore, I shall be content for our case to be judged on the verbatim reports that will be produced. But we failed.[31]

Straight after the conference, the TUC General Council's Industrial Committee, undaunted by the fiery speeches, again took up the task of persuading an unwilling government to make peace with the miners. On 1 May Walter Citrine wrote to Baldwin that the General Council was willing to open negotiations with the government immediately. Following the receipt of the letter, the prime minister invited the TUC representatives to meet him at 10 Downing Street at 8pm. The miners' leaders were kept in the dark. As A J Cook recalled in his best-selling pamphlet, **The Nine Days**:

I had arranged to keep in constant touch with the TUC, and to be at my office ready to give any information that was needed. To my surprise and alarm I heard quite by accident, on Saturday evening, at

about 9pm that the Negotiating Committee of the TUC were closeted
in Downing Street with the prime minister.
I could feel no other than apprehension, seeing I had not been
informed, and they were there presumably discussing the miners' case
in the absence of the miners' representatives. [32]

As a matter of fact, according to Cabinet minutes, the Negotiating
Committee had been discussing a formula for agreement that
signified a cut in miners' wages:

> The prime minister has satisfied himself, as a result of the conversa-
> tions he has had with the representatives of the Trades Union Congress
> that, if negotiations are continued (it being understood that the
> notices cease to be operative) the representatives of the Trade Union
> Congress are confident that a settlement can be reached on the lines of
> the report within a fortnight . . . in the view of the Trades Union
> Congress representatives the miners' representatives would agree to
> negotiate on the basis of the Report of the Royal Commission, recog-
> nising that this meant accepting a reduction of wags. [33]

The leaders of the TUC and Labour Party hoped — no, prayed, that
the government would come up with some face-saving formula that
would get them off the hook. But the government was totally
intransigent. The Cabinet minutes record of that Sunday evening,
when the Negotiating Committee met the prime minister and his
colleagues in private, states that:

> . . . the representatives of the Trades Union Congress had been asked
> what was the uttermost point to which they could go, and Lord
> Birkenhead had written down the following words of their reply:
> 'We will urge the miners to authorise us to enter upon a discussion
> with the understanding that they and we accept the report as a basis of
> settlement and we approach it with the knowledge that it may involve
> some reduction in wages.'
> As regards telegrams sent by unions to strike, 'they maintained that
> no irrevocable step had been taken, and said that all would be with-
> drawn at once if the conversations resulted in a resumption of
> negotiations'. [23]

The miners' leaders knew nothing of these negotiations. As
Cook recalls:

> I had my second surprise when, 'phoning to Eccleston Square [TUC
> headquarters], I learnt that the whole General Council was at Downing

Street, with Messrs Ramsay MacDonald and J H Thomas. I further
learnt from other souces that a small sub-committee were meeting the
prime minister and his colleagues. I believe this sub-committee consisted of Mr Pugh, Mr Citrine, and Mr J H Thomas. This again created
in the minds of myself and my colleagues a great deal of apprehension.
We waited some time at Russell Square until we were informed about
11 o'clock that we were wanted at once at Downing Street.

We arrived there to find the whole General Council with the Negotiating Committee. Immediately Mr Pugh, the chairman, placed before
us certain questions that they had been discussing, seeking our opinion
in regard to certain formulae, all of which would commit us to
reductions in wages. Again Herbert Smith, our president, with no
uncertain voice made it quite clear to the General Council that the
miners were not prepared to resume work on a reduction of wages or
any other sacrifices.[35]

The underhandedness and treachery of the Negotiating Committee
knew no bounds.

Although the Labour and TUC leaders had accepted that miners'
wages must be reduced, the government threw down the gauntlet
nevertheless, using the excuse that printers in the **Daily Mail**,
members of the union NATSOPA, had blacked an editorial entitled
'For King and Country' which attacked the miners. On 2 May
representatives of the General Council were asked to see the prime
minister. Baldwin told them that the negotiations must stop, and
handed them the following document:

> His Majesty's Government believe that no solution of the difficulties
> in the coal industry which is both practicable and honourable to all
> concerned can be reached except by sincere acceptance of the Report
> of the Commission.
>
> If the miners or the Trade Union Committee on their behalf, were
> prepared to say plainly that they accepted this proposal, the govern-
> ment would have been ready to resume the negotiations, and to
> continue the subsidy for a fortnight.
>
> But since the discussions which have taken place between ministers
> and members of the TU Committee, it has come to the knowledge of
> the government not only that specific instructions have been sent
> (under the authority of the Executive of Trade Unions represented at
> the conference convened by the General Council of the TUC), asking
> their members in several of the most vital industries and services of
> the country to carry out a General Strike on Tuesday next, but that

overt acts have already taken place, including gross interference with the freedom of the press.

Such action involved a challenge to the Constitutional rights and freedom of the nation.

His Majesty's Government, therefore, before it can continue negotiations, must require from the TUC Committee both a repudiation of the actions referred to that have already taken place, and an immediate and unconditional withdrawal of the instructions for a General Strike.[36]

Cook commented on the reaction of the leaders to the government's statement:

This created consternation among many of the General Council, and some of them were ready to immediately disown or to protest against the action of the **Daily Mail** printers. The Negotiating Committee were instructed by the General Council to again see the prime minister to explain to him the position, etc., but they found that he had retired. And we were politely informed that our presence was undesirable as everybody had retired, so at midnight or just after we left Downing Street for Eccleston Square.[37]

The grovelling of the Labour leaders did not stop. Worst were the speeches of Ramsay MacDonald, J H Thomas and Arthur Henderson in the House of Commons on 2 and 3 May. Henderson, secretary of the Labour Party, said on 2 May:

I was a witness, night after night . . . using all the influence I could and giving all the experience I have to assist those responsible in trying to bring about an avoidance of this great disaster . . . We all thought at 1 o'clock on Monday morning that they were just about to get that slight move forward which would have enabled us then to call off the whole thing, and to have called a settlement . . .

I am as alarmed about the position as any honourable member on the other side of the House. I have striven to advise and to avoid this catastrophe as much as possible.[38]

On 3 May MacDonald stated:

With the discussion of General Strike and Bolshevism and all that kind of thing, I have nothing to do at all. I respect the Constitution as much as the right honourable gentleman, the member for Hillhead [Sir Robert Horne, Minister of Labour].[39]

And Thomas surpassed all. When making his final effort in the House of Commons on 3 May, he stated:

> I am not going to make a party speech. I am not going to attempt to make party capital, nor do I believe that the prime minister has done so. Like him, I believe . . . the interests of the country and of those involved here are more important than any party.

He then went on to explain that over the previous weekend he had done his best to prevent public discussion of the issues:

> I did not want any ultimatum from the employers, and I did not want any speeches from the miners' side, because it might have rendered it more difficult to get peace.

The thought of a general strike filled Thomas with horror:

> I ask this House whether it is still too late to avert what I believe is the greatest calamity for the country.

Foreseeing a possible triumph for the workers, he added,

> I have never disguised that, in a challenge to the Constitution, God help us, unless the government won. That is my view.[40]

Years later, Thomas remembered this speech of 3 May:

> When I made that speech for peace, I felt in my heart that a general strike would do more harm to the cause of Labour than anything else. I don't mind confessing that when I left the House that night, realising that all had been in vain and that a strike was inevitable, I gave way to tears. It was like seeing the fabric you loved smashed to fragments.[41]

J R Clynes, deputy leader of the Labour Party, explained after the event how much he and other party leaders had detested the thought of the general strike:

> In an atmosphere of growing uneasiness and obstinacy, April drew towards its end. Thomas, Snowden, Henderson, MacDonald and I moved about behind the scenes, trying to find some way out of the *impasse*, hindered on the one hand by the armed preparations of the government, and on the other by the ferocious statements and wild promises of Cook and his following.
>
> No General Strike was ever planned or seriously contemplated as an act of trade union policy. I told my own union, in April, that such a stroke

would be a national disaster, and a fatal step to union prestige; and such it eventually proved to be.[42]

Clynes' actions were dictated by such beliefs. His grovelling reached a peak on 2 May when:

> With other union leaders, I sought an interview about midnight with the prime minister and his colleagues in a last-minute effort to show that the compositors' strike was isolated and unofficial, without our approval, and to plead, almost on our knees, for a less cruel arbitrament than he was now forcing upon us — an open fight between the workers and the Cabinet.[43]
>
> We, the leaders, had never sought the strike; our men to some extent ran away with us.[44]

Clynes implored the executive of his union, the National Union of General and Municipal Workers, to oppose the general strike, but failed. Thomas attempted to do the same at the NUR, where he

> urged and pleaded with the NUR executive to keep out of it. Many asked me afterwards why I did not resign my position as leader of the railwaymen when I realised that my advice would not be taken. I had to recognise that I was one of the strike leaders, and if I had resigned it would have given the impression that I sided with the government. That would have made matters worse for our men.[45]

At the beginning of the strike MacDonald declared:

> As far as we can see we shall go on. I don't like General Strikes. I haven't changed my opinion. I have said so in the House of Commons. I don't like it; honestly I don't like it; but honestly, what can be done?[46]

The same day he confided to Citrine: 'My hair has gone greyer than when I started this morning.'[47]

Until the last minute the Labour and trade union leaders continued to negotiate behind the backs of the miners, trying to avoid the 'catastrope'. Even after the General Strike had begun they did not stop plotting in an effort to put an end to the strike at the earliest possible moment.

So why did they call the General Strike at all if they did not want it?

First, they hoped that the call would serve as a ploy in new negotiations with the government. They did not understand that the government actually wanted the battle with the unions so that it could cut them to size.

Secondly, they saw in heading the strike a means of preventing the movement getting out of control. As Ernest Bevin later put it in his union journal, **The Record**:

> It must not be forgotten that apart from the rights and wrongs of the calling of a General Strike, there would in any case, with the miners' lock-out, have been widespread unofficial fighting in all parts of the country, which would have produced anarchy in the movement. [48]

Similarly, Ramsay MacDonald said:

> After the conduct of the government it was perfectly evident that had no general strike been declared, industry would have been almost as much paralysed by unauthorised strikes.

The TUC lefts may have been less vocal than the likes of Thomas or Bevin, but they in no way distinguished themselves from the right in the run-up to the strike. Trotsky's warning that in a crisis they would act no differently from the right was coming true in every respect.

The General Council as a whole was extremely wary of indulging in general strikes. These are by their very nature political as well as industrial acts. Victory would have demanded an all-out mobilisation of the trade union movement and a rigorous picketing of all scab transport. This would have challenged the government on the question 'Who rules?'. For the General Strike to succeed it had to be used as a revolutionary instrument — something which was obviously repulsive for the union leaders.

It was the government that had willed the confrontation, seeing in the defeat of a big stoppage the opportunity for a general attack on wages and the reduction of the trade unions to impotence. In May 1926 the union leaders' bluff was called. They staggered with heavy hearts into the strike.

PART THREE:
THE NINE DAYS

Chapter Sixteen

REVOLUTIONARY MASS STRIKE
OR BUREAUCRATIC NIGHTMARE?

ON THE OUTCOME of the 1926 strike depended the fate of millions of workers and their union organisations. The world had seen previous crises of this sort. Many had generated mass strikes in which the ruling class offensive was beaten off and the working class had made dramatic advances. Not all led to successful revolutions, but in the struggle the workers had been forged into a fighting unit. They had undergone a spiritual growth. They were changed so that they became able to change society. Even in defeat a substantial core of workers remained more class-conscious and determined than before.

By far the most brilliant exposition on such strikes is the classic work by Rosa Luxemburg, **The Mass Strike, The Political Party and The Trade Unions.** She sketches the rising wave of strikes in Russia in the ten years 1896–1905. In May 1896 a general strike of 40,000 textile workers took place in St Petersburg. This was followed by another general strike of the same workers in 1897. Following this, a whole number of small strikes took place until the next mass strike in March 1902 of the petroleum workers in the Caucasus. Then in November a mass strike of railwaymen in Rostov turned into a general strike. In May, June and July 1903, the whole of South Russia was aflame. Baku, Tiflis, Batum, Elizavetograd, Odessa, Kiev, Nikolayev, and Ekaterinoslav were in the grip of a general strike.

The year 1904 brought with it war, and for a time a pause in the strike movement, but this ended with the defeat of the Tsarist army and navy at the hands of the Japanese. In December 1904 a general strike broke out in Baku. Before this news had time to reach all parts of the Tsarist empire a mass strike broke out in St Petersburg in January 1905. This was the start of the Russian revolution of 1905. Rosa Luxemburg wrote in her book:

The sudden general rising of the proletariat in January under the powerful impetus of the St Petersburg events was outwardly a political act of the revolutionary declaration of war on absolutism. But this first general direct action reacted inwardly all the more powerfully as it for the first time awoke class feeling and class consciousness in millions upon millions as if by an electric shock. And this awakening of class feeling expressed itself forthwith in the circumstances that the proletarian mass, counted by millions, quite suddenly and sharply came to realise how intolerable was that social and economic existence which they had patiently endured for decades in the chains of capitalism. Thereupon there began a spontaneous general shaking of and tugging at these chains. All the innumerable sufferings of the modern proletariat reminded them of the old bleeding wounds. Here was the eight-hour day fought for, there piece-work was resisted, here were brutal foremen 'driven off' in a sack on a handcart, at another place infamous systems of fines were fought against, everywhere better wages were striven for and here and there the abolition of homework.[1]

Mass economic strikes led to confrontation with the Tsarist regime, its police and army, and this led directly to political strikes. The latter awakened previously dormant workers to undertake economic strikes to improve their conditions, and the economic strikes again gave new impetus to the political strikes. The mass strike overcomes the separation of economics and politics that is inherent in reformism (as well as in its symmetrical opposite, syndicalism). The mass strike fuses together the struggle for reforms inside capitalism with the struggle for the revolutionary overthrow of capitalism. The mass strike is a bridge between the here and now and the socialist future.

In the mass strike workers stop being onlookers of history, or a stage army; they step on to the historical arena shaping their future and forging themselves. Rosa Luxemburg writes:

In former bourgeois revolutions . . . the short battle on the barricades was the appropriate form of revolutionary struggle. Today, at a time that the working class must educate, organise and lead itself in the course of the revolutionary struggle, when the revolution itself is directed not only against the established state power but also against capitalist exploitation, mass strikes appear as the natural method to mobilise the broadest possible proletarian layers into action, to revolutionise and organise them. Simultaneously it is a method by means of which to undermine and overthrow the established state power as well as to curb capitalist exploitation . . . In order that the working class may participate *en masse* in any direct political action, it must first organise itself, which above all means that it must obliterate the boundaries between factories and workshops, mines and foundries, it must overcome the split between workshops which the daily yoke of capitalism condemns it to. Therefore the mass strike is the first natural spontaneous form of every great revolutionary proletarian action.[2]

Contrary to all reformists, who see a Chinese wall between partial struggles for economic reform and the political struggle for revolution, Rosa Luxemburg pointed out that in a revolutionary period the economic struggle grows into a political one, and vice versa:

The movement does not go only in one direction, from an economic to a political struggle, but also in the opposite direction. Every important political mass action, after reaching its peak, results in a series of economic mass strikes. And this rule applies not only to the individual mass strike, but to the revolution as a whole. With the spread, clarification and intensification of the political struggle not only does the economic struggle not recede, but on the contrary it spreads and at the same time becomes more organised and intensified. There exists a reciprocal influence between the two struggles. Every fresh attack and victory of the political struggle has a powerful impact on the economic struggle, in that at the same time as it widens the scope for the workers to improve their conditions and strengthens their impulse to do so, it enhances their fighting spirit. After every soaring wave of political action, there remains a fertile sediment from which sprout a thousand economic struggles. And the reverse also applies. The workers' constant economic struggle against capital sustains them at every pause in the political battle. The economic struggle constitutes, so to speak, the permanent reservoir of working class strength from which political struggles always imbibe new strength.

In a word, the economic struggle is the factor that advances the movement from one political focal point to another. The political struggle periodically fertilises the ground for the economic struggle. Cause and effect interchange every second. Thus we find that the two elements, the economic and political, do not incline to separate themselves from one another during the period of the mass strikes in Russia, not to speak of negating one another as pedantic schemes would suggest.[3]

The logical and necessary climax of the mass strike is

the open uprisings which can only be realised as the culmination of a
series of partial uprisings which prepare the ground, and therefore are
liable to end for a time in what looks like partial 'defeats', each of
which may seem to be 'premature'.[4]

For Rosa Luxemburg,

The most precious thing, because it is the most enduring, in the sharp
ebb and flow of the revolutionary wave, is the proletariat's spiritual
growth. The advance by leaps and bounds of the intellectual stature of
the proletariat affords an inviolable guarantee of its further progress in
the inevitable economic and political struggles ahead.[5]

And what idealism workers rise to! They put aside thoughts of
whether they have the wherewithal to support themselves and their
families during the struggle. They do not ask whether all the
preliminary technical preparations have been made. The mass
strike can 'generate such a tremendous volume of idealism among
the masses that they appear to become almost immune to the most
terrible privations.'[6]

Rosa Luxemburg's account concentrates on the great dis-
solving effect of the mass strike on the boundaries between
economics and politics in workers' struggles. But she is also clear
that it tends to dissolve other barriers as well — such as sectionalism and religion — at the same time as demonstrating the unbridgeable gulf between workers' interests and those of the bosses
and their state. Her description fits a number of mass strikes:
Russia 1905 and 1917; France and Spain 1936; Hungary 1956;
Poland 1980, and others.

However, there are many mass strikes that have little in common with Rosa Luxemburg's description. Where the workers are
highly organised in trade unions, the extent of their independence
from the conservative trade union bureaucracy is largely a function
of their confidence in facing the capitalists. The higher the level of
organisation and confidence of the rank and file in fighting the
capitalists, the more able are they to break the shackles of the trade
union bureaucracy, and vice versa. The extent to which a strike is a
product of rank-and-file initiative determines how near it is to the
norm of the mass strike described by Rosa Luxemburg.

The bureaucratically-administered general strike

Unfortunately, Luxemburg's analysis is sometimes used dogmatically, so that instead of comparing her concept with an *actual* mass strike the truth is obscured rather than enlightened. For the mass strike, like all social phenomena, is not a fixed absolute. Its character largely depends on the circumstances in which it takes place.

This applies particularly to the British General Strike of 1926 which, as we shall see, was very different from the romantic picture which has come down to us through left-wing folklore. It had little in common with the sort of revolutionary mass strike described by Rosa Luxemburg.

From the very beginning the TUC leaders made it clear that they intended to keep a tight grip on the strike. They took it upon themselves to decide who should stop work and who should not. A strong rank-and-file movement would not have tolerated the arbitrary decision to bring certain workers out but not others doing similar jobs. Without such a challenge the bureaucratic *fiat* held good, but the result was tremendous confusion.

Not all workers were called out. The TUC strategy was instead framed as a strike in 'waves' — one group of workers was to strike while others waited. This, it was hoped, would produce a satisfactory compromise before a total stoppage occurred. The first wave was to involve workers in the following industries:

Transport: including members of all affiliated unions connected with transport, in other words railways, sea transport, docks, wharves, harbours, canals, road transport, railway repair shops and contractors for railways, and all unions connected with air transport.
Printing: including the press.
Productive industries: iron and steel, metal and heavy chemicals, including all metal or other workers engaged to install plant to take the place of coal.
Building: all building workers except those engaged on housing and hospital work, together with all workers engaged in the supply of equipment to the building industry.
Power: electricity and gas workers were to co-operate with the object of supplying light but not power.

Workers in general engineering, textiles and light industry were not included, nor were those in the postal or telephone service, despite the fact that unions in these industries had voted as solidly for the strike as those whose members were called out.

Had all trade unionists been called out from the beginning, the impact would have been far greater. In the first 'wave', the first eight days of the strike, two million workers came out. The second 'wave' brought out another half-million: engineers, shipyard workers and textile workers. So altogether there were 2½ million on strike on the last day. In addition one million miners were locked out.

Thus the total number of trade unionists involved was 3½ million, who comprised two-thirds of all organised workers. This made the stoppage really a *partial* general strike since, with one in three workers unionised, only a quarter of Britain's labour force were directly involved.

The interdependence of different sectors of industry made nonsense of the hastily cobbled together idea of separate waves. To weaken the strike further, and increase the muddle, workers were not expected to act on the call of the TUC but wait for specific instructions to come from their own union:

> The General Council recommends that the actual calling out of the workers should be left to the unions, and instructions should only be issued by the accredited representatives of the unions participating in the dispute.[7]

The General Council's attempt to maintain the autonomy of individual union head offices prevented concentrated strike organisation and exacerbated the sectionalism that was endemic to the trade union movement.

Whereas the government had centralised the ruling class campaign, the individual unions rather than the General Council were the administrative machinery that ran the strike. The separate unions were left to interpret the TUC call in their own way. As a result confusion reigned supreme. Union branches received conflicting strike orders. Since there was no coordination at the top, there was no way for local union groups to resolve contradictory orders except through a terrible waste of time and effort — and still chaos prevailed.

The task of interpreting TUC guidelines involved some unions in countless problems, especially in industries such as electricity and building, of which only sections fell within the TUC lists. Take the example of electricity, where the TUC was asking for a discrimination between light and power, and between various kinds of power. On 7 May the General Council announced:

> Local strike organisations are authorised to offer to meet employers immediately and offer to supply light and power for such services as house, street and shop lighting, social services, power for food, bakeries, laundries and domestic services.[8]

It was an impossible selective process; and this on the fourth day of the strike. The London district of the electricians' union (ETU) pointed out that to divide power and light was a technical impossibility, and called on all members of the ETU in power stations to come out on strike. The General Council thereupon instructed them to go back to work![9] A sub-committee of the General Council dealing with electricity and gas suggested to the General Council that all workers in those industries should be called out, but this was still under consideration at the end of the strike.[10]

But this did not end the problems. Should workers *not* called out use electricity produced by scabs? This question was put to the National Strike Organisation Committee by the Northumberland and Durham Strike Committee. The reply given was: Yes, they should.[11]

A similar muddle was caused among building workers. The General Council's instructions were not at all clear:

> Building Trade — All workers engaged on building, except such as are employed definitely on housing and hospital work, together with all workers engaged in the supply of equipment to the building industry, shall cease work.[12]

Each union interpreted the instructions differently.

> The headquarters of the different unions provided conflicting guidelines on how to interpret the TUC's directives, so that the problem of deciding who ought to be on strike within each union was made more complicated by the fact that members of other unions on the same building site were working to different rules. This meant that on some building sites one set of workers had been ordered out and another ordered to report as normal.[13]

The secretary of a building workers' federation strike committee at Wellingborough described his problems:

> I called a mass meeting . . . each affiliated society secretary was on the platform with me, each with differently worded instructions, each of which called on the members to cease work and then went on to lay

down rules and regulations which no one could interpret, but which made it impossible for the members to do so.[14]

Similarly Charles Spraggs, the Birmingham district organiser of the housepainters' and decorators' union, had quite a struggle coping with the problem.

> Some men engaged on hospital and school building weren't called out and this caused no end of dissension and we had some lively meetings. At our biggest branch they all turned up and gave me an uncomfortable time. I won in the end but it was a very rough night. The men who were complaining wanted all out or none out. It was all black and white. They felt that if they were out then all should be out. Some wanted none out.[15]

The **Huddersfield Workers' Bulletin** of 11 May suggested the only logical solution to the muddle: 'A meeting of the Central Strike Committee in conjunction with the members of the unions in the building trades met, and it was jointly agreed to recommend that all members be withdrawn from the industry.'[16]

But this advice came too late to reverse the damage. Margaret Morris summed up the chaos of the strike in the building industry thus:

> In the building industry as a whole . . . although the general response was good, wrangling delayed the start of the strike and led to a yo-yo movement: some building workers did not come out until the middle of the strike, while others were sent back to work by their unions.[17]

Workers in other industries also suffered from muddled and contradictory instructions. According to James Jefferys, the historian of the engineering union, the contradictory instructions from Head Office created

> confusion among the engineers as to who was to come out and who was to stay in. Many members were engaged on motor-car manufacture and vehicle building, which was not clearly defined in relation to the instructions for transport workers. Some districts consequently interpreted motor-car manufacture as 'Transport', while others did not. Coventry settled the confusion in their area by calling out all motor-car workers and the Wolverhampton Strike Committee very quickly agreed upon a policy which brought the motor-car industry in that area to a complete standstill.[18]

In Sheffield

The 7,000 engineers, divided amongst various craft unions, working in anything from the largest steel firm to the smallest tool shop, were in receipt of confusing orders from the General Council. Most of them came out unordered on 3 May. The officials were horrified when they discovered on 5 May that they had misinterpreted the instructions and were now expected to send their members back to work. The AEU delegates reported to the [Central Dispute Committee] that they were 'in an extremely difficult position as all their men were out. The district committee believed it to be disastrous for them to return' . . . they were, they felt, being ordered to blackleg. The 2,000 foundry workers had waited for official instructions, but they found their position equally unacceptable, and their committee decided on 8 May to 'again visit our national executive council with a view to getting permission to withdraw all members.'[19]

Similar chaos prevailed in the Sheffield steel industry:

The several thousand cutlery workers in the NUGMW came out on 3 May but were ordered back to work on 5 May, where they apparently waited for their power and steel supplies to be cut off, so they could then claim benefit for being laid off . . . Along with union members who continued to work because their officials refused to authorise strike pay there were the non-unionists. As a result, all of Sheffield's major steel firms, with the exception of Hadfield's, and most of the small metal firms which had enough coal in stock, stayed partially open.[20]

At the beginning of the General Strike, the Sheffield Central Dispute Committee bemoaned the fact that the TUC's instructions 'tend to destroy morale and render sections of the strike ineffective on account of the numbers who are still at work and being sent to work.'[21] But the General Council was deaf to such complaints.

Another example of muddle came from the North-East:

One transport union had called out all men concerned with transport of food but given permits for transport of building materials; another had stopped all the latter but was giving some permits for transport of food . . . In Nottingham . . . two days were taken up with a dispute between the TGWU and the NUGMW because the former had called out its brewery men, the latter not, so the discussion turned on the question — 'is beer food?' Despite all efforts both local and national no settlement had been reached by the end of the strike.[22]

There was another very serious negative aspect of the partial strike: on 4 May the Glasgow Central Strike Co-ordinating Committee reported that engineers and shipbuilding workers were forced to use buses run by blacklegs — due to the TUC's instructions to go on working.[23]

Key sections of the trade union movement were kept completely uninvolved until the end of the strike: gas workers, post and telephone workers, those working directly for the government in naval dockyards, among others. On the other hand there was one section of workers called out who should not have been: printers working for the socialist press. Their stoppage considerably reduced the effectiveness of those arguing the workers' case.

Sectional narrow-mindedness led the printing unions to refuse to print Labour papers if their members working for the capitalist press were called out. In the majority of cases the Typographical Association refused to print local strike bulletins. Even when it came to printing provincial copies of the **British Worker**, the TUC's own strike paper, it demanded much coaxing and lengthy negotiations with the local branches of the print unions. Again with the London edition of the **British Worker**, narrow sectionalism reared its ugly head. 'The machine men . . . put in, to begin with, very large demands. They claimed more than they would have earned in ordinary times. They were pleaded with, but would not take less.'[24]

The government side had no scruples about fighting its corner. Apart from the **British Gazette**, which gave free reign to the unbridled class warrior instincts of Winston Churchill, it possessed a powerful propaganda weapon in the wireless, for the BBC was completely an arm of the government.

One final aspect of the British General Strike that made it unique among mass strikes must be mentioned. This was the issuing of strike pay to all workers out on strike — with the exception of the locked-out miners. This considerably strengthened the control of the trade union bureaucracy over the rank and file.

Chapter Seventeen

A SOLID STRIKE KEPT PASSIVE

THROUGHOUT the nine days (4–12 May) the strike was rock solid. Workers showed both massive enthusiasm and dogged determination. Thus one historian of the strike, Julian Symons, writes:

> The workers' reaction to the strike call was immediate and overwhelming. There can be no doubt that its completeness surprised the government, as well as the TUC. From district after district reports came into the TUC headquarters at Eccleston Square, sending the same message in various words: the men were all out, the strike was solid.[1]

On the first day of the strike, a TUC communiqué stated:

> We have from all over the country, from Lands End to John o' Groats, reports that have surpassed all our expectations. Not only the railwaymen and transport men, but all other trades came out in a manner we did not expect immediately. The difficulty of the General Council has been to keep men in what we might call the second line of defence rather than call them off. There are also no reports other than those of a quiet, orderly and good-tempered desire to keep the peace of all sections of the community.[2]

On the third day of the strike, the **British Worker** reported:

> The workers are growing more determined as the days pass. They are not 'drifting back to work'. On the contrary, the trouble everywhere is to keep those men at work who have not yet been ordered to strike.[3]

On the basis of the TUC's own local reports,[4] and the Cabinet's daily Intelligence Bulletins,[5] it is clear that everywhere the strike was solid and growing in power by the day. More and more industry was grinding to a halt.

On 11 May, the last day but one, the Minister of Labour, who had nothing to gain by exaggerating the strike's impact, told his colleagues that it was spreading to the flour-milling industry and would soon hit engineering and shipbuilding. Glasgow shows 'not the slightest sign of a break'; in Manchester 'there is no overall tendency of the men to resume and no likelihood of a change'; in London and the south 'there are indications of a growing spirit among the rank and file that they will stay out until they are forced back by hunger'; in Cardiff 'there is a definite tendency among printing trade workers and local authority employees, including tram drivers, to resume work, but not yet any indication of a breakaway among men in transport or the iron and steel industries'; Birmingham shows 'no sign of any break but the temperature is much lower'.[6]

The most solid group of workers were the railwaymen. As the historian of the National Union of Railwaymen, P S Bagwell, writes:

> From midnight on Monday 3 May, the engine fires were raked out, the wheels stopped turning, and the station platforms, signal boxes and goods yards were deserted. The response to the strike call was unprecedented. More railwaymen came out in sympathy with the miners on 4 May 1926 than had struck in support of their own demands on 26 September 1919. During the next ten days thousands of telegrams were received at Unity House reporting the transport situation in every part of the country. With almost monotonous consistency they told of the remarkable unanimity and loyalty of the membership. Sheffield, Cardiff, Newcastle upon Tyne and the Manchester District all reported 'Response magnificent'; Bristol, Grantham, Toton, Masborough, Huddersfield, Leeds and Aberdeen reported 'All solid', whilst Plymouth reported an 'Unexampled discipline' from the 2,000 railwaymen on strike in that area. . . . Among the membership of the ASLEF the response was, if anything, even more complete. According to the official journal of that society 'there were not fifty members out of 50,000 who failed to answer the call.'[7]

Bagwell goes on to say that:

> Whilst at no time in the strike there was a 100 per cent withdrawal of labour on the railways, the situation was not far short of this among the conciliation grades [drivers, firemen, guards, signalmen, shunters and porters] on 4 May, and had not changed appreciably by 12 May.[8]

This estimation is backed up by the government's own figures. Thus Ministry of Transport files[9] for the locomotivemen revealed no more than a paltry drift back to work:

		Men available for duty	
Railway	Total staff	5 May	12 May
Great Western Railway	6,206	79	104
London, Midland and Scottish	14,671	93	273
London and North Eastern Railway	11,500	94	127
Southern	7,044	?	238

The situation was virtually no different amongst signalmen:

		Men available for duty	
Railway	Total staff	5 May	12 May
Great Western Railway	4,843	384	584
London, Midland and Scottish	11,871	901	1,152
Southern	2,940	?	534

On the last day of the strike, 98.8 per cent of all engine drivers, firemen and motor men were on strike in the Great Western Railway. The equivalent figure for LNER was 99.3, LMS, 98.8, and Southern, 96.7. Guards: GWR, 95.5; LNER, 98; LMS, 98.8; Southern, 93.8. Shunters: GWR, 97; LNER, 89.9; LMS, 98.9; Southern, 96.3. Signalmen: GWR, 88; LNER, 92; LMS, 90; Southern, 82.[10]

On the first day of the strike, only 3 to 5 per cent of the passenger trains were running and far fewer goods trains. At the end of the strike, when passenger services (run by blacklegs) rose to 15 per cent or so of normal, goods trains remained at 2 to 3 per cent.

Other transport workers were less solid than the railwaymen. On the London underground 15 out of 315 trains ran on the first day of the strike, though these covered short distances only. Of London's 4,400 buses, 300 were run with scab crews on the first day of the strike, but the number was down to 40 by the end of the week. None of the capital's 2,000 tramcars were operating.[11] In most towns and cities public transport was paralysed. There were exceptions, however. In Birmingham, Edinburgh and Liverpool there were many scabs running transport, while other towns had a practically normal bus service — Bristol, Brighton, Southampton,

Portsmouth, Cardiff, Oxford, Chatham, Grimsby and Maidstone, for example.

The situation was worse in the area of road goods transport. This was a key weakness. The industry had employed 392,000 workers (many of these were self-employed) in 1921. At most only 60,000 were organised in trade unions in 1925–6.[12] But the poor response in road haulage must be offset against the solid response of the dockers. With them stood the building workers, iron and steel workers, those in the metal and heavy chemical industries, all of whom were firmly out by the morning of 4 May.

The bureaucracy had not simply caused chaos in organising the stoppage of those it wished to see strike. It was clearly holding back floods of workers who wished to be involved, for the chief problem the officials faced was not getting people out, but keeping numbers at work. As Postgate and others remark:

> This was a far more difficult task than the other, and the fact that it *was* the main task shows more than anything else what the spirit of the workers was.[13]

Evidence of this spirit was overwhelming.

Warrington's Central Strike Committee sent a telegram to Citrine on 6 May: 'Central Strike Committee urges withdrawal of *all* workers'. (Our emphasis.) York and District Trades and Labour Club wrote to Citrine on 7 May: 'Our greatest difficulty is to keep the men at work who should remain there, they all feel that they should be out helping in the struggle.' **Bradford Worker**, the official strike news bulletin, wrote: '*The trouble everywhere is to keep those men at work who had not yet been ordered to strike.*' Rotherham reported to Citrine on 8 May: 'Utmost difficulty in keeping uncalled men at work. Strong disposition to stop everything.' From Eccles a telegram to Citrine on 8 May: '100 per cent out. Our difficulty to keep others at work.'

Again and again engineers came out although not called. Thus Merseyside Strike Committee reported on 4 May that all engineers and shipyard workers on the Mersey were out. Preston Strike Committee reported in a letter to the General Council on 10 May: 'Engineering industry locally completely stopped, about 5,000 men being out. Also all at Leyland Motors and Vulcan Motors.'[14]

For Manchester we are told on the second day of the strike:

> The Amalgamated Engineering Union reports that its men had struck at works where members of other unions had been called out, including the railway shops, newspaper offices, and tramway sheds.[15]

In London:

> The militant London district of the Amalgamated Engineering Union did not wait for the TUC's 'second-line' instructions but called out all engineers in the first week except those engaged in health, sanitary and social services . . . Lewisham's main headache was in keeping in workers not called out.[16]

From Dundee we hear a similar story:

> 'Here as elsewhere our greatest difficulty in the first week was in preventing men ceasing work before being called upon to do so.' Almost identical comments were sent from Manchester, Bristol and Sheffield. In the latter town it was said that many non-unionists had ceased work, as well as AEU members.[17]

In North Lanarkshire 'by the end of the first week even second-line men came out before being officially called out by the TUC.'[18]

Altogether about 50 per cent of all engineers came out on strike before they were officially called out.[19]

One of the most encouraging things in the strike was that often non-unionists came out spontaneously. The textile workers were not called out but many cotton workers in Lancashire acted on their own initiative and struck. Thus Bob Edwards, a member of the Merseyside Council of Action, wrote:

> The amazing thing was Chorley, which wasn't a trade union town: I suppose 10 per cent of workers were in unions there. In fact, from a Socialist point of view, we used to say that it was as fertile as granite. But the whole of Chorley was closed.[20]

From Sheffield it was reported on 11 May: 'Large numbers of non-unionists have enrolled in their appropriate union and joined the strikers.'[21] Nearly two-thirds of all workers were not members of trade unions in 1926, but still a considerable number of non-unionists spontaneously joined the strike when their unionised workmates came out. Thus Postgate and others report:

> members came out enthusiastically and were followed by the 'nons' (or even preceded by them). At Chelmsford the 200 union men among

3,000 came out — at one shop (Crompton's) there were only six union men.[22]

The rock solid strike gives the lie to the TUC leaders' excuse for ending action on 12 May when they claimed it was on the verge of collapse. Their action was far more effective in damaging the strike than anything the government could muster.

In particular the OMS was far from a success. By the government's own admission it only marginally dented the industrial action. Thus Sir John Anderson, permanent under-secretary at the Home Office, wrote on 17 May:

> The OMS was a useful lightning conductor before the strike but apart from the fact that it trained a few drivers its practical utility was almost nil.[23]

Most of the OMS volunteers lived away from the industrial centres; they came mainly from the south east of England, which had a large middle class. The City of Westminster produced the highest number of volunteers — 7,734. Leeds, on the other hand, provided only 400, while Manchester and Liverpool did not appear on the OMS list at all.[24] By and large the OMS volunteers were unsuitable for industrial work. On 12 May it was reported from the North East that of the 18,000 people who had volunteered for service up to that date, only 1,000 had been actually given jobs. This is probably some indication of the remarkable small number of jobs in which volunteer labour was able to replace men on strike.[25] In London and Home Counties Division 114,000 volunteers had registered by 11 May, of whom only 9,500 were actually employed.[26]

The efficiency of volunteers was very low indeed. Thus we are informed from Liverpool that volunteer dock labour had, by official calculation, only one-fifteenth of the productivity of regular dockers. That is, each volunteer shifted less than half a ton per twelve-hour day, compared to five tons per eight-hour day for the regulars.[27]

Limiting the struggle

The trade union leaders did everything in their power to keep the strike inert. First of all the General Council kept rigid control over all avenues of information. It ordered that only material which it approved could be issued:

The Publicity Committee instructs secretaries and officers of local organisations to confine their statements on the situation to the material supplied by the committee and to add nothing in the way of comment or interpretation.[28]

The General Council exercised firm control over the **British Worker**. A group of censors from the Press and Publicity Committee, E L Poulton of the Boot and Shoe Union, J W Bowen of the Post Office Workers, and Will Henderson, the son of the former Labour Party leader, looked over every line of the paper. As its editor, Hamilton Fyfe, noted, their chief purpose was to keep out of the paper 'anything which might cause uncontrollable irritation and violence'.

Our task is to keep the strikers steady and quiet. We must not be provocative; our line is to be dignified, calm in our own strength; to make our statements forcibly, but with moderation of language. We shall print every day very prominently and in bold type, well displayed, this 'Message to All Workers':
'The General Council of the Trades Union Congress wishes to emphasise the fact that this is an industrial dispute. It expects every member taking part to be exemplary in his conduct and not to give any opportunity for police interference. The outbreak of any disturbances would be very damaging to the prospects of a successful termination to the dispute.
'The Council asks pickets especially to avoid obstruction and to confine themselves strictly to their legitimate duties.'[29]

In addition, to avoid inflaming passions, the General Council decided that all general news should be excluded from the **British Worker**.

The aim of such restrictions was to keep the strike, which the General Council had never wanted, in a state of inertia. The bureaucratic ideal of industrial action was summed up by the **British Worker**'s editor when he wrote on 7 May, day four of the strike: 'Meanwhile, the mass of the Labour Movement is sound, sensible, straightforward. It has folded its arms and quietly awaits the result.'[30] What a shame that the other side did not do the same.

Problems surrounded production of provincial editions of the General Council's news-sheet:

Separate editions were planned for publication in Leicester, Manchester, Cardiff, Liverpool, Glasgow, Newcastle and elsewhere, but difficulties were placed in the way of their production partly by the printing unions and partly by the General Council itself, which feared that rash statements might be inserted in these separate editions.

The multifold troubles involved in them is indicated by what happened in the cases of the Manchester and Glasgow editions. Fenner Brockway, secretary of the ILP, was asked to go up to Manchester and take charge of the local edition to be published there. Brockway was handed the copy and it was emphasised, both to him and to the local strike committee, that only material in the **British Worker** was to be used, with a different date-line. 'No alterations permitted', said the telegram to Manchester.

On Sunday 9 May arguments were still going on about the Glasgow edition, which had been set up with material not included in the original **British Worker** . . . 'We have a report lying on my desk now, saying that your people are wanting to extend the strike in all kinds of ways', Poulton said. 'Will you see that all that stuff is kept out and nothing provocative put in.' The Glasgow edition, again, appeared too late to be of much use.[31]

The first Newcastle edition of the **British Worker** did not appear until 11 May, the day before the strike ended.[32]

The General Council refused permission to publish for all labour papers except **British Worker**. Permits were sought by George Lansbury for **Lansbury's Weekly** and H N Brailsford for the ILP's **New Leader**. Although both these papers could be relied upon to support the trade union case, they were refused. Pleas were also made for the **Daily Herald**, the labour movement's only daily paper, to be allowed to continue. The General Council, however, decided to abide by its plans for a complete ban and turned a deaf ear to all pleas for exemption. G A Phillips writes:

> The **British Worker** afforded the General Council a powerful instrument of control over the conduct of the strike. It justified the attempted prohibition of any local publishing ventures and the silencing of the labour press, on the argument that competitors might promulgate conflicting and confusing orders or advice to the rank and file. 'The real reason for [the] close shut-down of all printing,' [Herbert] Tracey [of the TUC staff] told the London Society of Compositors on 6 May, 'was to enable [the] General Council through its Publicity Committee to maintain absolute control of all news or propaganda connected with the strike.'[33]

And what was the message of the **British Worker**? It is summed up by the list of things workers were expected to do:

> Do all you can to keep everybody smiling — the way to do that is to smile yourself.
>
> Do your best to discountenance any ideas of violent or disorderly conduct.
>
> Do the thing that's nearest — that will occupy you and will steady your nerves if they get shaky.
>
> Do a little to interest and amuse the kiddies now that you have the chance.
>
> Do what you can to improve your health, a good walk every day will keep you fit.
>
> Do something. Hanging around and swapping rumours is bad in every way.
>
> The General Council suggests that in all districts where large numbers of workers are idle sports should be organised and entertainments arranged. They will both keep a number of people busy and provide amusement for many more.[34]

Cardiff Strike Committee advised the men:

> Keep smiling. Refuse to be provoked. Get into your garden. Look after the wife and kiddies. If you have not got a garden, get into the country, there is no more healthful occupation than walking.[35]

The most extreme expression of the philosophy of the leadership, victory by folding arms, can be seen in the following quote from the **Bradford Worker**, the official strike news bulletin:

> Discipline, order, solidarity, confidence. Just the calm of it is fraying the nerves of our opponents. If there were riots and police charges and an excuse for machine-guns, they would understand. But this tremendous pressure of a power they cannot see, but which they can feel more and more intensely every hour, is unnerving. They cannot see what to do. There is nothing they can do. We have only to set out teeth and wait.[36]

When it came to instructions regarding picketing, the General Council's advice was diabolical. The government largely had a free run, especially in the crucial area of food supplies. This was because pickets were actively dissuaded from making their action effective. Instead of physically confronting the state's strikebreakers, friendly relations with the police were encouraged. For their part the police were only too ready to welcome the self-imposed docility of the strikers' pickets.

A survey carried out by Emile Burns for the Labour Research Department into the activities of 140 trades councils during the strike reported the following:

> Bath: '[pickets] have been complimented and thanked by Mayor and Chief Constable for maintaining perfect order; advised Mayor first day of strike to disband local specials as superfluosities.'
>
> Ilkeston: 'Police very good and sooner assisted than interfered with us.'
>
> Leyton: 'Very pleasant relationship with the police.'
>
> Lincoln: 'We had a fairly strong influence on city affairs, and the police asked us to supply the whole of the special constables — which we did.'
>
> Selby: 'Police assistance could not be improved upon; our strike police and local police worked in complete harmony.'
>
> Swindon: 'We worked so well with the police that when our autocratic Mayor sent two tramcars on the streets the police allowed our strike leaders to take charge of the situation. This was the only incident of excitement during the whole of the strike.'
>
> Yeovil: 'There was a good feeling exhibited by the town police throughout.'[37]

Bradford Worker reported 'police and strikers on best terms':

> If our men keep calm we are sure there will be no trouble with the Bradford police, who with their superiors know how to deal fairly in a crisis like this.

Grantham Joint Strike Committee, 7 May:

> We have given them an assurance that there shall be no violence on the part of our men, and the chief constable has promised to inform us before taking any action, of any probable grounds for complaint. At present we are pleased to say that there is absolutely no indication of any unrest amongst us.

Preston Strike News: 'We wish to thank the chief constable and his men for the courtesy and patience during this trying period.'

Victory Bulletin, Kingston and District Trades Council, 11 May: 'The police were simply splendid.'

Bow and Bromley Strike Bulletin of 6 May included a message from George Lansbury:

> Don't quarrel with the police. We can and will win without disorder of any kind. Policemen are of our flesh and bone of our bones, and we will co-operate with them to keep the peace.[38]

> Tilling's bus strikers of Brighton actually presented the chief constable with a silver salver after the strike; and, generally, the atmosphere was more often one of mutual tolerance and even amity.[39]

In Sussex more than a thousand strikers 'passed a vote of confidence on the local police sergeant and his constables which was received with musical honours.'[40]

Heeding official advice, pickets often showed consideration for the difficulties the state faced in undermining the strike! For example, at Newcastle on 5 May a government report described how about 5,000 pickets assembled outside the Central Railway Station:

> 'The crowd appeared formidable but at the request of the police superintendent they were addressed by a trade union secretary who advised them that disorder would hurt their cause. He said that these demonstrative tactics were putting an undue strain on the police. The crowd then dispersed.' Such cooperation by strikers with the police was entirely in line with the TUC's call to maintain order and discipline.[41]

To help good relations with the police, strikers were encouraged to engage in sport with them. The **British Worker** reported, under the headings 'sports for the Masses', 'Strikers beat Police at Football', 'Music and Drama':

> In many parts of the country excellent amusement and recreation facilities have been provided for the strikers and their families. Special football and cricket matches and a variety of other sports took place yesterday, while there were plenty of indoor attractions, such as concerts, dramatic entertainments and whist drives.[42]

From Plymouth we are informed:

> The sports committee were highly successful in their arrangements — concerts, billiard tournaments, card parties, cycle runs into the country districts, and football matches being arranged by them (on one occasion with the local police team, whom they defeated by 2 goals to 1 — this match being played at the request of our chief constable, whose wife kicked off). The local clergy were approached and asked to place their

Sunday Schools at the disposal of the sports committee, which many did very readily, and in addition daily religious services were arranged and well attended.[43]

At Peterborough the Mayor and Chief Constable gave use of the sports grounds at reduced prices or free of charge to Committees who were organising concerts and games of tennis, bowls and football.[44]

At Banbury joint concerts were arranged and both sides competed in a tug-of-war. At Norwich strikers and police organised a series of athletic matches under the auspices of the chief constable. In all of the eastern counties between London and the Humber, strike committees worked with police and civic leaders 'to keep the peace and organise recreations.'[45]

The Sheffield Forward, official publication of the Sheffield Trades and Labour Council, reported on 10 May under the headline 'Friendly Relations with the Police':

> At Lewes the police and strikers have organised a public billiards match, whilst the Forest of Dean have received a letter from the local trade union organisations saying that union members are open to assist the police in maintaining order in any way the police think fit.[46]

About a week after the end of the strike, a concert was organised by Coalville Miners' Committee, with an audience of 1,600. They were addressed by E Holmes, chief constable of Leicestershire. He spoke about 'the wonderful way in which the people behaved themselves in those trying times.'

> He was absolutely certain that there was in the country a great volume of sympathy with the miners in their struggle. (Cheers.) So he wanted to emphasise the importance of continued loyalty to the law by which they would increase that sympathy. (Cheers.)

J Smith, the local miners' agent, said he thought 'it was well that he should have a word at that meeting. They were really passive resisters and did not regard the police as a menace to the situation.'[47]

In a letter to the editor of the **Police Review**, the secretary of the Newton Heath branch of ASLEF conveyed the unanimously adopted resolution of the branch on 23 May: the branch

> hereby place on record its appreciation and offers its thanks to the superintendent and members of the staff of the Newton Heath Police Station, and to the members of the [Manchester] force who took part

in *assisting our members to effectively control themselves during the recent industrial dispute.*'[48]

One can see how successful the trade union leaders were in keeping the strike passive from the following fact: according to **Police Review** only 18 special constables were assaulted during the entire strike. 'One Special was stabbed with a chisel, another had a broken wrist and a third was cut about the face.' How tiny was the number is clear from the fact that the total number of Specials was 240,000, and that '43,800 truncheons were issued to Specials'.[49] The editor of **Police Review** pointed to the 'tact and commonsense displayed by both sides.'[50]

Because the officials encouraged workers to submit to state-organised blacklegging there were few arrests. The Home Secretary told the House of Commons that during the strike 632 people were imprisoned in England and Wales under the Emergency Powers Act and 409 in Scotland, making a total of 1,041.[51] This was a low figure, remembering the 3½ million workers involved in the dispute. The 9,000 arrested in the General Strike and the miners' lock-out that continued till December 1926 can be compared with the 9,778 arrested out of some 140,000 miners in the 1984–5 strike.[52]

As we shall see, the logic of the class struggle was stronger than the orders of the General Council, and relations with the police were far from harmonious at all times. Violence broke out again and again.

Besides participation in sport, the other main cultural activity of workers on strike, it seems, was churchgoing. In Battersea:

> On the second day of the strike the mayor approached several local churches suggesting that, 'to mitigate the unnecessary congregation of the public on the streets', churches and union halls should be opened to the public for rest purposes, and perhaps simple services or lectures could be given.
>
> One minister, the Reverend J W Harford at the Lavender Hill Congregational Church, declared that he and his colleagues 'unanimously fell in with the suggestion'. Not only would he open his hall and provide refreshments, but he would also be willing to give lectures. He suggested, under the heading 'Prophets and Priests of Democracy', lectures on Plato, Will Langland, John Wyclif and Thomas More. Other churches responded by opening their halls and, importantly, allowing their Sunday collections to be contributed to the Council of Action's fighting fund.

On Sunday afternoon the local NUR Transport Joint Strike Committee organised a church parade with banners, to march from Unity Hall in Falcon Grove to the nearby St Mary's Church. Having sung 'O God our Help in Ages Past', the congregation listened to a sermon. Subsequent events would suggest that, although there was some approval for what the vicar had to say, many present would have demurred had they not been in church when he said '. . . the railmen should remember that they are dealing with people with hearts. Why not get together and talk heart to heart.'[53]

Lansbury's **Bulletin** of 8 May reported:

> Tomorrow is Sunday. You will come to our meetings at night, but I would like you to attend the Church Services nearest your home . . . It is Christ's gospel of passive resistance which you are practising today.

From Newport on the Isle of Wight we are informed that prior to 'proceeding to a Special Brotherhood Service . . . 200 strikers filed past the Cenotaph and placed on it a wreath of laurels.' The Preston Strike Committee reported that on Sunday 9 May:

> Meetings took place simultaneously all over the country of inter-denominational bodies praying that the parties concerned be brought together with a view of negotiations being resumed . . . It is felt that the churches, irrespective of creed, have a golden opportunity in this crisis, of retaining the confidence of their respective followers.[54]

One can see how far many of the strikers were involved with pacifism, with non-violence towards employers, police and scabs, from events in Halifax. There management wanted the uniforms of the tramwaymen on strike to be returned so that they could clothe the scabs. The strike committee obliged!

> On Thursday [6 May] the tramwaymen, at the requst of the Tramway Committee, delivered up their uniforms. They marched in a procession supported by 4,000 strikers, and led by the local Labour mayor, Councillor W Smith, passed in their uniforms at the depot in perfect order and amid great enthusiasm.[55]

> In Wigan, where the railwaymen carried the burden of the strike on their backs, the editor appointed by them, on being chosen, 'knelt . . . acknowledged our weakness and asked for divine guidance,' and on Sunday he produced the curious bulletin reproduced here, inexplicable in any other country.

WIGAN JOINT STRIKE COMMITTEE.
LEGS OF MAN ASSEMBLY ROOMS

No. 2. Sixth day of strike. Sunday May 9th 1926.

MY DEAR PUBLIC,

Remember the Sabbath Day to keep it Holy.

Thou shalt love the Lord thy God with,
All thy heart, soul, mind and strength, and,
Thy neighbour as thyself.

Daily bulletin.
News from all points.
Situation magnificent.
Everywhere solid.

Public meetings well supported by eminent men of all shades of
thought and from all stations of life.

(*Wigan Strike Bulletin, Sunday 9 May*)

All St Albans railway strikers formed into procession on one day and
marched into the Abbey for a special service. And it was the same
railwaymen who on the 13th refused to go back and wired to the
General Council, cursing it and telling it to reimpose the strike.
Shrewsbury's official time-table one day began:
9.45 a.m. Intercession service at ——— Chapel.
10.45 a.m. Strike Committee meets. All strikers may attend and listen.
12.0 Noon. Service at St Mary's.

Postgate, Horrabin and Wilkinson commented on the above:
'Some of the strongest fighting centres proved to be also the most
religious . . . Foreign socialists were unable to understand the part
played by religion in the strike.'[56]
  The various religious activities during the strike remind one of
the reaction of Trotsky and Lenin to the influence of religion over
the British working class. Trotsky remembered:

I once visited, together with Lenin and Krupskaya, a 'free church' in
London where we heard socialist speeches interspersed with psalms.
The preacher was a printer who had just returned from Australia. he
spoke about the social revolution. The congregation begged God in
the psalms that he establish such an order where there would be

neither poor nor rich. Such was my first practical acquaintance with the British labour movement nearly a quarter of a century ago (1902). What role, I asked myself at the time, does a psalm play in connection with a revolutionary speech? That of a safety-valve. Concentrated vapours of discontent issued forth beneath the dome of the Church and rose into the sky. This is the basic function of the Church in class society.[57]

Religion has been one of the principal forms of bourgeois influence on the working class in Britain.

The atmosphere of calm was not disrupted, but was on the contrary encouraged by the activities of Labour-controlled local councils. Only a small minority of them refused facilities for the recruitment of OMS volunteers or restricted their use. The majority of Labour councillors, like the mayor of Birmingham — who chaired the city's Emergency Committee, saw their first duty as obedience to the law.[58]

To give respectability to the strike, to imbue it with patriotism, the TUC issued an instruction to strikers to wear their military decorations. Thus reverence for the law and God was matched by a patriotic regard for the British state. The **British Worker** of 9 May published an item under the heading 'Wear your medals', appealing

> to ex-servicemen strikers to wear their badges and decorations at all demonstrations and processions, thus showing the public that the men the government is fighting today are the same men who fought for that government yesterday.[59]

Transport workers, many of them wearing their war ribbons, attended services at St Luke's, West Norwood, and the clergy of that church were opening the men's branch meetings with prayer.[60] On 10 May we are informed from Poplar: 'War medals and service decorations are very common.' The **St Marylebone Bulletin** of 10 May reported:

> NUR members of the LNER at Marylebone have a grand array of medals and decorations covering every front from Mons to the end of the 'Great War for Civilisation' — France, Belgium, Greece, Turkey, Egypt, Gallipoli and Palestine. It is suggested that all men in the strike should wear their war medals.

Camberwell Strike Bulletin, 10 May:

On Sunday morning, about 400 strikers from the Nunhead Bus Garage paraded in military formation to the Central Hall, Peckham, where a Church Service was held. All the men wore 1914–18 War Decorations — many of them wearing as many as six medals.[61]

Chapter Eighteen

CONTROLLING FOOD SUPPLIES

ONE CRUCIAL AREA damaged most seriously by the bureaucratically-imposed passivity was control over food supplies. At the beginning of the strike the government's Supply and Transport Committee reported sizeable food stocks:

1. *Wheat and Flour*
Stocks between two to three weeks. Over country as a whole a maximum of six weeks' supply, including farm stocks, which are not readily made available.

2. *Meat*
. . . no shortage, so far as the country as a whole is concerned, is to be anticipated in the immediate future.

3. *Provisions*
a) Butter: . . . rather above the average.
b) Cheese: 3–4,000 tons in London and about 1,500 distributed between Liverpool and Bristol.
c) Bacon: Normal.
d) Sugar: Supplies in London heavy. Liverpool a little short. Bristol normal. Adequate supplies of raw sugar, but coal may stop supplies.
'Dealers' stocks of sugar are approximately three days and panic orders have been received for increased supplies. Co-operative Societies and the multiple shops have generally one or two weeks' extra supply on hand. London refiners were working all night on the night of 30 April/1 May on delivery and clearance of sugar.
e) Tea: 4–8 weeks' supply over the country.
f) Canned Milk: Fair stock with retailers, importers and wholesalers somewhat short.[1]

With ample food supplies in stock, the key problem for the workers on strike was who should control the movement of food in the country: should it be the government agency or the strike committees? As the Northumberland and Durham General Council Joint Strike Committee clearly saw:

> the problem of the general strike can be focussed down to one thing — the struggle for food control. Who feeds the people wins the strike![2]

However for the unions to control the feeding of the people, they had to challenge the power of the state by mounting mass pickets. Without them control over food distribution was impossible.

The TUC wanted to avoid confronting the state at any cost. On 1 May Walter Citrine, acting secretary of the TUC, wrote to Baldwin:

> Dear Sir — I am directed to inform you that in the event of the strike of unions affiliated to the Trades Union Congress taking place in support of the miners who have been locked out, the General Council is prepared to enter into arrangements for the distribution of essential foodstuffs.
>
> Should the government desire to discuss the matter with the General Council they are available for that purpose.
>
> The General Council will be glad to learn your wishes in this respect.
> Yours faithfully,
> Walter M. Citrine

The government naturally declined Citrine's offer to collaborate in food distribution. To accept dual control would have amounted to accepting dual power. On 3 May Winston Churchill, who was Chancellor of the Exchequer in the Baldwin government and editor of the **British Gazette** during the strike, told the House of Commons:

> I readily recognise the offer which was made to convey food and necessaries by the Trade Union Committee . . . It may have been a wise thing for the trade unions to have done, but . . . what government in the world could enter into partnership with a rival government, against which it is endeavouring to defend itself and society, and allow that rival government to sit in judgment on every train that runs and on every lorry on the road?[4]

Perhaps not many strikers used the term 'dual power', but local strike committees saw the importance of the issue. From the beginning permits to move food under union auspices were issued by local and national strike bodies. And if the strike was to be solid no road transport other than that with special permission from strike committees could be allowed. The Northumberland and Durham Joint Strike Committee reported: '. . . the mere rumble of wheels was something that weakened the morale of our men, and correspondingly cheered the other side.'

> In most towns, central strike committees set up their own permit committees and assumed the function of coordinating the policies of individual unions over the issuing of permits or exemptions. The General Council did not encourage this tendency and issued instructions limiting the issue of permits to individual unions or joint transport committees, but the natural way for unions to sort out conflicting decisions and avert chaos was to turn to the local Councils of Action or central strike committees for a ruling.[5]

Alas, too many abuses of the permit system took place.

> . . . the government forces had begun to practise forgery and evasion on a large scale. Toy rocking horses, bedding for blacklegs, and even coal were labelled FOOD ONLY, and local strike committee permits were being imitated. 'People are often found masquerading as loaves of bread,' remarked the **Westminster Worker**.[6]

The **Merseyside Council of Action Strike Bulletin** of 5 May stated:

> Permits issued are being abused and vans labelled 'Food Only' are being used to transport blacklegs, metal and machinery, etc. These abuses may compel council to withdraw permits already issued.

The **Doncaster Council of Action Strike Bulletin** of 11 May reported: 'A large number of brewery wagons conveying this beverage and marked "FOOD ONLY" pass through our streets.'[7]

The permit system was like a sieve. G A Phillips writes:

> . . . in the early stage of the stoppage, the movement of foodstuffs (and sometimes other commodities) by road from wholesalers to retailers and thence to customers was approved almost everywhere — whether by transport unions acting on their own behalf or by joint strike committees and their satellites. This was the practice of militant Councils of Action at Sheffield, Coventry, Preston, Cowdenbeath and the 'red village' of Chopwell in County Durham, as well as of organisations of more moderate complexion at Liverpool, Birmingham, Edinburgh and Cardiff. It seems probable that, at this juncture, local strike leaders in many centres hoped to demonstrate the impotence of

the government's emergency provisions . . . But the real objective of 'the struggle for food control' was not simply to secure a symbolic victory; if the unions could indeed establish the supremacy of their own permit system they would thereby be in a position to prohibit the movement of all 'inessential' commodities, and ensure that the General Strike established a stranglehold upon the whole economy.[8]

In only very few cases indeed did the permit system work effectively. On 7 May the National Strike Organisation Committee was told that the government system of distribution had broken down in Newcastle, Plymouth and Salford, and that in all three places the authorities had sought help in maintaining supplies,[9] but these were rare exceptions.

One factor could have aided union control over food movement: a firm agreement with the Cooperative Movement. The Co-ops had grown up as a movement for workers' self-help in the nineteenth century and retained links with the trade unions and Labour. However things were not encouraging. Discussions between the Industrial Committee of the TUC, the MFGB representatives and the Cooperative Union took place on 16 February 1926. The Cooperative representatives complained about their experience in the miners' dispute of 1921 when heavy financial advances were made that were still not repaid. They also referred indignantly to a statement by A J Cook in December 1925 at a meeting in South Wales, in which he said:

> In the coming struggle there would be a new trinity . . . a linking up of the miners' cause with the political, industrial and cooperative movements. The cooperative movement would be the victualling movement for the fighting forces of labour.

The secretary of the Cooperative Union immediately wrote the following letter to Walter Citrine:

> It is a great pity that Mr Cook cannot be 'muzzled'. See his statement again this week that an arrangement has been come to for the Co-operative Movement to deal with the question in case of a crisis. This is causing a lot of discussion in the Cooperative Movement, *because no such arrangement has been come to*, and I think he ought to be a little more guarded in his statements, as it is making our position more difficult every time statements like that appear in the press.[10]

Now the Cooperative Union's representative refused to guarantee any assistance to the unions unless the assets of the whole trade union movement were pledged in advance. Neither the Industrial Committee nor the General Council had the authority to give such a pledge.[11]

As no agreement had been reached, the Cooperative Wholesale Society issued a circular on 23 April warning its member societies not to grant credit. The estrangement of the Cooperative Movement from the strike led to a deputation of its directors going to see Sir Philip Cunliffe-Lister, President of the Board of Trade, on 8 May to ask for the assistance of government agencies where necessary to maintain services.[12] On its side the TUC made no ruling to give the Cooperative Societies favourable treatment on the issue of permits.

Despite the mutual distrust at the top, local relations between strike committees and Cooperatives were often very good indeed. Half the trades councils that responded to the Labour Research Department survey collected by Emile Burns reported that local Cooperative stores gave help to the strikers, usually in the form of credit.[13]

On 6 May, in face of the abuses of the permit system, Ernest Bevin declared on behalf of the TUC that no permits were to be issued by any individual trade union or trades council. A Joint Transport Committee was to be set up in every district, and 'all existing permits must be reviewed by the Transport Committee at once.'[14] It was also announced that a National Committee operating from Unity House (NUR headquarters) would deal with the release of foodstuffs. This announcement produced a sharp reaction in the government's **British Gazette**, which accused the TUC of trying to blackmail the nation by holding up food supplies:

> The situation is becoming more intense and the climax is not yet reached. Orders have been sent by the leaders of the railway and transport trade unions to do their utmost to paralyse and break down the supply of food and the necessaries of life.
>
> An organised attempt is being made to starve the people and to wreck the state, and the legal and constitutional aspects are entering upon a new phase.[15]

The alternatives facing the trade union movement were stark: either to impose its will on the movement of foodstuffs by effective mass picketing, preventing the movement of all vehicles without permits, or to give way. The trade union leaders tried after a couple of days to avoid making the choice.

What was the TUC's answer to the accusation by the **British Gazette** that it was aiming 'to starve the people and to wreck the state'? The General Council published in the **British Worker** a long statement denying the government's accusation, and including the following significant sentence: 'The General Council has done nothing to imperil the food supplies; on the contrary, its members were instructed to co-operate with the government in maintaining them.'[16] What pathetic crawlers!

Next day, 10 May, the General Council announced that it was giving up the struggle over the control of food supplies:

FOOD SUPPLIES

The General Council offered to assist in the distribution of food supplies in a letter sent to the prime minister before the strike was decided, but this offer was ignored. . . . several local [government] bodies made arrangements with local Strike Committees and permits were issued by the latter.

It has now to be reported that the government has ordered such permits to be withdrawn in many places. In order to avoid conflict between the authorities and men on strike, the Council has felt it necessary to withdraw its permits in these cases.[17]

This was a complete capitulation to the government, giving up any semblance of control over food movement.

If the General Council had been serious about winning the strike, its answer should have been a tightening of control over the movement of foodstuffs by organising effecting mass picketing. A glimpse of what was possible can be gleaned from what happened in the North East.

On 6 May Martin Connolly, Labour MP for Newcastle East, stated in the House of Commons

that the OMS has entirely broken down, that the authorities have approached the trade unions and asked them to take over the vital services, and that the trade unions have consented to do so on condition that all extra police, all troops, and the OMS services shall be withdrawn. This has been done, and the city is going on all right.[18]

This was later denied by the Attorney General. What are the known facts? The **Account of the Proceedings of the Northumberland and Durham General Council Joint Strike Committee** tells the story: On the evening of 5 May James Tarbit, of the National Union of General and Municipal Workers and a prominent member of both the General Council and the joint strike committee, informed the latter body that OMS volunteers had been brought on the quayside in order to unload foodstuffs. As a consequence, trade union labour already employed there under permit refused to continue working. An additional irritant was the mooring in the Tyne of two destroyers and a submarine. Later on the same evening, the Northern Division's Food Officer, General Sir R A Kerr Montgomery, telephoned a request from Sir Kingsley Wood, Civil Commissioner for the North East, that he would like a meeting with Tarbit. Following a second telephone call, a meeting was arranged between the Civil Commissioner and three representatives of the joint strike committee, C R Flynn, secretary of the joint strike committee, James White, its chairman, and James Tarbit.

After the meeting the three representatives reported back to the joint strike committee. A long extract from the minutes taken at the meeting with the Civil Commissioner is worth including.

> Wood had stated that his duty was to see that food supplies are maintained. There would, he said, be no interference if the trade unionists would continue to do the work. Tarbit had explained why the men had withdrawn their labour, [because of the presence of the OMS] . . . Tarbit raised the question of unloading ships, part of which only was foodstuffs, and stated that his men would equally object to working with the Emergency Organisation . . . if these people unloaded the other parts of the cargo. Wood asked what our proposal was in such cases. We made the suggestion to him that the ships could either go to anchorage in the river with their non-food cargoes on board, waiting the end of the dispute for complete discharge, or return to their port of origin. It was further represented by us to him, with the utmost emphasis, that he should take steps to have the naval contingent, which had been berthed alongside the quay, in a most provocative manner, moved back to the usual naval anchorage at Jarrow, as it was impossible for us to agree that our men should be forced to work under the shadow of their guns. Wood stated that he had no control over the Admiralty in this matter, but appeared to indicate that a suggestion from him to the commanders of the vessels might have the desired effect.

The following day's meeting was similarly reported:

Wood stated that they agreed to take steps to see that no outside people were brought in. He suggested that so far as the quay is concerned, the trade unions appoint an officer to work in conjunction with an officer appointed by him, Wood, to deal with any trouble which might arise and to supervise the work. Generally, they (Wood and co) agreed to the definition of foodstuffs as outlined by the TUC and felt that no disagreement could arise on this head. We asked what would be the position regarding non-unionists and blacklegs, as our men would only acknowledge permits issued to the trade unionists by the strike committee. Wood replied: 'They would welcome any suggestions which we can make inside the government scheme, but any questions of trade union labour loading and unloading vessels should be obviated by dual control.' We suggested that this could only be met by clearing off the quay altogether and leaving the men who usually did the work to carry on as usual. He replied that he could not abrogate his functions or act contrary to the instructions he had received. Montgomery stated that the full extent to which they would go, and they were anxious that this should operate, was that 'all men now doing their ordinary work should continue to do so.' Wood concurred and stated 'he would take any steps in conjunction with the executive here to see that this is carried out.' A general discussion then took place in reference to non-union labour, and Montgomery stated that they would go as far as to see that any chauffeur whose normal work is not to drive the lorries would be put off.[19]

So determined action by dockers had forced the government's representatives to offer the strike committee a share in the maintenance of essential services in the district. Whatever the strenuous denials by the government, the evidence supports the joint strike committee's statement.

The workers' initiative was to have further repercussions. Because the local rank and file had had a taste of their own power they were ready to fight when the government's representatives reneged on their deal. When workers battled to regain control of food movements in the Newcastle and Durham area the state faced its greatest difficulties and there was the highest level of arrests. We shall return to this subject shortly.

The events in Newcastle throw light on the real revolutionary *potential* inherent in the struggle for control of food supplies. Alas, with the tight bureaucratic control over every aspect of the General Strike, this opportunity was nipped in the bud. If the strike had continued for any length the government effort would have been in jeopardy, notwithstanding the generally half-hearted approach of union officials to control of food supplies. After the event, Colonel Strange, South Western Divisional Food Officer, admitted how close he had come to a major confrontation. He recorded that local food stocks ran very low and that the 'huge problem' of replacing rail by road-borne transport was never thoroughly tested. 'Had the General Strike lasted another fortnight or even another week', he warned, 'a very different story would have had to be recorded.'[20]

The idea of workers' control must have terrified the capitalists and the government. As one historian wrote:

> The sight of these [permits] posted on the windshields of cars and lorries was as maddening to the government's supporters as it was heartening to the strikers.[21]

What an inspiration to workers was even the limited power of giving or withholding permits can be seen from a letter of an Ashton sheetmetal worker in his union journal:

> Employers of labour were coming, cap in hand, begging for permission to do certain things, or, to be more correct, to allow their workers to return to perform certain customary operations. 'Please can I move a quantity of coal from such and such a place' or 'please can my transport workers move certain foodstuffs in this or that direction . . .' Most of them turned empty away after a most humiliating experience, for one and all were put through a stern questioning, just to make them realise that we and not they were the salt of the earth.
>
> I thought of the many occasions when I had been turned empty away from the door of some workshop in a weary struggle to get the means to purchase the essentials of life for self and dependents . . . I thought of the many occasions I had been called upon to meet these people in the never-ending struggle to obtain decent conditions for those around me, and its consequent result in my joining the ranks of the unemployed; of the cheap sneers when members of my class had attempted to rouse consciousness as to the real facts of the struggle . . . The only tactic practised by some of them was bullying, and that was no use in a situation such as this; some tried persuasion, referring to us as *Mr Chairman and Gentlemen*, but only a rigid examination of the stern facts of the case moved our actions. The cap-in-hand position reversed.[22]

Alas, the potential for workers' control was never actively developed and remained in its latent form. Many a chrysalis dies without turning into a butterfly.

Chapter Nineteen

LOCAL ORGANISATION OF THE STRIKE

THE LOCAL organisation of the General Strike was in the hands of councils of action or joint strike committees. Probably between 400 and 500 such organisations existed. In a great many cases these bodies were made up of the local trades councils, often with the addition of extra people.

Because of union leaders' efforts to run the strike through the machinery of their individual unions, there was often considerable confusion locally, and many trades councils were bypassed. In some places there were a number of different strike committees with conflicting powers. The Northumberland and Durham Central Joint Strike Committee, set up at a conference on 4 May, suffered from a number of defects. First, the Durham Miners' Association, patently the most influential union in the county, refused to join it. (It formed its own strike committee only two hours before the strike was called off.) Secondly, the joint strike committee had virtually no importance north of Ashington or South of Gateshead.[1]

In Darlingon there existed two strike committees: one was the Darlington Council of Action, a body centred on the local trades council; the other, representing far more workers, was the Rail and Transport Strike Committee.[2]

Leeds

> possessed no less than four rival strike committees, mutually jealous, and must have been the worst conducted town in England. The trouble was in part due to the possession by certain full-time officials of a direct telephone line to London. They clustered round this and remained isolated and superior.[3]

Frequently the representatives of the transport unions (or the railway unions alone) formed executives independent of the central strike committees, as for example in Birmingham, Glasgow, Darlington, Nottingham, Oldham, Crewe, Dunfermline, Gloucester, Stoke, Dorking and Llandudno.[4]

We have not been able to find one case of shop stewards being represented on the councils of action or joint strike committees.

So who were the key people in the councils of action — rank-and-file workers or full-time trade union officials? Margaret Morris sums up the situation thus:

> district officials or branch officers of the main unions were usually the leading members of the local trades councils.[5]

In the case of the Northumberland and Durham Joint Strike Committee mentioned above, the chairman was James White, area secretary of the TGWU, and the secretary was Charles Flynn, northern divisional officer of the National Union of Distributive and Allied Workers. Another prominent member was James Tarbit, the district official of the National Union of General and Municipal Workers.

Birmingham's strike organisation called itself the Trade Union Emergency Committee. Its leadership consisted of 'long-standing trade union officials of maturity, responsibility and moderation', according to the historian of the Birmingham labour movement.[6] The president, secretary and vice-president of the trades council occupied similar offices in the new committee. They were assisted by five executive members of the trades council, including one local magistrate. The nine union representatives had among their number another two magistrates, two local councillors and a former MP for the National Democratic Party. Two more people were co-opted to help with publicity.

> This, then, was the general staff. A mild and respectable group of men . . . four magistrates, two councillors and an ex-MP, amongst the score which made up the committee.[7]

Local strike committees were very much subordinated to the will of the TUC and the executives of their respective trade unions. The Northumberland and Durham Committee showed this clearly:

> the strike committee was subject to the decisions of the TUC General Council and to those of the trade union executives and not to any decisions which that particular conference might take.[8]

In the words of Robin Page Arnot, who played a central role in establishing and running this committee, the committee abided by the TUC's whole approach to the strike situation — and it was their watchword that where they had no discretionary power, they must 'carry out the Trade Union Congress decisions to the letter, no matter how many misgivings they might have'.[9]

In Sheffield the Central Dispute Committee saw its function as being:

> limited to interpreting how best to apply locally a strategy determined by the TUC, and not to determining the strategy itself . . . it saw . . . its *raison d'être* — in being a subordinate agent of the General Council of the TUC. It was certainly not pushing for the power to be a 'soviet' in even the limited sense in which that had been discussed in Sheffield in 1919. Nationally and locally, things had changed too much since then.[10]

Middlesbrough's strike body clearly conceived of its role as entirely circumscribed by bureaucratic red tape:

> the Central Strike Committee would not interfere with the domestic policy of any union, in any other than a constitutional way. Having regard to the discussion which took place on this point, it became evident that the Central Strike Committee could only hope to act as a co-ordinating and not a directional body at the outset, whatever may have been possible as the strike continued.[11]

In a number of areas the strike committees were mere shadows of organisation. As Emile Burns writes of the Central London Strike Committee: 'No effective contact was maintained either with the local councils of action or strike committees'.[12] Again, the official history of the London Trades Council sadly admits:

> The Central Strike Committee became an organ without real power, its functions limited to convening meetings of local delegates and giving advice and guidance which it could not enforce.[13]

Strike organisation in Glasgow, the heart of 'Red Clydeside', might have been expected to be different. The Central Strike Coordinating Committee did choose Peter Kerrigan, a prominent Communist, as its chairman, but it also had 23 members 'most of whom were full-time union officials'.[14] As its name implied, it saw its main function not as directing, but as *co-ordinating* the activities of the separate unions involved in the strike. The committee was prepared to criticise the TUC's decisions, but not to change the character of the strike from that determined by the TUC . . . despite its Communist leadership, the [committee] does not seem to have issued any propaganda for the Communist demand for a Labour government and coal nationalisation, nor did it try to set up a Workers' Defence Corps or Food Commissariat with the help of the Cooperative Societies.[15]

The Glasgow Central Strike Coordinating Committee did not even find it necessary to have a paper of its own separate from the official Scottish TUC paper, **The Scottish Worker**.[16] When Kerrigan suggested mass picketing, this was rejected by the committee, and he abided by its decision.[17]

Beneath this central coordinating committee were sixteen area committees. Divisional Labour Parties were asked to set these committees up, which they did. Many were chaired by Labour councillors. The central body

instructed the area committees to 'maintain discipline throughout the parliamentary division . . . prevent unauthorised propaganda . . . give effect to any instructions that may be forwarded by the TUC, the Scottish TUC, or the Central Strike Coordinating Committee.[18]

Indeed, at no point throughout the nine days was the TUC's authority questioned.[19]

Despite Kerrigan's leadership, the committee followed, practically slavishly, the line coming from the TUC. Many years later Kerrigan wrote:

For the nine days of the strike I was to be busy, almost to the exclusion of all other activity, with the work of the Central Strike Coordinating Committee, of which I was first vice-chairman and then chairman. People ask me today: did I expect the betrayal of the General Strike? I always have to reply that, amid the struggle, I never thought of it.[20]

The role of the Glasgow Central Strike Coordinating Committee was merely to act 'as a clearing house for information', so it 'issued bulletins, established a courier service, handled inter-union disputes and took up complaints with the police.'[21] Strike committees by and large showed little independence from the trade union bureaucracy and Glasgow was no exception:

It is sometimes said in discussion of the General Strike that towards its end control was passing out of the hands of the General Council into that of local left-wing militants. This does not appear to have been happening with the Central Strike Coordinating Committee . . . Indeed, at no point throughout the nine days was the TUC's authority questioned.[22]

And to think that it was Peter Kerrigan, future national industrial organiser of the Communist Party, who chaired this committee!

So local strike organisations did not tug particularly hard on the leash held by the General Council. One historian summarises the attitude of local committees in this way:

Taken as a whole, [the] mass of local evidence suggests that the majority of trades councils and strike organs were no more aggressive in temper or lawless in their behaviour than the General Council itself. They displayed on the contrary a strong determination to preserve discipline and demonstrate obedience.[23]

The core of the local strike committees were, as we said, the trades councils. These bodies had very restricted powers. Negotiations over wages and conditions in industry were carried out either nationally or at the workplace. Trades councils brought together representatives of different trade union branches in a locality, hence did not relate directly to the workplaces, and could play no significant part in bargaining over wages and conditions. Furthermore they had no financial or other sanctions to bind their members in any way, only playing a role in issues away from the workplace such as health, education or housing — acting as pressure groups in the community.

During the great industrial militancy of 1910–20 the trades councils had at best played a marginal role. Thus one historian, Alan Clinton, writes of their role in the rise of the shop stewards' movement during the First World War:

Trades councils were largely organisations of the trade union machinery itself, not in any way adapted to the workshop problems which arose in the period and expressed themselves in the shop stewards' movement. Though largely ignored at the time by trade union leaders, the trades councils as a whole reflected their policies and attitudes, if usually in a somewhat more radical form. Thus the relationship between the trades councils and the shop stewards' movement was one of occasional co-operation rather than active support.[24]

A book on the history of the Sheffield trades council states that the development of the wartime shop stewards' movement owed nothing to the trades council.[25] Similarly, Clyde shop stewards assiduously avoided the Glasgow Trades Council.[26]

Only on matters away from industry — such as agitation against the long food queues during the war — did shop stewards collaborate with trades councils. It was on this issue that both the Sheffield Workers' Committee and Coventry Engineering Joint Committee worked with their local trades councils.[27]

So trades councils, separated from the point of production, lacked the collective strength of rank-and-file organisations. Certainly they were geographically closer to the workers than the TUC, and their delegates were not primarily full-time functionaries, but they still saw themselves as part of the official machinery of trade unionism. Consequently they suffered from the sectionalism of the individual union delegations. The bureaucratic method was reproduced within them, just as it was in the TUC, though on a smaller scale.

Shortly after the General Strike, the executive committee of the Comintern came up with the ludicrous notion that trades councils were fully-fledged *soviets*:

> the councils of action organised by the trade unions actually developed into district *soviets*. The departments organised by the General Council already resembled in their structure and functions, the departments of the Petersburg Soviet in the period of so-called 'dual power' (February–November 1917).[28]

The attitude of revolutionaries to trades councils had not always been so inane. It was only with the collapse of the shop stewards' movement that leading Communists started to augment their opinion of the trades councils. Take the example of J T Murphy, the best worker intellectual of the shop stewards' movement during the First World War. He was once very clear that there was a *radical* difference between the trades councils and the workers' committees. In 1917 he wrote:

> . . . the trades council is only indirectly related to the workshops, whereas the workers' committee is directly related. The former has no power, the latter has the driving power of the directly-connected workers in the workshops.[29]

In 1920 Murphy was still dismissive of the idea that the trades councils could be a 'general staff' at local level:

> The trades councils are not the nuclei of *soviets*. Their ineptitude in all
> industrial disputes provides ample proof of this. They possess no
> executive power of the unions and action comes either through deleg-
> ates from the workshops, etc., or the local district committees of the
> unions, which bodies improvise strike committees composed of stew-
> ards . . . leaving the trades councils in the background or playing a
> reactionary part.[30]

But by 1922 Murphy and the rest of the CPGB leadership sang a
new song. They became convinced that:

> In times of crisis, these trades councils play a very important part . . .
> it is easy to see that the importance of capturing these councils by the
> revolutionists cannot be over-estimated . . . in the very near future
> the trades councils will play an ever-increasing part in the class war.
> Therefore our slogan must be: 'Capture the trades councils!'[31]

The same year Tom Quelch went as far as to describe trades
councils as infant *soviets*:

> This conception of the ultimate object of the trades council, or
> workers' council, is supported by the available evidence we have of
> the further development of our movement. The rise of the *soviets*, or
> workers' councils in Russia is the startlingly supreme example.[32]

In **All Power** Quelch wrote that trades councils

> are the local central bodies of the working-class movement. There is a
> permanent quality about them. Their *bona fides* are without question.
> They are the bodies best fitted to bring complete local working-class
> solidarity into being. They can easily become the most important
> bodies in the movement.[33]

In the crisis leading to Red Friday the Communist Party argued
that trades councils should set themselves up as councils of action.

The idea that trades councils could play a central role in class
struggle was linked historically with the idea of a labour 'general
staff' that dated back to Tom Quelch's articles in the BSP's newspaper a decade earlier.[34] The connection between the slogan of 'All
power to the General Council' and a call for councils of action was
an obvious one. If the TUC, a meeting of national trade union
officials, could establish a general staff to fight workers' national
battles, then a local meeting of union branch officials was a logical

corollary of this. The Councils of Action established in the 'Hands off Russia' campaign of 1920 were held to show the way forward. In reality they had done little more than issue propaganda or lead street demonstrations. The famous blacking of the *Jolly George*, a ship intended to transport armaments for use against Soviet Russia, was the act of rank-and-file dockers, and was unfortunately the unique example of industrial action in the Councils of Action 1920 campaign. Nevertheless the Communist Party threw itself into the trades council movement from 1922 onwards and played a leading part in the call for trades council representation at the TUC.

As the mining crisis drew nearer the idea of trades councils as Councils of Action received increasing attention. An article in May 1925 described what the Communist Party hoped for:

> A council of action is a fighting committee composed of delegates from all the trade union branches in a given district catering for miners, metal workers, railwaymen and transport workers. The purpose of such a Council of Action is to carry out an intensive propaganda to secure united action between these workers in the impending wage struggles . . . The necessity for Councils of Action is to unite all these workers in the localities and to exert rank-and-file pressure upon the officials.[35]

It became obvious in the General Strike that there was no practical alternative to the trades councils in terms of immediate broad strike committees. They became the natural *foci* for organisation. So there was nothing wrong in principle with stressing trades council work and the possibilities for agitation through them. The sad thing was that after the shop stewards' movement disintegrated, the Communist Party leaders made a virtue out of necessity. The problem was not so much the tactic of working through trades councils in itself, but the beliefs of the Communists in pursuing their tactic. In this case, while the party sought to revitalise the councils (they did mean Councils of *Action*), the idea was not to prepare the rank and file for the necessity of going beyond the existing organisations when the possibility arose, but of using them to 'exert rank-and-file pressure upon the officials'. So often when the party intervened, the action proposed was fine in itself, but the purpose to which it was turned led to dependence on the officials.

The tendency was underlined by the rest of the article quoted above:

> Firstly, a concentrated and intensive campaign must be carried on at
> the factory gates. Meetings should be arranged outside all the import-
> ant factories, workshops, garages, depots, at the pitheads, and at the
> docks. Every possible means of popularising the policy among the
> rank and file of a united struggle should be utilised.
> Short and concise handbills should be distributed and mass demon-
> strations and processions, with banners, should be organised wherever
> possible.
> Secondly, this factory gate agitation on behalf of joint action should
> also be utilised for a drive for 100 per cent trade unionism in the
> district.
> Thirdly, the question of the formation of factory, workshop, pit,
> depot, garage and docks committees must be made a prominent
> feature of the general agitation. These worker committees can be of
> tremendous assistance in rallying the rank and file around the policy
> of a fighting Industrial Alliance.[36]

The final point gives the whole meaning of Councils of Action.
They were not designed to replace union executives. Their aim was
to be the rallying of the rank and file around a policy of 'make the
leaders — lead', without warning of the risks of a sell-out. In 1925
an Industrial Aliance of selected trade union bureaucrats was the
intention. In 1926 the slogan became 'All Power to the General
Council'. We see the result of such a policy when tested in the
General Strike.

To recap: the Councils of Action or joint strike committees that
arose during the General Strike were not embryo *soviets*, but largely a
forum for bargaining between the different sectional interests of the
local union bureaucracy. Although, in many cases, the union strike
committees merged with the trades councils, this was never to the
exclusion of accepting orders from above. The General Council
successfully managed to restrict the role of local bodies to that of
supporting the strike committees of the individual unions, and thus
preserved the vertical, sectional, chains of command.

The low level of violence

The level of violence — in other words the degree to which
workers were organised to resist government-inspired scabbing
and challenge the state's monopoly of physical force — was low
during the General Strike.

Violence cannot be abstracted from its context. The October revolution in Petrograd was almost bloodless. This was the result of the overwhelming superiority of the workers' forces and the passivity and disarray of Kerensky's troops. In Britain in 1926 it was the TUC that sowed passivity and disarray, and the workers who lost as a result.

But it had not always been like this. Let us compare events in Liverpool in 1911, 1919 and 1926. In 1911, 70,000 seamen, carters and tramwaymen went on strike.

> Fourteen thousand troops were sent together with police from Leeds, Birmingham and Bradford, and two warships were brought into the Mersey. The outcome was that violence appeared where none had been before.
>
> A demonstration was held on the Plateau of St George's Hall on Sunday, 13 August, to celebrate the strike victories and to cement the newly won solidarity. Though authorised by the police, it produced one of the most unhappy incidents in Liverpool's history, an episode since commemorated locally as 'Bloody Sunday'.

Eighty thousand workers, men and women, went on the demonstration. They were met by a volley of rifle fire.

> Hundreds of people were practically shot out of the mouth of Lord Nelson Street, flying for their lives before a furious baton charge of dozens of policemen. People were knocked over like ninepins. Many were felled to the ground with blood streaming down their heads . . . Hundreds required hospital treatment and the Plateau resembled a battlefield.

Two days later, on 15 August, two strikers were shot dead by troops during an attack on prison vans taking convicted prisoners to Walton gaol.

In 1919:

> a strike of tramwaymen . . . stopped all trams for five days, and during the great rail strike of the same year a battleship was brought to the Mersey and the main railway stations were placed under 'military protection'. The difficulties of the authorities were increased still further when the police union went on strike in July 1919 in protest against the Police Bill, which had made trade unionism illegal in the force . . . Reinforcements drafted into the city after the 'orgy of looting and rioting' which resulted, consisted of 2,500 soldiers, four tanks, a battleship and two destroyers.

Several bayonet charges were made, occasional shots were fired, and some bloodshed occurred.[37]

In 1926 things were radically different. It is true that two battleships and three destroyers entered the Mersey, the former landing food supplies. A troopship arrived from Plymouth and two fully equipped battalions marched off under sealed orders,[38] but the navy and the army *did not* take an active part in the dispute. There were ugly scenes at the tram and bus depots on the Cheshire side of the Mersey, but these were isolated. Altogether in Liverpool there were not more than seven arrests under the Emergency Powers Act.[39]

Two thousand scabs worked in Liverpool's docks. 'They were met with hostility, but rarely with open violence',[40] and this at the same docks that had witnessed the most violent scenes in 1911 and 1919. 'In general, and again contrary to previous experience on Merseyside, the amount of violence and disorder in the area was minimal.'[41]

Further evidence comes from the **Police Review**:

> Liverpool has an unenviable reputation so far as strikes and labour troubles are concerned. But anyone visiting the city during the last great stoppage of work would have wondered where, when and how its bad name had been obtained.[42]

The reason: the high level of passivity inflicted by the discipline of trade union leaders from above. 'Whilst we are fighting for our very existence and liberty, we can still conduct ourselves like gentlemen,' said McLeod, secretary of the Bootle TGWU branch.[43] According to the local Labour MP, Jack Hayes, 'there was a large amount of co-operation between the authorities, the strike leaders and the strikers themselves.'[44]

Railwaymen, it seems, were everywhere amongst the most placid of workers:

> Of nearly 400,000 members of the NUR on strike only 174 were arrested. Of these, fifty-four had their cases dismissed, fourteen were found not guilty, fifty-four were given fines, mostly of £1 or £2, thirty-four were imprisoned, eleven bound over to keep the peace, whilst ten cases against the remainder were withdrawn.

The low level of arrests was the result of the non-aggressive nature of the picketing mounted by railwaymen. Thus the members of the Stratford Branch of the NUR were given the following instructions: 'Pickets' duties are that they must not lay their hands on anyone and they had best keep them in their pockets, they must not impede anyone, but they can converse with anyone by being at their side or walking at their side but not in front of them. If at any time they are interfered with by the police by (sic) carrying out the above duties, then they MUST not reply, but take the number of the policeman and report at this committee room or to the Chief Picket.'[45]

We have already looked at the low overall figures for arrests in 1926. It would be wrong, however, to assume that there was no violence. In certain areas it was highly significant. One historian of the General Strike, Patrick Renshaw, writes:

> The weekend of 8–9 May, with the strike six days old, saw police baton charges at a dozen places in London alone. Outside the capital there were ugly riots at Plymouth, Southsea, Swansea and Nottingham. Shots were fired at a passing train at the important railway centre of Crewe, while the Flying Scotsman, the nation's most important express, was derailed. At Preston, a mob of 5,000 people who tried to storm the police station and release an arrested striker were only beaten back by repeated baton charges. There were similar scenes in such important industrial centres as Middlesbrough, Newcastle and Hull, where there were 25 arrests and 41 hospital admissions. At York another mob tried to release a prisoner, while Edinburgh and Glasgow both saw violent scenes stretching over four or five nights with missiles being thrown and hundreds of arrests.[46]

Another historian, C L Mowat, writes:

> There were violent outbreaks in Glasgow, where buses were overturned and the police charged the crowds, on 5 May; there was trouble in Leeds and Barnsley over attempts to run buses. At Doncaster, on the last day of the strike, a crowd of about a thousand, mostly miners, interfered with traffic, and the police made several baton charges to clear the roads. In many other places, particularly in Scotland and the North of England, pickets interfered with the running of lorries carrying food. In London there were several clashes between police and strikers, in Canning Town, Poplar, Old Kent Road and elsewhere; in the provinces there was violence in Preston, Hull, Middlesbrough, Liverpool, and also in Edinburgh. The police retaliated with arrests . . . At Glasgow over 200 men were arrested, and 100 sentenced for impeding traffic to terms averaging three

months' imprisonment. After the fight at Doncaster 84 men got three months' sentences. Three men at Aberavon received two months' imprisonment at hard labour for having in their possession copies of the **Workers' Weekly** and other Communist literature . . .
At Birmingham the entire strike committee was arrested.

The highest level of violence was in the North East after the breakdown of the negotiations between the strike committee and Sir Kingsley Wood.

The Board of Trade daily bulletins are littered with examples of the problem which was presented by large scale picketing in the Northern Division. A few examples must suffice. On 7 May, the Home Office Situation Report noted that 'Police can protect the unloading of ships, but the difficulty is to get the convoys through the district just outside the city boundary.' Again, bus services were being withdrawn due to the activities of the strikers and 'in the North West area strong pickets have stopped private cars and refused them passage without a permit. Food transport was practically stopped at Consett last night but today the police organised convoys and got all traffic through successfully' . . .
On 8 May, both the **Northern Echo** and the **Newcastle Chronicle** were reporting the obstruction of traffic by strikers in the Stanley area of North West Durham and on the Newcastle to Consett road all vehicles were being turned back by a large crowd of miners thought to come from Chopwell. In the early hours of 10 May, 'an apparently organised attempt took place to stop road traffic on the main Newcastle–Durham road.' Baton charges by the police dispersed the crowds.
The police were informed that large crowds were assembling along the Great North Road at various points between Chester-le-Street and Low Fell. Consequently about a dozen policemen set out from Chester-le-Street in a lorry and were joined by other police at Birtley. Before Birtley was reached, however, a baton charge was made to scatter a crowd which threw stones at the police. Just north of Birtley, at the Teams colliery, a further use of police truncheons was made. At this spot, pickets had attempted to block the road with railway sleepers. During a fight between the police and pickets, three policemen were injured.[48]

In the House of Commons on 2 June, the Home Secretary reported that 1,389 of the arrests for offences under the Emergency

Regulations between 1 and 12 May came under the heading of actual disorder or violence. There were 583 cases of violence in England, of which 183 occurred in the County of Durham, and 103 in the County of Northumberland.[49] In other words, of all the cases of violence brought to court in England, 49.1 per cent occurred in Durham and Northumberland.

It was not only the number of arrests and prosecutions resulting from the General Strike that were low. So were instances of physical injury. On 13 May BBC radio was able to announce that during the whole period of the strike 'the total casualties arising from disturbances and accidents are less than those caused in the recent fracas between Royalists and police in Paris on Joan of Arc Sunday.'[50]

The relatively limited spread of violence by the police was a result and a cause of the restricted number of Workers' Defence Corps set up by strike committees. The Labour Research Department Survey reported the largest Workers' Defence Corps to be in Methil, Fife. It was 700-strong and organised in companies under former NCOs. Other Workers' Defence Corps were set up in the London boroughs of St Pancras, Willesden, Croydon and Battersea; at Selby and Sowerby Bridge in Yorkshire; at Denny and Dunipace in Scotland, and, more surprising, in the labour movement backwaters of Chatham, Aldershot and Colchester. Altogether only eleven out of some 140 strike committees examined by the Labour Research Survey had Workers' Defence Corps. Once formed, the Workers' Defence Corps created little trouble, and may actually have prevented it. The object of the Sowerby Bridge contingent, for example, was declared to be 'maintaining peace in the streets and highways'.[51]

The Battersea Strike Committee formed Special Pickets' Corps whose tasks were stated to be:

a) To see to the efficient picketing of those [places] where the individual organisations are unable to deal with same.

b) To prevent interference by irresponsible persons, with those who are permitted to work in accordance with the General Council instructions.

c) To assist in maintaining order at meetings and places where people on strike gather, and prevent any attempt to create disturbances.

d) For the purpose of acting as stewards at strike meetings and signing on centres.[52]

The Methil Workers' Defence Corps grew into a large organisation after a violent clash between pickets and police, during which arrests were made. As one participant recalled: 'There was an immediate demand that we assault the police cells in order to get the three lads out.'[53] Mass recruitment into the Methil Workers' Defence Corps served to divert this anger away from direct physical confrontation. It is true that henceforth picketing in Methil was very effective while the General Strike lasted: 'From the time that the Defence Corps became an organised body there was no more police interference with pickets.'[54] But this did not stop the increasing number of arrests of local militants. Even this most militant of Workers' Defence Corps stepped back from offensive action which challenged the right of the state to rule.

It was from such evidence that Postgate affirmed that:

> In no case were [the Workers' Defence Corps] armed, or intended for conflict with the police. They were of use, firstly, for keeping the labour forces steady and preventing a crowd going into conflict with the police unprepared; secondly, for stiffening and directing mass pickets.[55]

Postgate was probably unaware of the situation in Methil where pickets were armed with 'pickshafts, pokers, railway distance pieces and anything that would be useful in a dust-up',[56] but this was very much an exception to the rule.

To talk about maintaining order and preventing conflict at a time when the ruling class had gone on the offensive, locked out one million miners and systematically organised scabbing on the solidarity strike in their defence, is effectively to leave capitalist 'order' intact. Compare this to the Petrograd Soviet's slogan in 1905: 'Eight hours and a gun!'

In the major working-class areas of London, Glasgow, Edinburgh and many other cities there were cases where the police perpetrated vicious attacks on workers. The army, on the other hand, played a very small role — although the threat of direct army involvement was never hidden for a minute. All leave for soldiers was stopped:

> Army units were moved into, or near to, all the big industrial districts, and if a revolutionary situation had arisen no doubt they would have been used to deal with it; but the police and specials were able to handle all the outbreaks of violence that occurred, without army assistance. By deliberate government policy, the army remained in the background. They trained for the possible violence to come.[57]

The army played only a small part in the strike. Naval ratings were used in considerable numbers at the docks and power stations; the RAF provided, among other things, a shuttle service for urgent documents; but the army's role, with one or two exceptions of which the most notable was the London docks convoy . . . was passive.[58]

This is what happened in the case of the London docks convoy:

The first convoy of 105 lorries moved out of Hyde Park in the cold wet dawn of Saturday morning. The convoy was escorted by twenty armoured cars manned by men of the Royal Tank Corps, and men of the Welsh Guards and Coldstream Guards were on the lorries . . .
The breaking of the docks blockade was of great practical and moral importance. Practical, because the exercise, once performed, was repeated and extended — on the second night the convoy numbered 267 lorries, and after two or three days lorries went to some of the docks without escort; moral, because of its effect on the dockers and on the trade union leaders.[59]

But this demonstration of force was in fact a sham, as no real opposition met the convoy. The **British Worker** of 9 May carried the following entry:

CREATING PANIC
A convoy of 140 flour and other food lorries was taken yesterday from the London docks to Hyde Park. For no reason whatsoever except to delude the public mind, the Cabinet gave those lorries an 'escort' of sixteen armoured cars, cavalry and mounted police. There was no risk of attack whatever. The lorries were as safe as at ordinary times. The object of making this ridiculous, unnecessary demonstration was clear. It was to make people afraid, by making them believe that the strike has violent revolutionary aims.[60]

Next day the paper reported:

The men, whose normal work is to handle thousands of tons of such cargo each day, lined the streets with arms folded, smiling and chatting, some waving a greeting to the soldiers.[61]

A few days earlier it had carried the following item:

GREAT SILENT CITY OF DOCKLAND
PEEP AT EAST LONDON: STRIKERS' FINE DISCIPLINE
KEEP CALM. KEEP COOL.
DON'T CONGREGATE

. . . The police are having a very easy time — no traffic whatever to attend, no crowds to move on. I saw many of them chatting to the strikers, the best of friends, and with the best of good humour.[62]

If anything, the above items from **British Worker** make it crystal clear that the General Council had no serious intention to impose its authority over anyone except the rank and file.

What about the Royal Navy?

During the period of the strike the navy manned power stations, operated docks and cold storage plants, maintained the mail service across the Irish Sea, protected and distributed gasoline supplies, carried the essential commodity of yeast to English ports (to the amount of 250 tons daily), and provided war vessels of different sizes in the various ports, canals and harbours, for aid to the civil powers if required.[63]

As the strike tightened its grip at the end of the first week and the economy was grinding to a halt, there was clear evidence of a hardening-up of police measures throughout the country:

Wholesale arrests, mounted and foot-police charges, and a general increase in severity of sentence dealt out to those brought into court, in the last few days of the strike, all pointed to more than accidental or local action by the authorities.[64]

The most fundamental weakness in the strike was created by large-scale blacklegging in the commercial road transport services. This was the bloodstream of the government emergency scheme. It could have been stopped only by mass picketing, obstruction and the use of direct force. Thus the success of the General Strike would have demanded a physical challenge to the state — a revolutionary political struggle. Restricting the strike to the economic field inevitably meant its defeat. Had the strike gone on much longer than its nine days, it would either have raised the level of police and army action against the strikers, or the violence of the strikers against the police and army, or both. However the sudden ending of the strike after nine days set both alternatives aside.

Chapter Twenty

CONSPIRING FOR A DEFEAT

FROM THE BEGINNING of the strike, while the trade union and Labour leaders were expressing in public their resolute determination to struggle, in private they were moaning about the strike and looking for an escape route. It was not long before a saviour appeared, in the form of Sir Herbert Samuel.

On 6 May Samuel rushed back from Italy hoping he could help to solve the crisis. A phone call to Jimmy Thomas elicited a warm welcome. Thomas promised to arrange a meeting with the TUC Negotiating Committee. Samuel's intervention was exceedingly well-timed, because by Friday Bevin as well as Thomas was urging the General Council 'to get negotiations going somewhere'.[1]

On Friday afternoon, 7 May, the Negotiating Committee met Samuel in the plush Bryanston Square home of Sir Abe Bailey, South African mining millionaire and friend of Thomas. Samuel asked whether the miners were now prepared to face the prospect of wage cuts. Yes, replied the Negotiating Committee, provided the Samuel Report proposals of reorganisation of the mining industry were implemented.[2] In fact the miners did not express their agreement at all. They knew nothing of the negotiations.

Thomas had other irons in the fire besides Samuel. On the same day the Negotiating Committee met Samuel, Citrine wrote in his diary:

> Thomas . . . raised the possibility of members of the General Council getting into conversation with influential businessmen who might be able to exert some power to achieve a settlement. The Council agreed that . . . we should lose no opportunity of getting on to negotiations. Thomas apprised us of a conversation he had had with Lord Londonderry [a leading coal owner]. He also mentioned that he had seen Mansfield, the vice-president of the Federation of British Industries.[3]

Other Labour leaders also got into the act of negotiation. According to Tom Jones, the assistant secretary to the Cabinet, Ramsay MacDonald went secretly to Downing Street on Friday morning, 7 May, with Sir Allan Smith, chairman of the Engineering and Allied Employers' Federation, to press for a settlement based on a temporary wage cut of 10 per cent, and the establishment of a Tribunal 'with S W Mackenzie, chairman, to fix the permanent wage'. Baldwin turned the scheme down.[4]

Nevertheless MacDonald's negotiating efforts served the main thrust of government policy. Jones explained that MacDonald

> had suggested an interview between Pugh and the PM to which there were obvious objections. My policy was to split Eccleston Square in two with the aid of a gesture from the PM which would help the moderates. Even if it did not split the executive it would weaken loyalty in the country and induce men to return to duty.[5]

Next day, 8 May, yet another Labour leader, Harold Laski, contributed his bit to the secret wheeling and dealing. Jones records what Laski told him:

> 'I spend all day at Eccleston Square. I take Pugh home every night. I think I know their minds there. Of the twenty-six known to me not more than three are out-and-out revolutionists.' . . . Thomas . . . has won the confidence of Herbert Smith by the way he has fought for the miners. Herbert Smith would consent to 15 per cent off the wages of the hewers and 10 per cent on an average off the rest.' [Laski's] scheme was a conditional withdrawal of the strike with arbitration on unsettled points in the [Samuel] Report . . . I told him I would show the document if he liked to the PM, leaving his name out.[6]

Here was a Judas who did not even ask for his pieces of silver!

The same day as Laski's proposition was made, Thomas carried on negotiations with Lord Wimborne and friends. The destiny of millions of families already at near-poverty level provided an agreeable topic for after dinner chit-chat at Lord Wimborne's sumptuous Arlington Street residence. Wimborne was a landowner and industrialist and former Lord Lieutenant of Ireland. Thomas's fellow guests included the mine-owners Lord Londonderry and Lord Gainford (former Viceroy of India), Lord Reading, a former Liberal Attorney-General, and Ethel Snowden, wife of Philip Snowden, the former Labour Chancellor of the Exchequer.

Thomas came to an agreement with Wimborne which was conveyed to Baldwin on 10 May.

> If some assurance could be given that negotiations would be resumed for the purpose of bringing the recommendations of the [Samuel] Report into operation without delay, it is possible that the TUC might call off the General Strike and indicate that miners accept the Report unconditionally with all its implications, including the question of possible adjustment of wages as the basis of a settlement. This assurance might be accepted if it were made by some person of influence, not a member of the government.[7]

The General Council as a whole was kept in the dark about these negotiations, but the Cabinet were aware of them from the outset, Churchill, Birkenhead and Tom Jones all being informed of the first meeting, and the latter channelling information to Baldwin on subsequent transactions. These secret negotiations went on and on; indeed, until the strike was brought to an end.

While all this was happening, the General Council pretended in public that the strike would not end until victory. Thus the **British Worker** of 10 May stated:

> ALL'S WELL
> The General Council's Message to Trade Union Members
> We are entering upon the second week of the general stoppage in support of the mine workers against the attack upon their standard of life by the coalowners.
> Nothing could be more wonderful than the magnificent response of millions of workers to the call of their leaders. From every town and city in the country reports are pouring into the General Council headquarters stating that all ranks are solid, that the working men and women are resolute in their determination to resist the unjust attack upon the mining community.
> The General Council desire to express their keen appreciation of the loyalty of the trade union members to whom the call was issued and by whom such a splendid response has been made . . .
> The General Council's message at the opening of the second week is: 'Stand Firm. Be Loyal to Instructions and Trust your Leaders.'[8]

To encourage the same spirit, the paper also published the following item:

GLAD TO BE ALIVE
Veteran, Leader, Cheered by Splendid Solidarity
'I am pleased I did not die last year,' says Mr Harry Gosling MP in a
letter to members of the Transport and General Workers' Union.
'Even if I do not live to see the end of the struggle, my life would have
been worth while. I am glad I have lived to see this splendid demonstration of solidarity that is the first of its kind in the world's history.'[9]

Such a scale of bureaucratic cretinism was indeed 'the first of
its kind in world history'! But still rank-and-file solidarity shone
through. On 11 May — one day before the strike was called off —
the **British Worker** announced:

SPIRIT WONDERFUL
'All solid — spirit wonderful — conduct of the men leaves nothing to
be desired,' is the purport of messages which continue to pour into the
headquarters of the Transport and General Workers' Union from
branches around the country.[10]

Then came the following statement:

Message from the executive council and officers to our members:
The might of the governments cannot defeat men who are in the right.
Remain calm and undaunted.
Do not be provoked to disorder.
Our passive resistance is invincible.
We shall continue steadfast in our stand for justice and right.
Hold fast. We must see the Miners through.
(Signed) H. Gosling. Ernest Bevin.[11]

With the weekend over, the General Council was faced with
the alternatives: either bring the strike to an end by negotiation, or
extend it. Characteristically, they did both. On Friday 7 May the
General Council issued instructions to trade union executives to
bring out all the engineers, shipbuilding and textile workers so far
unaffected by the strike, the order to be effective from Tuesday
night, 11 May. The General Council used this intensification of the
struggle as a ploy to end it.

While publicly the General Council was speaking about extending the struggle, completely different intentions were expressed in
the diary of Walter Citrine. Here again and again we read that the
strike *must* be brought to an end. Thus on Sunday 9 May, he wrote:

It was evident to me that the General Council were coming to the conclusion that it was simply hopeless to continue the strike if the intention was that in no circumstances and in no conditions would the miners accept any reductions. We cannot see any possibility of winning on this negative issue.[12]

On the same day, 9 May, Thomas declared at a public meeting in Hammersmith that 'he had never disguised and did not disguise now that he had never been in favour of the principle of a general strike.' He concluded:

The responsibility is indeed a heavy one. But there will be a graver responsibility on whichever side fails to recognise the moment when an honourable settlement can be arrived at. The moment must be accepted, and everyone must work to that end.[13]

The significance of these words was not lost on the government: they were quoted on the BBC's 9pm news bulletin, and given prominent coverage in two consecutive issues of the **British Gazette**. Thomas's speech, and press speculation generally about secret negotiations, began to feed the miners' suspicions.

An agency report in Thursday's **Manchester Guardian Bulletin** stated: 'It is understood Mr Baldwin and Mr Thomas are again in formal conversation with a view to seeing whether some understanding can be reached without delay.' More newspaper speculation was inspired by MacDonald's indiscreet comment to reporters that he was 'keeping in continual touch with the government side, and was hourly in conference regarding settlement of the strike'.[14]

This led the General Council to deny categorically that any negotiations were taking place. On 7 May the **British Worker** stated:

It is being persistently stated that Mr Ramsay MacDonald, Mr Herbert Smith, Mr Arthur Cook, and other trade union leaders have been engaged in an attempt to reopen negotiations with a view to ending the General Stoppage.

The General Council wish it to be clearly understood that there is no truth in this assertion. No official or unofficial overtures have been made to the government by any indiviual or group of individuals, either with or without the sanction of the General Council.[15]

But the miners' leaders did not trust this denial. On Saturday 8 May they heard that contact had been made with Samuel — though it was not the TUC that told them this. A J Cook and Herbert Smith asked why the negotiations with Samuel had been started without them. There was a fiery scene. John Bromley, the ASLEF leader, told Smith:

> By God, we are all in this now, and I want to say to the miners in a brotherly, comradely way, but straight — but *straight* — that this is not a miners' fight now. I am willing to fight right along with them and suffer as a consequence, but I am not going to be strangled by my friends.

Smith rose to this:

> I am going to speak as straight as Bromley. If he wants to get out of this fight, well I'm not stopping him.

The quarrel was smoothed over by explanations that it was only a conversation that had been held with Samuel, not negotiations.[16]

Next day, 9 May, the miners' leaders nevertheless became alarmed at what seemed to be going on. A J Cook described their feelings:

> On Sunday 9 May it was quite evident that these discussions and pow-wows had reached a stage when the Negotiating Committee and the leaders of the Labour Party felt that something tangible had been secured to justify a move towards calling off the General Strike . . . we were again pressed by certain individual to consider proposals for a reduction of wages. Attempts were being made by the Negotiating Committee to draft new formulae — to use the expression of our president, 'to provide a new suit of clothes for the same body' . . . It did seem terrible that we had to fight, not only the government and the coal-owners, but certain Labour leaders as well.[17]

A meeting between the miners' executive and the General Council took place at which the first draft of Samuel's proposals was produced. The proposals took for granted that there must be wage cuts. Citrine described the meeting:

> Herbert Smith was just as dour and dogged as ever. Miner after miner got up and, speaking with intensity of feeling, affirmed that the miners could not go back to work on a reduction of wages. Was all this sacrifice to be in vain?[18]

After the miners left, Samuel revised the draft and it was then submitted to the miners with a recommendation by the General

Council to accept. In the early hours of the following morning, Tuesday 11 May, the miners replied to the General Council saying that they could not accept the proposal.

Later that same day the General Council decided to call off the strike on the basis of the Samuel Memorandum, even if the miners did not agree. The miners' leaders were furious. Herbert Smith declared:

> 'I don't understand what has been going on in these conversations . . . I protest about the miners not being consulted. Why should a decision be taken tonight? Have you committed us to anything?' He was indignant at being presented with a finalised document without any opportunity for amendments.[19]

Cook wanted to know what guarantee there was that the government would accept Samuel's proposals — including the reorganising of the mining industry. Thomas replied: 'You may not trust my word, but will you accept the word of a British gentleman who has been Governor of Palestine?'

Members of the General Council were livid with Herbert Smith and A J Cook. Citrine reports that Arthur Hayday

> pointed out that the miners were not aware of the general industrial situation. They were not trade unionists in the general sense. They were ignorant of the position. They lived in villages, and they thought in the mass. They did not realise that we could not keep people out much longer. They would never understand that all there would be left to sacrifice in a few days would be the broken-hearted best of our members.
> Thomas followed and said that Hayday had put his hand right on the spot. The miners were not big enough. They were not trade unionists in a proper sense, and did not understand or very much care about what happened to the rest of the movement.[20]

George Hicks, the 'left' darling of the Communist Party, said:

> You cannot ignore the action of the miners. They have put us in the soup. They have no regard at all for the thousands of people who have sacrificed their jobs.[21]

Thomas's reassurance to Cook notwithstanding, Samuel never pretended that the government accepted his memorandum. Baldwin, J R Lane-Fox, the Minister of Mines, and Arthur Steel-Maitland, the Minister of Labour, saw Samuel on 8 May and told him that the abandonment of the strike must *precede* any negotiations. Steel-Maitland went so far as to write a letter emphasising that the government could not possibly agree to

> procure the end of the general strike by a process of bargaining . . . I am sure that the government will take the view that while they are bound most carefully and most sympathetically to consider the terms of any arrangement which a public man of your responsibility and experience may propose, it is imperative to make it plain that any discussion which you think proper to initiate is not clothed in even a vestige of official character.[22]

In a letter to the General Council after the strike Samuel stated:

> I have made it clear to your committee from the outset that I have been acting entirely on my own initiative, have received no authority from the government and can give no assurances on their behalf.[23]

So the perfidious Thomas, Bevin, Pugh and the rest were lying through their teeth to the miners' leaders.

The General Council made one last effort to carry the miners with them. In his pamphlet, **The Nine Days**, Cook describes how on Wednesday morning, 12 May, Labour Party and TUC leaders met miners' officials once more. During an interlude

> Ramsay MacDonald approached me and asked if he could come to see us and help us in this business as this 'was a tragic blunder'. I replied: 'No, you have already taken your stand in appealing to us to consider reductions and the full acceptance of the Samuel Report, which meant reductions. That has been your attitude throughout, and we do not want you to come to our meeting.'[24]

Although during the meeting the miners' leaders refused to inflict a humiliating settlement on their members, the General Council went ahead with its sell-out anyhow. The decision to surrender was *unanimous*. The two miners' representatives on the 32-strong council were absent. Tom Richards was ill and Robert Smillie stayed in Scotland to assist his members there.

Later Ben Turner, a right-winger on the General Council, made this highly significant comment in a letter to the Communist Party-influenced **Sunday Worker**:

> I don't think you were just to the General Council of the TUC. You divided us into left-wingers and right-wingers . . . [But] the absolute

unanimity of the General Council in declaring the General Strike off did not divide us into left-wingers and right-wingers.[25]

From surrender to rout

On Wednesay evening, 12 May, the General Council issued the following statement to affiliated unions, trades councils and strike committees:

> The General Council, through the magnificent support and solidarity of the trade union movement, has obtained assurances that a settlement of the mining problem can be secured which justifies them in bringing the general stoppage to an end. Conversations have been proceeding between the General Council representatives and Sir Herbert Samuel, chairman of the Coal Commission, who returned from Italy for the express purpose of offering his services to effect a settlement of the differences in the coal mining industry.
>
> The government had declared that under no circumstances could negotiations take place until the General Strike had been terminated, but the General Council feel, as a result of the conversations with Sir Herbert Samuel and the proposals which are embodied in the correspondence and documents which are enclosed, that sufficient assurances had been obtained as to the lines upon which a settlement could be reached to justify them in terminating the General Strike.
>
> The General Council accordingly decided at their meeting today to terminate the general stoppage in order that negotiations could be resumed to secure a settlement in the mining industry, free and unfettered from either strike or lockout.
>
> The General Council feel, in taking the last steps to bring the crisis to an end, that the trade union movement has given a demonstration to the world of discipline, unity, and loyalty without parallel in the history of industrial disputes.
>
> Yours fraternally,
>
> Arthur Pugh, *Chairman*. Walter M. Citrine, *Acting Secretary*.[26]

The decision of the General Council to call off the strike was taken without consulting the miners. Only after the decision was taken were the miners' representatives notified of it. As Cook describes:

> In a long speech, Mr Pugh solemnly and seriously declared that the General Council had decided that these proposals [the Samuel

Memorandum] must be accepted by the miners' representatives as a
basis for negotiations, and that they would call off the strike. They
had guarantees that satisfied them that the government would accept
these proposals, and that on the strike being withdrawn the lockout
notices also would be withdrawn, and the miners should return to
work on the status quo (with, of course, a reduction in wages to come
after resumption of work). We were told these proposals were unalter-
able, could not be amended, that we had to accept them en bloc, as
this was the unanimous decision of the TUC.[27]

Cook's comment on the behaviour of the General Council was apt:

Before myself and my colleagues an abyss had opened. It was the
culmination of days and days of faint heartedness. It had begun even
before the General Strike with the attempt to use this magnificent
expression of working-class solidarity as a mere bluff — albeit, gigantic
bluff.

To prevent that bluff being called they had been prepared (on Saturday
and Sunday and Monday, from the 1st to the 3rd of May) to give away
all the TUC had stood for. They had been prepared to force *us* to
retreat in order that *they* might carry out the retreat they longed for.
When the truculence of the Tory Cabinet thrust them willy nilly into
the General Strike they had not ceased in their endeavour to 'smooth it
over'.[28]

None of the editions of the **British Worker** revealed the crucial
fact that the Miners' Federation had issued a statement that they
were 'no party in any shape or form' to the calling off of the strike.
The evening edition of the **British Worker** on Wednesday 12 May
ran banner headlines: 'Strike Terminates Today: Trade Union
Congress General Council Satisfied that Miners Will Now Get a
Fair Deal'.

On Thursday evening, 13 May, the **British Worker** published
the following statement:

The General Strike is ended. It has not failed. It has made possible the
resumption of negotiations in the coal industry and the continuance
during the negotiations of the financial assistance given by the government.[29]

There was not a word of truth in this: the government *did not*
promise the continuation of subsidies to the mining industry. The
historian Allen Hutt writes:

Comment on the misleading nature of these communications can be left to the reader. How some unions were deluded may be seen from the circular letter addressed by the Railway Clerks' Association to its branches on 12 May. Signed 'Yours in the Victory' by general secretary A G Walkden, this letter ran in part: 'I am very glad to say that the efforts of the TUC General Council during the stoppage have resulted in ensuring for the miners the inauguration of the large measures of reorganisation which have long been overdue in their industry, and the adoption of reforms which will bring for them a brighter and better future' while they 'also brought about an undertaking for the withdrawal of the lockout notices and the continuance of the subsidy for such reasonable period as may be required for completing the negotiations.' Mr Walkden added that 'it was part of the understanding on which the General Strike was concluded that there should be no victimisation on either side.' At no single point did this letter bear any sort of relation to the facts.[30]

The telegram sent by Cramp to members of the NUR claimed not only that the lock-out notices had been withdrawn but that 'There are to be no wage cuts whatever for the miners.'

Some strike committees took these bogus declarations at face value. Birmingham, for instance, printed a special 'Victory Bulletin' and even the militant committees in Islington and St Pancras thought there was cause to celebrate. Others were puzzled but felt certain that, in the words of the Wealdstone committee, 'whatever the conditions, it means that justice has triumphed.'[31] The **Altrincham Express** strike sheet reported on 13 May a huge victory meeting:

> The portions of the settlement message that gave the greatest pleasure to the trades unionists of the district, were the following two sentences: *The General Council have terminated the strike because they are convinced that the miners are now assured of a square deal* — and — *The miners wish to thank the General Council, the trades union movement, and all who have supported them, for their splendid help.*
> It was generally felt, that so long as the settlement seemed to be satisfactory to the miners, whatever it might be, it was satisfactory to the rest of the movement, for the fight had been waged on behalf of the miners.[32]

The employers' vendetta

The headlines of the last issue of the **British Gazette** demolished whatever illusions remained: 'Unconditional withdrawal of

notices by TUC. Men to return forthwith. Surrender received by
Premier in Downing Street'. The **Daily Mail** of 13 May exulted:
'Surrender of revolutionaries'. Further headings were 'For King
and Country' and 'Revolution routed'.

The workers who went on strike were now facing victimisation
and reprisals. On the railways, in the docks, in passenger transport
and the print, employers were taking advantage of the end of the
strike to put the boot in. Threats of reduced wages and longer
hours faced the workers. Humiliating documents were thrust before
them for signature.

The General Council left each union to organise the return to
work of its own members. These had to do the best they could to
secure the reinstatement of members on the previous terms, and
they found this difficult. Many of the men returning to work on
Wednesday night and Thursday, including engineers who had only
entered the strike at midnight on Tuesday, were refused employment. Others were offered terms which might include wage cuts,
loss of seniority and pension rights, and a ban on union membership.

The reaction of the trade union leaders was pathetic. The TUC
official **Bulletin** issued by the General Council on 13 May stated:

> Those employers who are refusing to reinstate their workers unless
> wage reductions are accepted, are deliberately and maliciously defy-
> ing His Majesty's appeal for peace.[33]

Workers were so angry that, without waiting for an instruction
from their own union executive, they refused to accept the degrad-
ing terms the employers tried to impose:

> . . . the General Council [was] inundated with indignant telegrams
> and phone calls from strike committees . . . All over the country
> strike committees were [calling] for a continuation of the struggle
> independently of national union leaderships. In some areas a rent strike
> was developing; in others, which had hitherto been peaceful, there were
> oubreaks of violence. There was, for instance, a major riot at Swindon
> on Thursday when a crowd of thousands, including women with aprons
> full of stones, prevented the first trams from returning to the streets.
> The Intelligence Committee reported on Thursday: 'Feeling is running
> frightfully high all over the North.' Desperate to regain the initiative,
> the executives of the three rail unions ordered their members not to
> resume work until previous agreements were recognised and the Gen-
> eral Council issued a belated 'Stand Together' appeal of its own.[34]

Workers refused to give up the strike. The Postmaster General, as Chief Civil Commissioner, reported on 13 May at 11am:

> Broadly speaking, the general strike still continued in all parts of the country, largely owing to the unwillingness of workers to return unless employers would take back the whole of the men who had gone on strike.[35]

J H Thomas told the House of Commons on Thursday, 24 hours after the General Council had declared the strike terminated, that the number of workers on strike had increased by 100,000.[36]

> In Hull the railway and tram workers, and the dockers, refused to go back on Friday because 150 tramway employees were threatened with dismissal. On the same day a demonstration of 30,000 railway workers was held in Manchester, which affirmed a demand for unconditional reinstatement. On this day the BBC reported that there had been no general return to work, on Saturday railwaymen were still out everywhere although an agreement had been signed on Friday, and not until the weekend were terms of settlement reached for the printing workers and the dockers.[37]

The terms were very harsh. The railway unions were compelled to sign humiliating agreements, which did not, however, include wage reductions.

> The trade unions admit that, in calling a strike, they committed a wrongful act against the Companies, and agree that the Companies do not, by reinstatement, surrender their legal rights to claim damages arising out of the strike from strikers and others responsible.
> The unions undertake —
> a) Not again to instruct their members to strike without previous negotiations with the Company.
> b) To give no support of any kind to their members to take any unauthorised action.
> c) Not to encourage supervisory employees in the special class to take part in any strike.[38]

> These terms were described as 'eminently satisfactory' (Thomas) and 'very satisfactory' (Bromley), while Mr Walkden spoke of the 'managers' magnanimous spirit'.[39]

The agreements reached by the TGWU for the dockers were similar to those made by the railway unions:

The Union undertakes:

a) Not in future to instruct their members to strike, either nationally, sectionally, or locally for any reason without exhausting the conciliation machinery of the National Agreement.

b) Not to support or encourage any of their members who take individual action contrary to the preceding clause.

c) To instruct their members in any future dispute to refrain from any attempt to influence men in certain supervisory grades (to be specified hereafter) to take strike action.[40]

What about the press?

Settlement terms in connection with the strike on the press were, perhaps, more serious in the losses to the unions than in many of the other trades. In Glasgow the whole of the Outram Press, controlling four daily newspapers, turned 'non-union', enforcing its decision so strictly that its journalistic staff were forbidden to meet their union colleagues at a dinner. In Manchester the **Manchester Guardian**, famed for its tolerance, changed its habit of years and formed a 'company union'.

In general, however, the settlement made between the Newspaper Proprietors' Association and the unions concerned, for the London press, was largely copied in other provincial cities, with occasional local additions or alterations. The London terms included an agreement by the unions that there should be 'no interference with the contents of the newspapers' or with any of the members of the staffs who remained at work or returned to work during the period of the strike. No union interference was to be tolerated with the process of employment or discharge of members of the staff, nor were private secretaries or managers of departments necessarily to be union members. No 'chapel' meetings (meetings of the local union members in the newspaper office) were to be held during working hours, and strictest observance of agreements was henceforth to be 'a matter of honour affecting each individual employer or employee'.

The government's own printing plant posted a notice declaring that His Majesty's Stationery Office would henceforth include non-union workers alongside union employees, and that any unionist returning to work must recognise that the plant would not be a union shop thereafter.[41]

The engineers were particularly bitter, facing victimisation after being called out on 11 May, although the General Council had by then already decided to call off the strike the next day.

> Regional reports show that most of the AEU officers spent the whole of June dealing with victimisation problems: in Edinburgh, 'immediately after the very precipitate and badly arranged calling off of the strike, we were in a sea of trouble in connection with the complaints of members who had failed to secure reinstatement'; in Glasgow, 'many members have lost their employment, directly or indirectly because of the strike'; in Preston the organiser reported, 'I feel it a crime that these men who were loyal in every degree should have been left without any safeguard against victimisation'; in Bristol it took until 27 May to sort out the terms of restarting work for all firms and even then eighty members were not back; . . . on the Yorkshire coast 'many members' were still out of work at the end of May. [42]

The vindictiveness of the railway companies continued for many months after the strike. In October 1926, at the Labour Party Conference, Thomas stated that the NUR 'had 45,000 men out of work who had not gone back to work since 1 May, and 200,000 who were working three days a week.' [43] To some extent these figures reflect the general decline in railway freight transport due to the continuing coal lock-out, but there was also deliberate victimisation by the railway companies.

Chapter Twenty-One

THE ENDING OF THE STRIKE: FACT AND FICTION

MANY EXCUSES were given by the TUC leaders for calling off the General Strike. The most common was that if they had not acted the strike would have crumbled. Thus John Bromley, general secretary of ASLEF, said on the night of 10 May that unless the General Strike was called off, there would be 'thousands of trains running'.

'It is not good, we cannot go on any longer,' Ben Turner of the National Union of Textile Workers and a member of the TUC General Council, wrote in his diary during the closing hours of the strike:

> During Monday night spoke to Cramp at top of steps about it being desirable strike should not go on above the week out. He declared also it must not go on much longer. Tuesday, Thomas saying ditto. Our reports are weakening: 4,000 trains running, etc. Report Bristol docks weakened, Southampton strikers weakening, etc.[1]

After it was all over Thomas said: 'The criticism is — Why did we not go on? We could not have gone on.' In an article he contributed to **Answers** magazine in January 1927, he wrote that 'there was a wonderful service of trains on all lines in the kingdom within a short while of the strike being called.'[2]

The argument was completely phoney. Thus P S Bagwell, historian of the NUR, writes:[3]

> The belief that the volunteers were on the point of re-establishing the train services to something like their normal pattern was, however, a myth. The following figures issued by the railway companies themselves show the extent to which volunteer labour had been able to meet the nation's needs for goods and passenger services:

| | Passenger trains as a percentage of normal | | Goods trains as a percentage of normal |
Company	First day of strike	Last day of strike	Last day of strike
London, Midland and Scottish	3.8	12.2	3.0
London and North Eastern Railway	3.5	12.8	2.2
Great Western Railway	3.7	19.2	8.4
Southern	5.1	19.1	?

So the railway companies had failed completely in their attempt to run the railway system without railwaymen.

We have already seen the government's estimation of the continuing strength of the strike on 11 May, when the Minister of Labour reported to the Cabinet that it was still spreading in many areas. On the day the strike was called off the TUC Intelligence Committee submitted the following appraisal to the General Council:

> The reports received from all quarters . . . show a remarkable spirit in the country . . . The numbers who are standing continue to grow. Every day adds to the number of idle factories and workshops . . . The government has endeavoured to impress the country with the improvement in railway facilities. The actual improvement, though real, is very small . . . The reports to hand from local strike committees and independent observers indicate no real breach in the solidarity of the strike . . . The reports coming into this office do not confirm or explain the government's claims . . .
>
> Some of the reports with regard to railwaymen returning to work are clearly quite untrue . . . The **Slough Observer** issued Monday evening stated that the local station master reported 'A steady flow of our men back to work', and this was broadcast over the wireless, according to a report from Slough . . . This steady flow consists only of one signalman and one porter (father and son) and one platform inspector. It may be that the government are making big claims on the basis of a staff consisting in the main of supervisory grades, clerks, and more or less isolated railwaymen in the rural areas . . . There is no real evidence of wavering on the part of the trade unionist core of the strike . . . As a whole, the strike is perfectly solid . . . While there are no indications of any important tendency on the part of men on strike to

resume work, many reports show that the strike is extending and the factories and workshops not directly involved are slowing down or shutting down . . . many factories are stopping owing to shortage of fuel, shortage of raw material, lack of power, or inability to get their output transported.[4]

The **British Worker** on Tuesday evening, 11 May, one day before the strike was called off, asserted in block type on its front page:

The number of strikers has not diminished; it is increasing. There are more workers out today than there have been at any moment since the strike began.[5]

On the same day the TGWU issued the following summary of typical reports from the districts:

LONDON AND HOME COUNTIES. Mass meetings held throughout the area were well attended, great enthusiasm being displayed. Out of 40,000 passenger workers employed in the metropolitan area not one has returned to work.

SOUTH OF ENGLAND. Central Strike Committee perfectly satisfied with the position. Wonderful enthusiasm was displayed at a series of highly successful meetings.

WEST OF ENGLAND. The general position is more than satisfactory, the workers displaying a great spirit of determination.

SOUTH WALES. Everything is as solid as ever.

MIDLANDS. The position continues satisfactory. Successful meetings have been held throughout the area.

LANCASHIRE AND PART OF CHESHIRE. Position as solid as ever.

SCOTLAND. Position as solid as ever.

NORTH OF ENGLAND. Spirit and determination good.

YORKSHIRE. Position as solid as ever. Good order everywhere.

EAST COAST. The position is even better than when the strike began.

LIVERPOOL AND DISTRICT. The position is as solid as ever.

BRADFORD. The BBC rumour to the effect that tramwaymen had gone back to work is denied by the trades council, the secretary of which body says that the situation is as sound as a bell.

EAST GRINSTEAD. Still going strong. Earl de la Warr and miners' MPs have been addressing large and enthusiastic demonstrations.

DIDCOT. Morale exellent. 99 per cent solid.

LEICESTER. Solid and enthusiastic response in all places.

EASTLEIGH. 3,600 members solid in the fight.

CARLISLE. Spirit excellent. Support for TUC assured.

DERBY. The arrangements are working well and the men are in good spirits.

SWANSEA. About 40,000 out. Wonderful spirit generally.

SWINDON. The position is unchanged. No news of any wavering.

POPLAR. The spirit of the workers is intensifying rather than diminishing. The government's display of armed force has been met with amusement and contempt.[6]

The Cabinet on 12 May reported that as far as London was concerned:

The general position is very little altered save that there are more people out, many, of course, through force of circumstances.[7]

Another excuse for calling off the strike was its cost. The General Council had no qualms about spurning a £26,000 donation from the Russian unions,[8] but they still begrudged every penny drawn on their precious union funds. Ernest Bevin complained bitterly of the strain of the strike on the TGWU's finances:

With almost all the members drawing strike pay, the nine days' General Strike and its aftermath cost the union close on £600,000, a financial set-back from which it took years to recover. But for the support which they had given the miners, Bevin reflected bitterly, the TGWU would have been the second wealthiest union in the country. Now he had to start again from the beginning in order slowly to build up its financial strength to the point it had reached in April 1926.[9]

Bevin forgot what he had said at the Memorial Hall when he spoke on behalf of the General Council recommending the General Strike:

Even if every penny goes, and every asset is swallowed up, history will write that it was a magnificent generation that was prepared to do this rather than see the miners driven down like slaves.[10]

The NUR spent £1,100,000 on strike benefit to its members. The total cost of the strike to union funds, stated Citrine, was nearly £5 million.[11] Here were complaints about the cost of the strike when one million miners and their families, who *weren't* receiving strike pay, were being starved and brought to their knees!

After the excuse about the cost came the argument that the miners were far too selfish — they were not grateful for all the help we, the union leaders, had given them. Thus John Bromley, in ASLEF's **Locomotive Journal**, gave the General Council's verdict: 'After all the sacrifices made by other unions the miners both deserted their comrades who were fighting for them, and themselves.'

How was this extraordinary conclusion reached? The miners were in fact being accused of deserting the true bureaucratic path of shoddy compromise:

> The General Council never had any reason to doubt that, had the Miners' executive accepted the advice of the General Council to adopt the Samuel Memorandum, and joined with the General Council in calling off the strike, the lock-out notices would have been withdrawn, negotiations set on foot, and an acceptable arrangement arrived at.[12]

The vile charges that the union leaders were prepared to heap on the million miners still facing lock-out and starvation were aptly expressed in an entry Citrine made in his diary:

> *Thoughts on the Termination of the General Strike* . . . Had the miners risen to the appeal that Pugh made them last night, in one of the most earnest addresses I have ever heard, they would have come along and said to us: 'We are disappointed with the result. It is not what we had hoped for, but we realise that your men have made a sacrifice for us. We cannot expect you to do more. We will go back to our members and tell them that, on our own responsibility, having placed our case in your hands, we had called the strike off.' But not they!
> They had neither the loyalty to the Congress, nor to their colleagues, nor the appreciation of the sacrifices of the movement, to enable them to rise above their restricted vision of their own coalfields.[13]

How strange it was for Citrine to talk of loyalty. Throughout the strike, he and his colleagues showed a respect only for the laws, institutions and religion of the class enemy. They had demonstrated nothing but contempt for the miners and for their own members by their back-door negotiations and by their surrender without such elementary preconditions as the full reinstatement of all strikers.

Of course, if all else failed there was one further way of excusing the disaster that had befallen the movement: pretend that the General Strike had not been sold out at all! Only the TUC lefts were brazen enough to employ this stratagem. Thus on 13 June Purcell wrote in the **Sunday Worker** that the stoppage was merely a 'preliminary encounter' and:

> More real working-class progress was made in those few days than has
> been made in as many years previously . . . Those who talk about the
> failure of the General Strike are mentally a generation behind the
> times in which we live.[14]

An even more startling re-write of events came from the pen of
Hicks in the same issue:

> Was the General Strike a victory or defeat?
> I reply: Who has gained the most from it? The working class has
> gained infinitely more from the General Strike than has the capitalist
> class . . . 'A Great Victory'.
> Of course the General Strike has been a success — a great victory.
> Those who talk about the General Strike being a failure and of the
> uselessness of the General Strike as a weapon must be living in a world
> of their own imagining.[15]

It is clear who ought to have been in an asylum.

Was Cook, the miners' general secretary and another notable
left, exempt from criticism? Even though the miners' leaders
refused to compromise their demand of 'Not a penny off the pay,
not a second on the day', they were prisoners of bureaucratic
methods. Cook's account shows that he resented the behaviour of
the General Council, but he took no effective measures to counter
their policies of passivity and then surrender.

To have turned the tide would have taken a direct appeal to
the rank and file and a serious mobilisation of miners to prevent
scab food transport and the like. Cook did not call for such things
because he looked to his fellow union leaders to guarantee
solidarity. The miners' leaders left their members as passive
spectators to the doings of the bureaucracy. They stopped their
own pits and strengthened pickets in mining areas but did not go
beyond the limits set by the General Council. Cook's anger and
dismay at the outcome were genuine enough, but this was not
turned into positive action. Clear evidence that the bureaucratic
straitjacket affected *all* officials in 1926 was Cook's willing
participation in a cover-up of the TUC's crime after the end of the
strike.

In June 1926 Cook wrote the pamphlet **The Nine Days**, which
was a damning indictment of the TUC. Regrettably he contradicted
the spirit of the whole pamphlet in his last sentence:

We hope still that those leaders of the TUC who feel that a mistake has been made will rally to our cause and help us to victory.[16]

Some hope!

One example of the bewildering speed with which Cook was ready to change from sharp criticism of the TUC General Council to covering up for it is the following. There was to be a Conference of Trade Union Executives on 25 June. However, two days before this the General Council of the TUC and the Miners' Federation issued a joint statement postponing the meeting

> so that a united policy may be adopted to resist to the fullest possible extent the government's action'.
>
> The General Council and the Miners' Federation regard it as of the greatest importance at this juncture that all sections and parties should avoid statements, either in speech or writing, which create friction and misunderstanding and which divert attention from the purpose in view.[17]

To show his full support for this agreement Cook withdrew **The Nine Days** from circulation. In justification he wrote: '*Both the industrial side of the movement and the parliamentary Labour Party are now absolutely with the miners.*'[18]*

In September the TUC Congress was held in Bournemouth. An attempt was made by Jack Tanner of the Minority Movement to refer back paragraph 13 of the General Council's report dealing with the mining situation and the General Strike. Speaking in the name of the AEU, he said:

> We feel that an attempt is being made to prevent the workers, and the delegates here particularly, from knowing the whole truth in respect to the national strike . . . The General Council have been traitors, cowards and weak fools . . . the General Council sold the miners in calling off the national strike when they did call it off.[19]

---

*This was not Cook's only activity at the time. On 3 July 1926 he conducted secret negotiations behind the backs of the MFGB executive with S Seebohm-Rowntree, the chocolate magnate, Sir William Layton, editor of **The Economist**, and F D Stewart, Rowntree's private secretary, and came to compromising conclusions. (See further, Tony Cliff, 'The tragedy of A J Cook' in **International Socialism**, second series, number 31.)

W C Loeber of the NUR seconded the reference back. Cook intervened:

> I do hope Congress will recognise that we have over a million miners out at the present moment, and we are more concerned just now to get an honourable settlement for those million men, than we are in washing dirty linen in this Congress. Whatever our feelings may be, whatever view we may take of the mistakes made, this is a mutual arrangement arrived at while our men are on the road. The Miners' Federation do not burk inquiry. They welcome it. But that inquiry must come when our men are working.[20]

Cook's intervention put an end to the debate. His prestige was very high and Congress gave him a standing ovation. The reference back was heavily defeated: 775,000 to 3,098,000.[21] The MFGB sided with the General Council.

But Cook's salvation of the General Council's reputation did not help the miners one bit. For the TUC never once, during the gruelling six-months' lock-out that followed the General Strike, put an embargo on coal. Cook was trapped in the bureaucratic machine like all the rest.

Why did the TUC really back down?

From the beginning the government treated the General Strike as a constitutional and political issue. 'It is not wages that are imperilled,' declared Baldwin solemnly, 'it is the freedom of our Constitution.' Trade union leaders were 'threatening the basis of ordered government and going nearer to proclaiming civil war than we have been for centuries past.'[22]

On 6 May the **British Gazette** published a statement by Baldwin: 'Constitutional government is being attacked . . . The General Strike is a challenge to parliament, and is the road to anarchy and ruin.'[23] On 10 May its front page carried the following:

LORD BALFOUR DEFINES THE ISSUE
Attempted Revolution — Its Purposes and Results
. . . it is what I have called it — an attempted revolution. Were it to succeed the community would thenceforth be ruled not by parliament, not by the parliamentary Labour Party, not by the rank and file of the trade unions, not by the moderate members of the Trade Union Council, but by a revolutionary small body of extremists who regard

trade unions not as the machinery for collective bargaining within our industrial system, but as a political instrument by which the industrial system itself may be utterly destroyed.

. . . From such a fate may the courage and resolution of our countrymen save the civilisation of which they are the trustees.[24]

For their part, the General Council was frightened to accept the challenge that the strike was industrial *and* political. It went against the whole concept of trade union leadership as part of the Establishment. For decades the incorporation of trade union leaders into government-sponsored conciliation machinery had run parallel with the incorporation of Labour Party leaders in parliament. To accept that the General Strike was a political challenge to the state would undermine both. Throughout the strike the General Council repeated again and again that the dispute was purely economic.

Four of the seven issues of **British Worker** published before the strike was called off carried an identical declaration from the General Council, that it did

> not challenge the Constitution. It is not seeking to substitute unconstitutional government. Nor is it desirous of undermining our parliamentary institutions. The sole aim of the council is to secure for the miners a decent standard of life. The council is engaged in an industrial dispute. In any settlement the only issue to be decided will be an industrial issue, not political and constitutional. There is no constitutional crisis.

The three remaining issues carried an identical 'Message to All Workers!':

> The General Council of the Trade Union Congress wishes to emphasise the fact that this is an industrial dispute. It expects every member taking part to be exemplary in his conduct — not to give any opportunity for police interference. The outbreak of any disturbance will be very damaging to the prospects of a successful termination of the dispute. The council asks pickets especially to avoid obstruction and to confine themselves strictly to their legitimate duties.

The trade union MPs repeated the same in their speeches in the House of Commons. They used every opportunity to state that the strike was not aimed at the Constitution. John Bromley, speaking in the House on 5 May said: 'Any suggestion that the dispute is a challenge to the Constitution, or an endeavour to overthrow the government is quite wrong.'[25] Thomas, on 8 May, went as far as to declare in the House: 'I have never disguised that in a challenge to the Constitution, God help us unless the governent won.' This dispute, he contended, 'was merely a plain, economic, industrial dispute.'[26]

It was part and parcel of their position in not challenging the state that the General Council encouraged football matches between strikers and police.

As daily reports from the regions showed, from the first the strike was solid and as it spread it paralysed the national economy more and more. So the question of power rose inevitably as a logical extension of the strike. To render the strike effective, the trade unions had to challenge the emergency organisation of the government by using mass pickets. The logic of the mass strike demanded an open challenge to the state, and this was becoming increasingly clear during the final days before the strike was called off.

But the trade union leaders had no intention whatsoever of overthrowing the government through industrial action. To challenge the state was to put a dagger in the heart of the trade union bureaucracy. Take the following vignette from Aneurin Bevan's **In Place of Fear**:

> I remember vividly Robert Smillie describing to me an interview the leaders of the Triple Alliance had with David Lloyd George in 1919 . . . 'He said to us: "Gentlemen, you have fashioned, in the Triple Alliance of the unions represented by you, a most powerful instrument. I feel bound to tell you that in our opinion we are at your mercy. The army is disaffected and cannot be relied upon. Trouble has occurred already in a number of camps. We have just emerged from a great war and the people are eager for the reward of their sacrifices, and we are in no position to satisfy them. In these circumstances, if you carry out your threat and strike, then you will defeat us.
> ' "But if you do so," went on Mr Lloyd George, "have you weighed the consequences? The strike will be in defiance of the government of the country and by its very success will precipitate a constitutional crisis of the first importance. For, if a force arises in the state which is stronger than the state itself, then it must be ready to take on the functions of the state, or withdraw and accept the authority of the state. Gentlemen," asked the prime minister quietly, "have you considered, and if you have, are you ready?" From that moment on,' said Robert Smillie, 'we were beaten and we knew we were.'[27]

If Lloyd George had told *revolutionary* leaders, 'You are stronger than the state', the simple reply would be: 'Excellent. Move over.' But the trade union leaders were not revolutionaries.

In 1926 the government knew very well what a spineless bunch of people the union leaders were. The assessment of Tom Jones, assistant secretary to the Cabinet, was very acute indeed:

> The General Strike could not succeed because some of those who led it did not wholly believe in it and because few, if any, were prepared to go through with it to its logical conclusion — violence and revolution.[28]

In a mass strike, if there is no leadership capable of posing correctly the question of power and leading the working class to an assault on the state, then the strike must inevitably retreat, leading to defeat and demoralisation.

The converse of the trade union bureaucracy's kowtowing before the state is its fear of the unruly rank and file, its fear of workers' rebellion against the incorporation of the trade union leaders into the establishment, as well as the incorporation of the Labour Party leaders into parliamentary institutions. During the General Strike the leadership trembled at the very idea of rank-and-file independence, even though at no stage did that become an actuality. They suffered from deep paranoia on this subject. Thus Thomas told the House of Commons the day after the strike ended:

> What I dreaded about this strike more than anything else was this: If by any chance it should have got out of the hands of those who would be able to exercise some control, every sane man knows what would have happened. I thank God it never did. That is why I believe that the decision yesterday was such a big decision, and that is why that danger, that fear, was always in our minds, because we wanted at least, even in this struggle, to direct a disciplined army.[29]

An even franker admission of the same fear was given by Charles Dukes, secretary of the National Union of General and Municipal Workers, at the Special Conference of Union Executives, held in January 1927:

> Every day that the strike proceeded the control and the authority of that dispute was passing out of the hands of responsible executives

into the hands of men who had no authority, no control, and was wrecking the movement from one end to the other.[30]

Of course, this was a fantastic exaggeration. But for the bureaucracy even a shadow of revolution is a frightening sight.

Chapter Twenty-Two

THE LEFT PARTIES AND THE STRIKE

THE TUC committed a disgusting act of betrayal when they dropped their public face of defiance and called the strike off, but the Labour Party did not even rise to mouthing defiance, so craven was its attitude. At no time did it come out clearly in support of the strikers nor even the million miners who faced poverty wages or longer hours. Thus Ramsay MacDonald's reaction to Red Friday was:

> The government has simply handed over the appearance, at any rate, of victory to the very forces that sane, well-considered Socialism feels to be its greatest enemy. If the government had fought their policy out, we should have respected it. It just suddenly doubled up. The consequence has been to increase the power and prestige of those who do not believe in political action.[1]

Throughout the General Strike itself Labour leaders showed the utmost hostility to the whole idea of action. The defeat and the victimisations that followed did not soften their attitude. Thus MacDonald wrote in June 1926:

> The General Strike is a weapon that cannot be used for industrial purposes. It is clumsy and ineffectual. It has no goal which when reached can be regarded as a victory. If fought to a finish as a strike, it would ruin trade unionism, and the government in the meantime could create a revolution; if fought to a finish only as a means to an end, the men responsible for decisions will be charged with betrayal . . . The real blame is with the General Strike itself and those who preached it without considering it and induced the workers to blunder into it. It was not (because of its nature it could not be) of help to the miners . . . I hope that the result will be a thorough reconsideration of trade union tactics. Large industrial operations of either offence or

defence cannot be planned by platform speeches. If the wonderful unity in the strike which impressed the whole world with the solidarity of British labour would be shown in politics, labour could solve mining and similar difficulties through the ballot box.[2]

The most venomous attack on the General Strike is to be found in the diary of Beatrice Webb, mother of Fabianism. On 3 May, the eve of the General Strike, she wrote:

> The General Strike will fail . . . We have always been against a General Strike . . . The failure of the General Strike of 1926 will be one of the most significant landmarks in the history of the British working class. Future historians will, I think, regard it as the death gasp of that pernicious doctrine of 'workers' control' of public affairs through the trade unions, and by the method of direct action . . . On the whole I think, it was a proletarian distemper which had to run its course and like other distempers it is well to have it over and done with at the cost of a lengthy convalescence.[3]

A few days after the strike, on 18 May, she added: 'The failure of the General Strike shows what a *sane* people the British are.'[4]

Beatrice Webb's special fear was that workers might discover industrial action to be more effective than the dead-end of electoral politics. So for the Webbs the sad defeat of the General Strike was of benefit, since it pushed people towards parliamentary activity. On 31 May she wrote:

> The parliamentary Labour Party will again dominate the situation. After the unconditional surrender there was despair of industrial action; to this has been added renewed hopes in salvation through the ballot box.[5]

Then on 21 August she made this entry in her diary:

> So far as I can see the only organisation that comes out stronger for this disaster is the parliamentary Labour Party — for the simple reason that the prestige of the General Council of the Trade Union Congress has been destroyed and the strike as a weapon has been discredited . . . the agony of the Miners' Federation *might* mean a Labour government after the General Election.[6]

For 19 October we read the following:

> The victory of the coal-owners or of the miners would be deplorable

— one hardly dare say which of the two would be most destructive to the commonwealth.[7]

In the next few months Beatrice Webb's wishes came true. The miners went down to a crushing defeat from which it took half a century to recover, but as a reward Labour did well in the municipal elections! **The Times** of 3 November 1926 reported:

> The success of the Labour Party in the municipal election was widespread, and in some places sweeping . . . The principal successes were in the coal-mining areas and industrial towns and boroughs which have been suffering from depression.

Why did the Labour Party leaders have such an antagonistic attitude towards the General Strike?

The Labour Party is sustained by the trade unions, from which it gets a vast proportion of its membership and finance. However, as Lenin explained, the Labour Party does not reflect the trade unions' membership, but its bureaucracy. The unity of the two wings of the movement — the Labour Party and trade unions — is based on the fact that both are incorporated into the establishment, the first into the parliamentary establishment, the second into conciliatory arrangements with employers and government.

Ideologically the Labour Party has never been an exclusively working-class party. At its founding conference, it threw out a motion calling for 'a distinct party . . . based upon the recognition of the class war'. It has represented itself as a *national* party whose aim is to integrate the demands of the working class with those of the nation.

Ramsay MacDonald, who was undoubtedly the major intellectual and political figure in the Labour Party in its first three decades, associated the party in his writing with the rejection of Marxism.

> 'Neither Marx nor Engels,' he wrote, 'saw deep enough to discover the possibilities of peaceful advance which lay hidden beneath the surface . . . any idea which assumes that the interests of the proletariat are so simply opposed to those of the bourgeoisie as to make the proletariat feel a oneness of economic interest is purely formal and artificial'. Instead he offered a definition of socialism that drained it of its class content in favour of a higher 'organic' social unity. 'Socialism

marks the growth of society, not the uprising of a class. The consciousness which it seeks to quicken is not one of economic class solidarity, but one of social unity and growth towards organic wholeness.' 'Socialism is no class movement . . . It is not the rule of the working class; it is the organisation of the community.'[8]

In similar vein Keir Hardie wrote: 'The propaganda of the class hatred is not one which can ever take root in this country . . . Mankind in the main is not moved by hatred but by love of what is right.'[9]

Morgan Phillips, then secretary of the Labour Party, wrote in an election pamphlet before the 1945 general election: 'Let us remove at the outset any lingering impression of the outworn idea that the Labour Party is a class party.'[10] Similarly,

Harold Wilson warned the 1961 Conference: 'We shall . . . as a national party and a nationally-based government, be frank in condemning all who shirk their duty to the nation. The professional fomentors of unofficial strikes and those who easily follow them, equally with businessmen who cling to out-of-date methods and out-of-date machinery because it yields them a profit.[11]

The synthesis of opposition to class war and acceptance of the need to articulate workers' needs is founded on the assumption that there are no irreconcilable differences in society, that politics is about making compromises, that consensus is desirable. The Labour Party is a contradictory phenomenon. It expresses both workers' opposition to the social *status quo* and at the same time blunts that opposition. The party's task is to inculcate the workers with the idea of 'national' rather than class interest, reshaping working-class demands and integrating them in terms of national values. Thus the British capitalist system is 'our economy', the people who protect the bosses' property are 'our boys in blue'.

Labour's nation/class synthesis is not a stable one. It depends above all on the state of the economy and how far concessions to workers can be achieved without challenging the system. So it involves compromise between workers and capitalists. The Labour Party aims at social reform within capitalism. But the ability of capitalism to sustain such reforms is not constant. A time of slump is different to when the system prospers. If the Labour Party is in power it comes into conflict with workers who are forced to defend their living standards, often in defiance of the policies of the government they elected.

This was the experience of the 1924 Labour government. It will be repeated again and again. The rhetoric may change: whether the emphasis is put on maintaining capitalism and class collaboration, or on expressing workers' needs, is determined by whether Labour is in opposition or in power. But whatever the current tone, in opposition the party is impotent, and in office it is managerial, hence in conflict with workers' interests.

The attempted synthesis of 'nation' and 'class' make for a policy of gradualism. To achieve progress within the system, the party dare not go so far as to antagonise all other classes in society. 'Softly, softly' is the watchword; building a consensus is the aim.

Accepting the national interest as a point of reference leads the Labour Party to accept parliament as the expression of the nation, as the highest peak of national achievement. Hence the party's 'parliamentary cretinism':

> the Labour Party has always been one of the most dogmatic — not about socialism, but about the parliamentary system. Empirical and flexible about all else, its leaders have always made devotion to that system their fixed point of reference and the conditioning factor of their political behaviour.
>
> . . . the leaders of the Labour Party have always rejected any kind of political action (such as industrial action for political purposes) which fell, or which appeared to them to fall, outside the framework and conventions of the parliamentary system . . . And in this respect, there is no distinction to be made between Labour's political and its industrial leaders. Both have been equally determined that the Labour Party should not stray from the narrow path of parliamentary politics.[12]

Between the Labour Party and the trade unions, there is not simply unity, but also a contradiction. Both are reformist, both accept the synthesis of 'nation' and 'class', both accept gradualism and parliamentarism. But the two wings of the Labour movement have different *functions*. The Labour Party is purely electoral. Hence it relates to its supporters as a multitude of individuals. The trade union bureaucracy must relate to groups of workers as collectives. With this separation of politics and economics, the Labour Party leadership is always an outsider to the industrial struggle. In contrast to this, the trade union bureaucracy can never completely avoid heading the industrial struggle, even if only in order to restrain it.

The union bureaucracy can be, and is, incorporated into capitalist state institutions — but this incorporation cannot be absolute. If it were, the unions would cease to be unions, and the bureaucracy would lose its *raison d'être*, its role as intermediary between capitalism and workers, between the capitalist state and the working class.

For the leaders of the Labour Party the industrial struggle must be subordinate to parliamentary activity. Ramsay MacDonald put it thus in 1912:

> 'Any project of social reconstruction which founds itself upon reality must begin with the facts of social unity, not with those of class conflict, because the former is the predominant fact in society'. As to parliament, it was 'essential to social coherent life'; ultimately, industrial disputes would have 'at length to be settled by the House of Commons as representative of the common interest of consumers and as guardian of social order and peace.'[13]

And this was written at the time of the first national miners' strike, and in the midst of the 'Labour Unrest'.

How estranged the leaders of the Labour Party were from the industrial struggle is clear from the words of C D Buxton, President of the Board of Trade, informing the Cabinet after the end of the 1912 miners' strike of

> the almost complete collapse of the Labour Party in the House of Commons as an effective influence in labour disputes. They were not consulted with regard to, and had no share in the Seamen's or Transport Workers' movement last summer. During the railway strike, they attempted to act as a go-between for the men and the government. But they had very little influence over the actions of the men, or on the result. During the Miners' Strike . . . the Labour Party exercised no influence at all.

Furthermore, he said, 'Their elimination is a distinct loss to industrial peace.'[14]

J R Clynes, future deputy leader of the Labour Party, told the 1914 Labour Party Conference: '. . . too frequent strikes cause a sense of disgust, of being a nuisance to the community.'[15]

Above all Labour leaders oppose industrial action for political aims. This was expressed strongly by J McGurk in his presidential address to the 1919 Labour Party Conference:

> Referring to the movement 'that was already afoot to employ the strike weapon for political purposes', he said that this 'would be an

innovation in this country which few responsible leaders would welcome . . . We are either constitutionalists or we are not constitutionalists. If we are constutionalists, if we believe in the efficacy of the
political weapon (and we do, or why do we have a Labour Party?) then
it is both unwise and undemocratic because we fail to get a majority at
the polls to turn round and demand that we should substitute industrial
action.'[16]

After the General Strike, Clynes, who was also secretary of the
National Union of General and Municipal Workers and had been a
minister in the 1924 Labour government, wrote:

> We learnt that a national strike could not be used as a weapon in a
> trade dispute . . . There is one way, and one only, to alter unfair
> conditions in Britain. It is through the ballot box, and not through
> violence or resistance.[17]

For the Labour Party leaders the industrial struggle is at best
of secondary importance, and at worst a diversion from the *real*
important activity — elections. The fact that the two wings of the
movement are intertwined ideologically, as well as structurally,
does not prevent conflict between them, especially when the
Labour Party is in office. When union leaders had the gall to
oppose cuts in wages and unemployment benefit in 1931, Sidney
Webb told his wife: 'The General Council are pigs. They won't
agree to any cuts.'[18] In fact every time the Labour Party has come
into office sharp clashes have taken place between trade unions on
the one side and the Labour government and Labour
Party on the other. This was the case in 1924, 1931, 1950, 1968–9
and 1979.

The pattern of conflict between the two wings of the movement at such times is quite complex. One finds some union
leaders supporting the Labour Party and government, while
others clash with them. To add to the complexity, in some cases
one and the same person is both a leader of a union and a Labour
MP — as were Thomas, Clynes, Bromley and Purcell in 1926.
Furthermore the various unions do not enter into conflict with
government policies to an equal extent. Much depends on the
specific situation, on the ideological influence of Labourism on
different union leaders, and above all on the pressure of the rank
and file on those leaders.

The tail that failed to wag the dog

The members of the Communist Party showed great enthusiasm, energy and self-sacrifice throughout the strike. One measure of this is the high proportion of Communists among those arrested. Of 5,000 persons prosecuted for acts committed during the strike, 1,200 were members of the Communist Party, and 400 of these were sent to prison.[19]

The political lead given to the members, however, was poor.

Throughout the nine days of the strike, the leaders of the party tail-ended the General Council. One can see this clearly by reading through the daily **Workers' Bulletin**, the party's publication, during the strike. The first issue of 4 May is summed up by its own slogans:

HOLD TIGHT — THAT'S RIGHT
All it needs is for every man to stand fast and the fight is won . . .
Every man behind the miners!
Not a penny off the pay! Not a minute off the day!
No government has the right to order men and women to starve!
An injury to one is an injury to all![20]

The General Council could not have taken exception to one word of this.

The second issue of **Workers' Bulletin** did differentiate itself from the **British Worker** by making clear that in its view the General Strike was not only industrial but also political. It included a statement by the executive committee of the Communist Party, headed 'The Political Meaning of the General Strike':

The first watchwords of the General Strike . . . have been and remain: 'All Together Behind the Miners. Not a Penny off the Pay. Not a Second off the Day!'

But now that the struggle has begun, the workers have it in their power to put an end once and for all to this continued menace to their living standards and working conditions. Simply to beat off the employers' present offensive means that they will return to the attack later on, just as they did after Red Friday last year. The only guarantee against the ravenous and soulless greed of the coalowners is to break their economic power.

Therefore let the workers answer the bosses' challenge with a challenge of their own: 'Nationalisation of the mines, without compensation for

the coalowners, under workers' control through pit committees!' . . .
If the strike ends, though it be with the defeat of the coalowners, but
with the government's power unshaken, the capitalists will still have
hopes of renewing their attack. Therefore the third essential slogan of
the General Strike must be:
'Resignation of the forgery government! Formation of a Labour
government!' . . .
'Not a penny off the pay: Not a second off the day!'
'Nationalise the mines without compensation under workers' control!'
'Formation of a Labour government!'[21]

What practical steps did the CPGB suggest?

The Communist Party continues to instruct its members and to urge
the workers to take every practical step necessary to consolidate our
position against the capitalist attack. Such essential steps are: to form
a Council of Action immediately; to organise able-bodied trade unionists in a Workers' Defence Corps against the OMS and *Fascisti*; to set
up feeding arrangements with the Cooperative Societies; to hold mass
meetings and issue strike bulletins, and to make their case known to
the soldiers.[22]

And that is all! Not a word of criticism is to be found of the
bureaucratic way the strike was run, nor any practical suggestions
for what to counterpose to the General Council's instructions. In all
the eight issues of the **Workers' Bulletin** published during the
strike, the most important aspects of the struggle were totally
excluded. There was nothing about the partial nature of the strike
or the way that the engineers, shipyard workers and textile workers
were kept at their posts to the last day of the strike. No mention was
made of the fact that the gas, post and telegraph workers were
never brought out at all. There was not a word about the mess
caused by calling on power workers to stop power, but not light;
nor about the mess created for building workers.

The **Workers' Bulletin** passed over the passive nature of the
picketing in silence, as it did over the General Council instructions
to keep strikers off the streets, to be involved in concerts, sports
and country walking. It did not talk about the strikers' games with
the police, or the church events in which strikers were involved.
There was no discussion of the composition of the Councils of
Action or joint strike committees, which were dominated in the
main cities by full-time officials. There was not even a word about

the way the Councils of Action or Central Strike Committees completely abided by General Council instructions.

The last issue of **Workers' Bulletin** during the strike was number 8, of 12 May. It published the following item without comment:

> Labour JPs in court
> A sensation was caused at Birmingham on Tuesday, following a police raid on Monday night on the offices of the Birmingham Joint Trade Union Emergency Committee. The principal defendants were Frederick William Rudland JP, secretary of the Birmingham Trades Council, George Haynes JP, secretary of the Midland Bakery Co-operative; Charles F Barett JP, who contested the Ashton Division at the last election. Defendants were remanded on bail.[23]

What a crime — arresting respectable magistrates!

The most significant omission from the **Workers' Bulletin** was of practically any criticism of the General Council. As late as 11 May, one day before the strike was called off, we find the demand for 'All Power to the General Council' repeated as the key to victory for the struggle:

> THE COMMUNIST PARTY LEAD
> The Trades Union Congress at Scarborough refused to grant further powers to the General Council. The **Workers' Weekly**, the organ of the Communist Party, commenting on the decision, stated candidly that such powers would not be granted by the endorsement of a formal resolution but that economic conditions would enforce such powers being taken by the General Council. Only a few months have elapsed and the whole of the trade union movement is in accord with the General Council acting as the National Strike Committee. All the executives of national unions have agreed to place the conduct of the struggle in their hands. The Communist Party is right in its slogan of *All power to the General Council.*
> *Join the Communist Party and stiffen the militant action of the Trade Union Movement.*
> *Down with the forgers' government — form a Labour government.*[24]

The Communist Party did not take a position of general opposition to the right-wing and centrist leadership of the TUC, but acted as fellow-travellers of the left on the General Council, and at best as ginger groups at local level. As George Hardy, acting secretary of the Minority Movement, remembers:

. . . we sent out from Minority Movement headquarters instructions to our members to work for the establishment of Councils of Action in every area. We warned, however, that the Councils of Action were under no circumstances to take over the work of the trade unions . . . *The Councils of Action were to see that all the decisions of the General Council and the union executives were carried out.* [25]

Because of the soft line taken by the Communist Party during the nine days, Hamilton Fyfe, editor of the **British Worker**, could write:

The Communists have . . . kept very quiet . . . On the Continent, in America even, it is the extremists who come to the top in crises. Here they have sunk out of sight. [26]

For the same reason, one finds not a mention of the 'red bogey' in the diary kept by Citrine throughout the strike.

Communist Party members were active on the great majority of Councils of Action or joint strike committees. They were heavily represented in South Wales and industrial Scotland, in Merseyside, Middlesbrough, and around Manchester. Party fractions were active in all but ten of London's seventy Councils of Action, and Communists dominated those in Battersea, Poplar, Stepney, Bethnal Green, West Ham, Islington, St Pancras and Camden Town. The secretary of the London Trades Council was a Communist Party member, Duncan Carmichael. In Glasgow, the chairman of the Central Strike Co-ordinating Committee, was the leading party member Peter Kerrigan, and there were another four Communists on this committee. In the Northumberland and Durham committee a leading role was played by Robin Page Arnot, a member of the Communist Party executive. [27]

It is one thing for a revolutionary to sit on a council or committee, but it is quite another to get that body to follow a revolutionary policy. From what we know of the General Strike one has to make quite a leap to arrive at the conclusion of the Eighth Communist Party Congress which, in October 1926, claimed that

in actual practice the Councils of Action in nearly all the industrial centres more or less followed the party lead in one form or another

. . . and events were forcing them closer and closer to our line as time went on.[28]*

Following in the footsteps of the Eighth Congress, James Klugmann, in his official history of the CPGB, goes on to point out a number of Councils of Action of special virtue. We shall remind ourselves of a few of these examples.

Klugmann asserts that of all the local strike bodies, the Northumberland and Durham General Council and Joint Strike Committee showed 'probably the most effective exercise of power.'[29] Yet as we have already noted it was top-heavy with officials: the chairman and secretary were respectively area secretary of the TGWU and northern divisional officer of the National Union of Distributive and Allied Workers. The committee's third most prominent member was a district official of the National Union of General and Municipal Workers. And how did it work? Anthony Mason, historian of the committee, tells us that when it met in conference 'no really important decisions were taken.'[30]

Most members of Glasgow's Central Strike Co-ordinating Committee were full-time officials and 'at no point throughout the nine days was the TUC's authority questioned'.

At Middlesbrough, Klugmann tells us, 'there were four party members and a number of close associates of the party on the Central Strike Committee. This was an extremely effective committee.'[31] But as we saw, Middlesbrough's Central Strike Committee 'would not interfere with the domestic policy of any union . . . [and] could only hope to act as a co-ordinating and not a directional body.'[32] Emile Burns threw further light on this 'extremely effective committee' when he described its financial arrangements:

> The financial position of the Central Strike Committee has been materially helped by a grant which was received on 7 May from the Darlington and District Labour College (£7) . . . The expenses

---

*This view conforms with the statement we have already quoted from the Executive Committee of the Comintern, 8 June 1926, which said: 'the Councils of Action organised by the trade unions actually developed into district *soviets*. The departments organised by the General Council already assembled in their structure and functions, the departments of the Petersburg Soviet in the period of so-called "dual power" (February–November 1917).'

exceeded this grant, and it has been decided to ask the trades council to meet the deficit.[33]

Finally, as regards the Central London Strike Committee, we have already quoted the following statement: 'The Central Strike Committee became an organ without real power, its functions limited to convening meetings of local delegates and giving advice and guidance which it could not enforce.'[34]

If the Communist Party really had such a lot of influence on the Councils of Action, the question must be asked: why did the strike develop so badly and end so catastrophically?

The 'Theses' of the Eighth Congress of the CPGB went on to contradict their earlier claim that there was decisive Communist influence in the Councils of Action:

> The presence in most regions of trades councils and strike committees dominated by the right-wing elements was . . . a factor militating against the effective extension and defence of the strike and its regional co-ordination.[35]

To lead is to foresee, and the Communist Party leaders foresaw nothing. After the strike they had to admit that they did not expect the betrayal by the General Council. George Hardy wrote:

> Although we knew of what treachery the right-wing leaders were capable, we did not clearly understand the part played by the so-called 'left' in the union leadership. In the main they turned out to be windbags and capitulated to the right wing. We were taught a major lesson; that while developing a move to the left officially, the main point in preparing for action must always be to develop a class-conscious leadership among the rank and file.[36]

The **Workers' Weekly**, in aggrieved surprise, said:

> We warned our readers of the weakness and worse of the right wing on the General Council — but here we confess that reality has far exceeded our worst forebodings . . . The Communist Party had in fact consistently warned the workers that such was likely to hapen, but even the Communist Party can be forgiven for not believing it to be possible that once the struggle had begun these leaders should have proved themselves such pitiful paltroons as to surrender at the very moment of victory.[37]

Only after the strike ended, in a flash of insight, did the party leadership understand the role of the 'Left' on the General Council. On 13 May the Communist Party issued a statement stating, *inter alia*, the following:

> . . . most of the so-called left wing have been no better than the right. By a policy of timid silence, by using the false pretext of loyalty to colleagues to cover up breaches of loyalty to workers, they have left a free hand to the right wing and thus helped to play the employers' game. Even now they have not the courage to come out openly as a minority in the General Council and join forces with the real majority — the workers — against the united front of Baldwin-Samuel-Thomas.[38]

The Eighth Congress of the CPGB repeated: the 'Lefts' were

> apologists for the General Council . . . aiders and abetters of the right-wing during the strike . . . unashamed agents of the Trade Union Congress . . . a set of phrase-mongers who had won easy fame as 'revolutionaries' on the issue of international trade union unity.[39]

There was no mention of who had assisted the 'Left' to gain this 'easy fame'. And for many months there was no word of self-criticism for the CPGB or the Comintern line.

Only after the strike did the Communist Party suddenly find out how bureaucratic and inefficient was the leadership of the strike. The Eighth Congress declared:

> The partial calling out of workers caused confusion, and the strike was not extended rapidly enough. The refusal to call out workers in public services and the stoppage of the workers' press along with the capitalist press, weakened the strike.[40]

The party still apologised, however, for the Comintern's mistakes. The continued policy of sucking up to the Judases on the General Council was defended by pretending that: 'The Anglo-Russian Committee is not a union between the leaders, but a union between the millions of trade unionists of Russia and Britain'.[41] By an irony of history it was the General Council that a few months later talked of sticking to its principles(!) and decided to break off relations with the Russian unions.

Because the Eighth Congress assiduously avoided self-criticism it prepared the party very badly for the difficult times ahead. Instead of facing up to the impending collapse of the miners' struggle, at a time when some 150,000 miners had already been starved back to work, the congress put the following scenario forward for the miners' struggle:

> This congress emphatically declares that victory is possible. The lock-out is undermining the whole economic and political position of British capitalism . . .
> What is called for?
> 1. Undertake in conjunction with the MFGB a campaign to secure 100 per cent stoppage in the wavering districts.
> 2. Carry out all over the country an energetic campaign in favour of the embargo and the levy.
> 3. Demand the dissolution of the present government.[42]

The Communist Party totally failed to understand the impact of the massive defeat represented by the General Strike and the disintegration of miners' resistance, and hence the move of the whole trade union and labour movement to the right. There was but a tiny minority of workers who learnt important lessons and moved leftwards. The vast majority were demoralised. Yet the Eighth Congress declared: 'The General Strike and the mining lock-out have awakened the class consciousness of the rank-and-file workers who are moving to the left.'[43]

Worse was to come. After the miners caved in, the perspective for revolution became even rosier. Thus in December 1926 William Gallacher prophesied that 'the day will soon come when the oppressed and exploited working class will form a workers' republic in Britain.'[44]

Such blinkered optimism continued to flourish in 1927 and 1928, and made the CPGB leadership all too ready to accept Stalin's stupid policy known as the 'Third Period'. Now the reformist allies of the past were discovered to be no more than 'social fascists', an analysis as bad as trusting them to be 'good proletarians'.

Again, it was the optimism of the CPGB leadership which led the Eighth Congress to put forward fantastic targets for party growth. After declaring that the party membership had more than doubled over the months May to October 1926, from 5,000 to 10,730, the task was now 'once again to double our membership'.[45] In fact party membership fell consistently: from 10,730 in October 1926 to 7,377 in October 1927; from 5,500 in March 1928 to 3,200 in December 1929. It finally reached 2,555 in December 1930.[46]

Trotsky superbly summed up the CPGB and the 'British experiment' as follows:

The Minority Movement, embracing almost a million workers, seemed very promising, but it bore the germs of destruction within itself. The masses knew as the leaders of the movement only Purcell, Hicks and Cook, whom, moreover, Moscow vouched for. These 'left' friends, in a serious test, shamefully betrayed the proletariat. The revolutionary workers were thrown into confusion, sank into apathy and naturally extended their disappointment to the Communist Party itself, which had only been the passive part of this whole mechanism of betrayal and perfidy. The Minority Movement was reduced to zero; the Communist Party returned to the existence of a negligible sect. In this way, thanks to a radically false conception of the party, the greatest movement of the English proletariat, which led to the General Strike, not only did not shake the apparatus of the reactionary bureaucracy, but, on the contrary, reinforced it and compromised Communism in Great Britain for a long time.[47]

Chapter Twenty-Three

THE END OF AN ERA

THE GENERAL STRIKE was a decisive turning point in British history. Hardly had it ended than C T Cramp of the NUR cried 'Never again!'. This was to echo throughout the trade union and Labour leadership for years. The miners, abandoned, fought on alone for another six months, only to be broken. The immediate aftermath of the strike was the Trades Disputes and Trade Union Act of 1927, which aimed to curb strike action and weaken the bargaining power of trade unions.

Lack of confidence among demoralised workers increased the independence of the trade union bureaucracy from rank-and-file pressure, and both union and Labour Party leaders moved massively to the right. The sell-out brought to an end a long, although not uninterrupted, period of working-class militancy.

The change was especially marked in the case of the Miners' Federation, which hitherto had been very much to the left in the trade union movement. Not only was the union defeated in the lock-out, it was weakened by the right-wing breakaway union run by George Spencer in the Nottingham coalfield. At the 1927 MFGB Conference, its president, Herbert Smith, went on an offensive against the Communist Party and the Minority Movement. Turning on Arthur Horner, the leading Communist in the union, Smith said:

> You are doing as much harm as Spencer . . . I want to give some advice to Horner or anybody else that unless they are prepared to stand four square and carry out the policy of this federation, then you have to get out.[1]

Others sang the same tune: J Hobson of Durham said: 'I can tell my friends here, Mr Horner in particular, that where the Communists and Minority Movement is strongest in Durham, there we have the weakest position.'[2]

This attack on the Communist Party took place less than a year after the end of the lock-out when the sacrifice of party members was so impressive.

The September 1927 TUC Congress witnessed the Miners' Federation joining a witch-hunt against the Communist Party and the Minority Movement. The General Council's Report to the Congress included the following resolution of the General Council of February 1927:

> That those trades councils which are affiliated to the Minority Movement . . . shall not be accorded recognition by the General Council nor allowed to participate in any work carried on under the auspices of the General Council.[3]

Herbert Smith, in supporting the resolution, said: 'I am not going to be dictated to by Moscow through the Minority Movement.'[4] An attempt to refer back this part of the General Council's Report was defeated heavily: 148,000 to 3,746,000.[5] The MFGB voted with the right.

Along with the General Council's ban on trades councils sympathetic to the Minority Movement came the Labour Party's disaffiliation of a number of local parties which persisted in maintaining Communist connections.

Now class collaboration and not class struggle was all the rage. The miners' lock-out ended at the end of November 1926. Less than two months later, in January 1927, Lord Weir, head of one of the largest contracting firms in the country, wrote to Ernest Bevin suggesting talks between employers and trade union leaders. A meeting followed in March which included, besides Bevin, Arthur Pugh and George Hicks — the former 'left' and now chairman of the TUC.[6] In his presidential address to the 1927 TUC, George Hicks called for collaboration with employers 'in common endeavour to improve the efficiency of industry and to raise the workers' standard of life.'

The offer of collaboration with employers was picked up in November by Sir Alfred Mond, chairman of ICI, a former Liberal MP who had joined the ranks of the Tories. Along with a group of big employers from a number of industries, including Lord Weir, he approached the TUC General Council with a proposal that they should meet and discuss a drive for 'rationalisation of industry' which would be carried through more smoothly if there were harmony with the trade unions. The General Council, of which

Ben Turner was chairman, accepted the invitation, and in July 1928 an Interim Report was agreed and issued. It supported rationalisation and cooperation between the trade unions and their employers.

The Report proposed the establishment of a National Industrial Council, composed on the one hand of the General Council, and on the other of an equal number of employers nominated by the National Conference of Employers Organisations and the Federation of British Industries. Together they would appoint joint standing committees which would operate a system of compulsory conciliation. That is to say, the General Council would waive the workers' right to strike if an employer applied for a case to be heard before the joint conciliation board. The agreement fitted the mood of the TUC leadership following the General Strike. After all, the only alternative they had to collaboration with the employers was to organise the defence and resistance of workers to the employers' offensive while building up forces for a renewal of struggle.

For the next quarter of a century, the unions were dominated by an openly class-collaborationist right wing who also held absolute sway in the Labour Party.

The defeat of the strike was the result of betrayal by the leaders of the trade unions and Labour Party. They did not want a strike: at most they were willing to make a gesture in defence of the miners, hoping this would be enough to bring the government to the negotiating table. But the government did not want a compromise. It wanted to defeat the unions, so that it could impose its own terms not only on the miners but along the line. Baldwin, a shrewd politician, wanted to break the strength of the unions, while at the same time using the leaders to discipline the rank and file.

A general strike is the sharpest form of the class struggle. It is only one step from general strike to armed insurrection. In modern society no one can hold power without controlling the railways, power stations, coal and communications. In 1926 striking workers again and again showed discontent with the trade union bureaucracy, pressing against the ideological and organisational barriers of the conservative trade union apparatus. Workers groped towards the principle of workers' control over the strike action. Alas, the General Strike did not shake the union apparatus. It was a bureaucratically regimented strike and there was little opportunity for workers to escape even temporarily from the grip of the bureaucrats.

Chapter Twenty-Four

IN CONCLUSION

IN MAJOR CLASS STRUGGLES all social and political theories are put to the ultimate test of practice. Ideas and beliefs that persist long after they have ceased to explain the world around them are suddenly illuminated by the light of practical struggle. Those that pass such a rigorous examination are validated more surely than any words could do.

The General Strike of 1926 was one such test. It has long been encrusted by myths that obscure the real lessons. These serve both to shield the vicious ruling-class attack on British workers and the trade union leaders who betrayed them in the midst of battle.

The most enduring myth which the General Strike has reinforced is that violent class war is somehow foreign or 'un-British'. Both Tory and Labour politicians subscribe to this idea since it justifies and reinforces their self-importance as members of parliament, where such conflict is 'resolved'. The events of 1926 are given as proof that not even in times of major disputes do the British lose their sense of fair play or forget the rules of civilised behaviour.

The truth is entirely different. The miners' lock-out, the mass victimisation of strikers, the wage cuts and longer hours were a barbaric reminder of what capitalism will do if workers allow it. The dole queues of the 1930s, still remembered with sorrow today, were the result. The general passivity of the strike made its defeat and the demoralisation that followed all the more certain and was the deliberate outcome of the trade union bureaucracy's cowardly policies. There was nothing especially British about this. Reformists the world over have behaved as appallingly (though usually with less effect).

There is an opposite reading of the General Strike which was put forward by Leon Trotsky, who saw the event as a missed revolutionary opportunity. Was Britain in a revolutionary situation in 1926?

First of all, we must make it clear that not every revolutionary situation leads to a revolution. Without a revolutionary party, even the most revolutionary situation can end in defeat of the working class and counter-revolution. Secondly, the revolutionary situation itself depends on a number of basic factors. Society must be in an economic, social and political *impasse*. All sections of society must feel more and more that it is impossible to go on in the old way. The working class finds its situation intolerable. The ruling class loses confidence that it can go on as before and splits, one section being inclined to crush workers' opposition with an iron fist, another section trying to buy the workers off. The division in the ruling class increases the confidence and combativity of the working class — while the struggle of the working class deepens the split in the ruling class. The workers are encouraged to fight even harder. And so it goes on, the crisis in one camp feeding the strength and confidence of the other.

The 1926 conflict was real enough. The stoppage involved millions of workers; the army and navy were deployed; armoured cars rolled through the streets. But to judge if there was a feeling of insecurity among the ruling class, one can best compare the Cabinet papers of 1926 with those of 1919–1920, or compare the entries in the Whitehall diaries of Tom Jones, deputy secretary to the Cabinet, for the same period. As we have seen, there was turmoil in government ranks in 1919–1920. We find nothing like that in 1926. The public statements of the government did not reflect its real feelings and the use of troops was mostly for show.

In 1919–20, while the government feared an outbreak of revolution, they showed complete calm in public. In 1926 they deliberately fostered alarm about the usurpation of constitutional authority. In 1919–20 there was no open talk about revolution. In 1926 dire warnings of revolution were the fashion.

What about the working class?

The workers showed great solidarity and readiness to fight. But this largely took the form of *passive* endurance.

So the General Strike neither showed that class war was alien to British politics, nor was it a failed revolution. The working class lacked that crucial subjective element needed to turn a defensive action into an offensive one, a ruling-class attack into a revolutionary upheaval.

After the event many complained of the workers' passivity. But the leaders who later complained, including those of the

Communist Party and the Minority Movement, were not free from blame for this. Is workers' activity like a revolver that can be kept unused for years in the leaders' pocket and then taken out and fired at will?

To overcome this inertia, the product of lack of control over their working lives and the debilitating effect of 'leave it to us' reformist leadership, workers have to win confidence in themselves and in the party that organises and leads them. Class consciousness, and the confidence of workers that they can control and change things, is the product of workers' own activity, of the collective interaction of people and parties in the objective world of the class struggle. The reformist bureaucracies can never be expected to provide the catalyst for this vital self-activity of the working class. The tragedy of 1926 is that the leadership of the Communist Party also completely failed to lead the workers — and so provided nothing either.

If the Communist Party had given the correct leadership, could it have broken the shackles imposed by the trade union bureaucracy? Such a question cannot be answered with certainty. In the final analysis it is the class struggle that decides, but the failure of the Communist Party to challenge the trade union leadership in the months before the strike and during it ensured that this class struggle did not take place.

Yet one thing is beyond doubt: while the victory of the strike could not have been guaranteed even with correct leadership from the Communist Party, at least the nature of the defeat would have been radically different. Defeat *can* educate substantial sections of the working class and strengthen their revolutionary ideas, whatever the effects of conservative bureaucratic inertia. The inheritance of the past can be challenged by the living forces of the present. But nowhere was this challenge articulated, whether by word or deed, in 1926.

The General Strike was the classic example of bureaucratic methods of trade union action. It entirely confirmed Trotsky's statement that

> If there were not a bureaucracy of the trade unions, then the police, the army, the courts, the lords, the monarchy would appear before the proletarian masses as nothing but pitiful ridiculous playthings. The bureaucracy of the trade unions is the backbone of British imperialism. It is by means of this bureaucracy that the bourgeoisie exists . . . The

Marxist will say to the British workers: 'The trade union bureaucracy is the chief instrument for your oppression by the bourgeois
state. Power must be wrested from the hands of the bourgeoisie and
for that its principal agent, the trade union bureaucracy, must be
overthrown.[1]

In a revolution hundreds of thousands, indeed millions of
people are swept up into struggle and the unfolding of events is
decisively shaped by their action. The twists and turns of the fight
are thoroughly unpredictable. The same could certainly not be said
of the General Strike. Its broad outlines — the very date of the
conflict, the initial rhetorical support of the miners by the TUC, the
government's determination to call its bluff, and the calculated
betrayal — all these things could have been discerned after Red
Friday.

The government openly admitted that its climbdown in
July 1925 was a device which it needed to win time in order to
marshall its forces for a concerted attack. In granting the nine-
month coal subsidy in 1925 the government set a timetable which
was there for all to see, yet when time ran out no group on the side
of the workers was politically prepared. In many ways this fact is
more remarkable than the course of the General Strike itself. For
on the face of it there should have been no failure to foresee the
sell-out.

With a correct revolutionary policy the Communist Party
could not guarantee the conquest of power by the proletariat — the
logical outcome of the mass general strike — but at least it could
have guaranteed the conquest of a large section of the proletariat to
the ideas of workers' power and communism. It is not the objective
situation that explains the devastating impact of 1926 on the working class for decades to follow. It was the subjective element: the
bankruptcy of the Communist Party, who served as cheer leaders
for the 'left' bureaucrats — Purcell, Swales and Hicks — while
these acted as cover for the Thomases, Bevins and MacDonalds.

The 1926 stoppage was one example of the mass strike, which
has a long history dating from 1842 to the present day. In her
pamphlet on the subject Rosa Luxemburg used the spontaneous
struggles of Russian workers in 1905 as the basis for an analysis of
mass strikes. The British General Strike must be considered as
very different, the summit of bureaucratic manipulation.

Even so the reality of class war did appear on the stage,

although it was heavily disguised. For example, the relationship of economic struggle to politics was much discussed. But it was not the workers' movement that used it to advantage, as the Petersburg Soviet had done. It was Baldwin's government that attacked, roundly denouncing the strike as a threat to the Constitution, while the TUC energetically denied it was anything more than an industrial dispute. By pretending the strike was purely economic the whole field of ideological and physical force was left free for the ruling class.

But even this was not enough to break the spirit of the workers. It took a sell-out from the top.

The key to understanding the 1926 strike, its half-hearted engagement and callous betrayal, is the trade union bureaucracy. The role of this group as a brake on workers' struggles is a theme which runs throughout this book. It is not simply a question of denouncing the very obvious sell-out. Many other questions have been discussed: how the bureaucracy arises and under what laws it functions.

For example, in the period between 1919 and 1926 we saw how the bureaucracy's freedom of manoeuvre was relative. Its behaviour was never a simple reflection of the wishes or pressure of the rank and file, nor was it at liberty to act as it liked. The General Strike was a classic case. The TUC had to lead when the lock-out notices were served, or it would have lost control altogether. But that leadership was designed in every detail to paralyse the rank and file and prevent a decisive challenge to the ruling class.

The bureaucracy acted just a like a safety valve on a boiler. If pressure builds up too much it opens and the necessary steam is released. But the *purpose* of a safety valve is not the release of steam, but the prevention of the boiler from exploding.

Beneath the surface events lay the problem of mass reformism. Why did the officials — a group supposed to represent and serve the interests of the rank and file — become the polar opposite: a bureaucracy which pursued its own separate goals and had the rank and file serve its interests?

Under capitalism the working class is exploited and oppressed. If it is not forged into a self-confident force through collective struggle, its individual members are made to feel weak in the face of the monopoly of the forces of violence maintained by the state and the concentrated power of capital — the foreman, the threat of the dole, and so on upwards. Unless a crisis overtakes them, workers' mass organisations, the unions, seek only to negotiate within the system. Given time they develop a group of specialists who make the power entrusted to them by the rank and file their own personal property. Now all relations appear inverted. The union machine becomes an end in itself, the rank and file its stage army. The funds are to be conserved, not wasted in upholding action. The bureaucracy blames the rank and file for letting it down, not *vice versa*. The trade union discipline, born of a felt need for class solidarity, is used, as it was in 1926, as a means of holding back workers' action. If the rank and file remains alienated from its collective power and does not reclaim this through its own activity, then the rank and file will remain dominated by the bureaucracy.

The historical roots of the bureaucracy and its role have also been discussed at length. Our comparison of British and Russian trade unions showed that the key to the bureaucracy is not the officials themselves, but the general situation of the working class, and in particular its consciousness as a class. We looked at the revolutionary trade union movements of Britain in the 1840s and Russia in 1905–17, and saw how different these were from the British unions of the 1850s or 1926.

It was in these latter periods that the bureaucracy was able to rise up and consolidate its position. The bureaucracy (and reformist leaders in general) can play a key role in maintaining, or more often retarding, the workers' movement, but they do so within the general framework set by the balance of class forces and workers' consciousness. Nevertheless they can, by their influence, dramatically alter that balance.

To put it another way. The bureaucracy is not the only explanation for the failure of the British working-class movement to realise socialism. The question of political organisation and consciousness is also of paramount importance. Take the example of craft unionism. The skilled labour aristocratic unions grew up after the defeat of Chartism and during economic boom. Though they had conservative policies they were not dominated by bureaucracy in the early days, because at that time the skilled rank and file were self-reliant in face of their employers. The later 'new unions', after 1889, were politically left-wing (thus they supported founding a Labour Party to oppose the Liberals), but had a strong bureaucracy — because the rank and file lacked sectional strength and needed a strong centralising force to make an impact. That is why the two strong right-wing bureaucrats of 1926 were J H Thomas, of the largely unskilled NUR, and Ernest Bevin of the TGWU, which owed its origins to the new unionism of 1889.

So a Marxist analysis of the trade union bureaucracy cannot make do with appearances, but must show how the surface events are constructed from the deeper forces that are at work. And crucial among these is the balance of class forces at the point of production and the political consciousness of the working class.

A history of bureaucratic crimes is not enough. Though a necessary first step, this cannot break the vicious circle that has led successive working-class revivals to defeat. Socialists can no more ignore the internal debates and issues of trade union struggle now than they could in 1926, for the mass of advanced workers are still there.

For as long as socialists have lived in this country they have argued about trade unionism. The pioneering efforts of analysis of Marx and Engels are as valid today as when they were written. Nevertheless they left many detailed issues unanswered. This was inevitable, given the period when they were writing. The chief features of modern trade unionism were barely visible. The same goes for the writings of Russian revolutionaries who, though they made great advances in many fields of Marxism, had practically no experience of mass reformist unions.

There were other traditions, such as the South Wales Unofficial Reform Committee and the workers' committee movement during the First World War. These were both extensions of syndicalism. In terms of general analysis these currents were far weaker than Marx, Engels or Lenin. But the latter had approached the problem of unions largely from the outside. Despite their lack of theory, these British revolutionaries had been involved from the inside — ranging from the Cambrian Combine strike of the pre-war 'Labour Unrest' to the fight of munitions workers against government war-time attacks on conditions.

For this reason they stressed some of the essential features that the more important thinkers had overlooked. In particular they recognised the conflict betwen the interests of the rank and file and the bureaucracy. They went further, putting forward practical measures to overcome the official stranglehold. When circumstances were favourable unofficial movements were built. These are still relevant today since they are among the few models we have of a serious alternative to the rule of the officials.

However, exclusive emphasis on the rank and file/bureaucracy

divide led such movements not only to reject reformist politics of
the Labour Party kind or official union methods, but to deny *all*
politics, including the revolutionary party. Indeed the concept of
any type of leadership was repudiated. This attitude was soon seen,
even by its promoters, as false. But the question remained — what
kind of leadership *is* needed in the class struggle — both in terms of
a revolutionary party and inside the unions?

The first problem began to be solved when the Communist
Party was set up in Britain in 1920. But the trade union problem
was more difficult. It was through the Russian revolution and the
Comintern that real steps towards a *Marxist* strategy for working
inside trade unions became possible. This does not mean that there
were no revolutionaries in trade unions before then, but until
economic and political action could be fused by the linking of trade
union work with the building of a revolutionary socialist party,
progress was inevitably limited within the narrow horizons of trade
unionism.

The British Communist Party was the product of a marriage
between the ideas of the Communist International and home-grown
socialist organisations. The weakness of the Comintern in matters
of trade unionism was a serious handicap. The establishment of the
RILU as a Communist split from the reformist union movement
itself symbolised the mistakes of those early years. But as 1926
approached, the attempt to ditch RILU and form alliances with left
union officials pushed the party in the opposite direction — towards
accommodation with reformist bureaucrats. This accommodation
was part and parcel of the massive move to the right by the increasingly Stalinist Comintern leadership, which not only led to errors in
Britain at that time, but to the massacre of the Chinese Revolution.

Domestic factors were also important in shaping CPGB policy.
The party inherited two ideas from the past. On the one hand there
was the syndicalist attitude, which viewed socialist parties as a
propaganda outlet for purely industrial activity. On the other hand
many former British Socialist Party members brought with them to
the new party the idea that politics had nothing to do with trade
unions. Up to Black Friday 1921, these two factors coexisted in the
party and led to a propagandist view of its role, both politically and
industrially.

The crisis that followed Black Friday forced a questioning of
old positions and an awareness of the need for intervention. The
unrealistic policy of calling for workers' committees was dropped

and party work in the unions stepped up. The tactical questions asked at the time are still of the utmost relevance: how important is the official machine (conferences, the passing of formal resolutions, union branch work and so on), or is the rebuilding of shopfloor organisation in the factories the sole concern? How can a real leadership in the unions be created? Are left bureaucrats a useful ally, or should agitation be organised only under party auspices?

Unfortunately, while there were many path-breaking ideas put forward, the final results of the discussion led to serious mistakes. On the one hand the weaker aspects of the South Wales mining tradition were used in creating the National Minority Movement. The party centred its work on working among the rank and file, but in order to influence trade union branches and officials *at the expense* of rank-and-file struggle. Even worse, the Anglo-Russian Trade Union Unity Committee led the Communist Party to place great faith in the TUC lefts. The valuable work of the party's factory cells and the agitational impact of the **Workers' Weekly** newspaper were squandered in such enterprises.

The idea the party now held, that the fundamental division in the unions was between right and left, was as false as the old one which ignored politics and saw only the division between rank and file and bureaucracy.

This does not mean that the differences between right or left ideas amongst workers is not important. It is upon this difference — this unevenness in consciousness — that revolutionary parties are established as separate from reformist ones. But just as important is the fact that *objectively*, rank-and-file workers — whether reformists, centrists or revolutionaries — have a common interest in opposing and overthrowing the system (whether they are aware of it or not!). In contrast union bureaucrats — reformist, centrist or verbally revolutionary — have a common group interest which means they must confine workers' struggle within the system.

Reformist workers can become revolutionaries through struggle, officials *cannot*. The proof is 1926. Despite the massive issues, the General Council learnt nothing. Instead it wanted to limit the strike and invented the nonsensical idea of separate 'waves' of action which caused utter confusion. The bureaucracy wished union head offices to retain control and so reinforced sectionalism. They feared to challenge the state and abandoned control over food, while encouraging football with the police, churchgoing and the wearing of medals. Most significant of all, in 1925 the left bureaucrats Purcell, Hicks and Swales, discovered in the heat of class struggle that their identity of interest lay with right-wingers like Thomas, Pugh and Bevin.

So how should revolutionaries approach the two divisions in the workers' movement — between the left and right or between the rank and file and the bureaucracy? Unevenness in workers' consciousness makes necessary the building of a revolutionary party in conscious distinction to reformism. Its politics must be based on rank-and-file self-activity and distrust of bureaucrats. This party can and must be argued for even in periods of minimal class struggle, though at such times these ideas may appeal to only a tiny minority and activities may be largely confined to propaganda. But at times of intense industrial militancy a far wider group will be open to revolutionary politics, and many will be drawn to the party through direct experience of struggle. In such a period the principle of workers' self-activity needs to take the form of direct agitation for independent rank-and-file organisation, and political leadership by the party.

Between these two extremes there can be a whole range of different levels of party activity, balancing propaganda against agitation, work inside the union machine against opportunities for action beyond it and so on. The right/left split among union leaders may at times be exploited to take the fetters off rank-and-file action. But this split must be understood as one internal to the bureaucracy. Despite the differences between left and right-wing officials, they form a common social group. Workers too hold a wide variety of opinions, yet are of a single class. It is the clash of interest between the bureaucracy and rank and file that overrides any superficial similarities between, say, a left union official and a militant worker.

Many such political questions were raised in 1926 and before. In the Communist International there was the polemic of Trostky against the central leadership of Zinoviev and the rising star of Stalin. British issues were very much to the fore in this debate. The dominant trend in the International hoped that a mass revolutionary party would come in Britain through alliances with left-wing union officials and Labour Party politicians. British Communist leaders accepted this viewpoint. Trotsky, however, argued that there was no alternative to the building of a principled revolutionary party sharply critical of reformists of every hue.

In Britain J T Murphy and R Palme Dutt were occupied with similar qustions. Red Friday, the left resolutions of the TUC Congress at Scarborough and the Left Wing Movement, all posed the question of the revolutionary attitude to reformism and bureaucracy in an acute form.

So the period up to and including 1926 is important for several reasons. The General Strike itself was a textbook demonstration of bureaucratic methods and the harm they can do. The path that led to this catastrophic defeat posed the problem of how a revolutionary party should function in a non-revolutionary situation and orientate towards trade unionism.

The issues raised in this book — the hold of officialdom, the building of a Marxist party, rank-and-file action and trade unions — are still with us today. Their solution is hinted at here; but the real answer can only be realised in practice, by the moulding of a revolutionary organisation with a clear concept of how to combat mass reformism. A knowledge of the events of 1926 can hopefully assist in this task.

NOTES

Chapter 1: TRADE UNIONS IN RUSSIA AND BRITAIN

1.   S A Smith, **Red Petrograd** (Cambridge 1983) pages 57–8.
2.   Tony Cliff, **Lenin** (London, four volumes, 1975–79) volume 1, page 331.
3.   Smith, pages 105 and 109.
4.   Smith, pages 107–8.
5.   Smith, pages 109–110.
6.   Leon Trotsky, **1905** (New York 1971) page 196.
7.   Sidney and Beatrice Webb, **A History of Trade Unionism** (London 1920) page 31.
8.   Webbs, page 1.
9.   Webbs, page 217.
10.   Webbs, page 199.
11.   Webbs, page 190.
12.   Webbs, page 489.
13.   Webbs, page 204.
14.   Webbs, pages 577–8.
15.   Webbs, page 466.
16.   Webbs, pages 468–470.
17.   Webbs, page 594.
18.   Webbs, page 636.
19.   Webbs, page 180.

Chapter 2: MARXISM, BUREAUCRACY AND THE TRADE UNIONS

1.   Friedrich Engels, **The Condition of the Working Class in England** (1844) in Marx and Engels, **Collected Works** (London 1975 onwards) volume 4, page 507.
2.   Engels, page 512.
3.   Karl Marx, **The Poverty of Philosophy** (1847) in Marx and Engels, **Collected Works**, volume 6, pages 210–211.
4.   Marx and Engels, **The German Ideology**, in **Collected Works**, volume 5, pages 204–5.
5.   M Jenkins, **The General Strike of 1842** (London 1980) page 21.
6.   Jenkins, page 23.
7.   Jenkins, page 15.
8.   Jenkins, page 148.

9.   J Foster, introduction to Jenkins, **The General Strike of 1842**, page 13.
10. Marx, **Wages, Price and Profit** (1865) in Marx and Engels, **Selected Works** (Moscow 1958) volume 1, pages 446–7.
11. Quoted in Hal Draper, **Karl Marx's Theory of Revolution** (London 1978) volume 2, page 107.
12. Quoted in Draper, volume 2, page 107.
13. Vladimir Lenin, **Collected Works** (Moscow 1965) volume 8, page 92.
14. Lenin, volume 10, page 32.
15. Rosa Luxemburg, **The Mass Strike** (London 1964) page 48.
16. Lenin, volume 5, page 384.
17. Alex Callinicos, 'The Rank and File Movement Today', in **International Socialism**, second series, number 17, page 5.
18. Tony Cliff, 'On Perspectives', in **International Socialism**, first series, number 36.
19. A Bullock, **The Life and Times of Ernest Bevin** (London 1960) volume 1, page 31.
20. Bullock, volume 1, page 116.
21. Trotsky, **Writings 1932–3** (New York 1972) page 170.
22. Clyde Workers Committee leaflet in the Beveridge Collection, British Library of Political and Economic Science, section 3, item 5.
23. Trotsky, **Writings on Britain** (London 1974) volume 2, page 191.

Chapter 3: LENIN'S CONTRIBUTION ON TRADE UNIONS

1.   Lenin, volume 5, page 400.
2.   **Internationaler Sozialisten-Kongress zu Stuttgart, 1907** (Berlin 1907) page 106.
3.   Quoted in Lenin, **On Britain** (London 1959) page 582.
4.   Lenin, volume 21, page 223.
5.   Lenin, volume 21, page 223.
6.   Lenin, volume 21, page 242.
7.   Lenin, volume 22, pages 193–4.
8.   Tony Cliff, 'The Economic Roots of Reformism', in Tony Cliff, **Neither Washington Nor Moscow** (London 1982) pages 110–111.
9.   Lenin, **On Britain**, pages 326–7.
10. Quoted in J Riddell (editor), **Lenin's Struggle for a Revolutionary International** (New York 1984) pages 492–3.
11. Quoted in Riddell, page 482.
12. **The Second Congress of the Communist International** (London 1977) volume 2, page 62

Chapter 4: THE COMMUNIST INTERNATIONAL AND TRADE UNION STRATEGY

1.   Adler (editor), **Theses, Resolutions and Manifestoes of the First Four Congresses of the Third International** (London 1980) page 33.
2.   Lenin, volume 31, pages 53 and 55.

3.   Radek, quoted in **The Second Congress of the Communist International**, volume 2, page 62.

4.   **Second Congress**, volume 2, page 67.

5.   **Second Congress**, volume 2, page 67.

6.   **Second Congress**, volume 2, page 66.

7.   **The Worker**, 31 January 1920.

8.   **The Worker**, 31 January 1920.

9.   **The Worker**, 31 January 1920.

10.   Degras, **The Communist International 1919–1943: Documents** (London, three volumes 1956–1965) volume 1, pages 89–90.

11.   E H Carr, **The Bolshevik Revolution**, volume 3 (London 1966) page 397.

12.   E H Carr, **Socialism in One Country** (London 1964) page 545.

13.   **Communist Review**, March 1922.

14.   **Communist Review**, October 1921.

15.   O Flechtheim, **Die KPD in der Weimarer Republik** (Frankfurt-am-Main 1969) page 170.

16.   For details of the complicated negotiations, see D Horowitz, **The Italian Labour Movement** (Cambridge, Massachusetts, 1963) pages 162–4.

17.   Carr, **Socialism in One Country**, volume 2, page 690.

18.   Degras, volume 2, page 258.

19.   Degras, volume 2, page 645.

20.   Quoted in **Communist Review**, April 1922.

21.   **Bericht über den IV Kongress, Petrograd-Moskau vom 5 November bis 5 Dezember 1922** (Hamburg 1923) page 395.

22.   **Communist Review**, March 1923.

23.   **International Trade Union Unity**, with introduction by Harry Pollitt (London 1925) pages 17–18.

24.   **Second Congress**, volume 2, page 175.

25.   **Second Congress**, volume 2, pages 81 and 175.

26.   Degras, volume 1, page 145.

27.   Degras, volume 1, page 96.

28.   **Theses, Resolutions and Manifestoes**, pages 264–5.

29.   **Second Congress**, volume 2, page 71.

30.   **Second Congress**, volume 2, pages 64–5.

31.   **Second Congress**, volume 2, page 89.

32.   **Second Congress**, volume 2, page 78. Our emphasis.

33.   **Second Congress**, volume 2, page 167.

34.   **Theses, Resolutions and Manifestoes**, page 265.

35.   **Moskau gegen Amsterdam** (Hamburg 1921) page 58.

36.   **Moskau gegen Amsterdam**, page 53.

37.   **Second Congress**, volume 2, page 175.

38.   Duncan Hallas, **The Comintern** (London 1984) page 66.

39.   **Thèses et Résolutions adoptée au Deuxième Congrès de l'Internationale Syndicale Rouge, Novembre 1922** (Paris, no date) page 2.

40.   Cliff, **Lenin**, volume 4, pages 45–6.

Chapter 5: BRITISH SOCIALISTS AND INDUSTRIAL STRUGGLE

1.   Quoted in H Collins, 'The Marxism of the Social-Democratic Federation', in A Briggs and J Saville (editors), **Essays in Labour History, 1886–1923** (London 1971) page 55.
2.   Cliff, **Lenin**, volume 4, page 80.
3.   T Rothstein, quoted in W Kendall, **The Revolutionary Movement in Britain** (London 1969) page 12.
4.   **Vanguard**, publication of the Scottish area of the British Socialist Party, July 1913.
5.   **Proceedings of the Socialist Unity Conference, 30 September and 1 October 1911**, (no date or place of publication given) page 18.
6.   **Socialist Unity Conference**, page 12.
7.   **The Industrial Syndicalist**, December 1910 (reprinted with an introduction by G Brown, Nottingham 1974).
8.   **Industrial Syndicalist**, July 1910.
9.   A G Tufton, speaking at the Industrial Syndicalist Education League's founding conference, **Industrial Syndicalist**, December 1910.
10.   **Industrial Syndicalist**, December 1910.
11.   **The Socialist**, March 1910.

Chapter 6: TWO RANK-AND-FILE MOVEMENTS

1.   Beveridge Collection, section 3, item 5.
2.   J T Murphy, **Preparing for Power** (London 1972) pages 129–130.
3.   J T Murphy, **New Horizons** (London 1941) page 44.
4.   Donny Gluckstein, **The Western Soviets** (London 1985) page 70.
5.   **Solidarity**, February 1918.
6.   Murphy, **Preparing for Power**, pages 152–3.
7.   Murphy, **The Workers' Committee** (London 1972) page 14.
8.   **Solidarity**, July 1917.
9.   For details of the structure of engineering trade unionism, see B Pribicevic, **The Shop Stewards and Workers' Control** (Oxford 1959) page 27.
10.   **The Miners' Next Step** (London 1973) page 26.
11.   M G Woodhouse, 'Rank and File Movements among the workers of South Wales, 1910–26' (Oxford PhD thesis, 1969).
12.   Woodhouse, page 76.
13.   **The Worker**, 4 September 1920.
14.   **Glamorgan Free Press**, 1 March 1912, quoted in Woodhouse, page 82.
15.   **South Wales Worker**, 10 January 1914, quoted in Woodhouse, page 95.
16.   **South Wales Worker**, 13 June 1914, quoted in Woodhouse, page 112.
17.   **The Pioneer**, 13 July 1918, quoted in Woodhouse, page 149.
18.   **Rhondda Socialist**, 1 May 1912, quoted in Woodhouse, page 74.
19.   Woodhouse, page 142.
20.   **Labour Leader**, 10 October 1918.

Chapter 7: THE MISSED OPPORTUNITY

1.   The Worker, 1 February 1919.
2.   Murphy, Preparing for Power, pages 176–7.
3.   Solidarity, January 1919.
4.   British Government Cabinet Papers, CAB 23/9, WC 514/9.
5.   CAB 23/9, WC 518 (6).
6.   CAB 23/9, WC 522.
7.   CAB 23/9, WC 525 (1).
8.   British Labour Statistics, Historical Abstract 1886–1968 (London 1971) table 196.
9.   G A Phillips, 'The Triple Alliance in 1914', in Economic History Review, February 1971, page 63.
10.   G Blaxland, J H Thomas: A Life for Unity (London 1964) page 121.
11.   Allen Hutt, The Post-war History of the British Working Class (London 1972) page 18.
12.   F Hodges, My Adventures as a Labour Leader (London 1925) page 90.
13.   N Edwards, History of the South Wales Miners Federation (London 1938) page 116.
14.   TUC Annual Report 1919, pages 263–6.
15.   Robin Page-Arnot, The Miners' Year of Struggle (London 1953) page 339.
16.   Hutt, page 62.
17.   Murphy, Preparing for Power, pages 213–4.
18.   Murphy, Preparing for Power, pages 207–8.
19.   Fourth Congress of the Communist International (London 1923) page 62.

Chapter 8: THE FIRST FEW YEARS OF
THE COMMUNIST INTERNATIONAL

1.   Lenin, On Britain (London 1973) page 363.
2.   Official Report of the Communist Unity Convention held in London, 31 July to 1 August 1920 (London 1920), page 7.
3.   Communist Unity Convention, page 32.
4.   Communist Unity Convention, page 50.
5.   The Communist, 5 August 1920.
6.   Tom Bell, in The Communist, 30 September 1920.
7.   The Communist, 7 October 1920, article signed by A MacManus and A Inkpin.
8.   See for example The Communist, 9 April 1921.
9.   The Communist, 30 April 1921.
10.   Communist Review, December 1921.
11.   The Worker, 17 September 1921.
12.   The Communist, 1 April 1922.
13.   Communist Review, 4 February 1922.
14.   Solidarity, December 1919.
15.   The Communist, 30 September 1922. Our emphasis.
16.   All Power, June 1922.
17.   Harry Pollitt, Pioneering Days (London 1940) pages 159–160.

18.   **The Worker**, 16 September 1922.
19.   **Labour Monthly**, October 1922.

Chapter 9: THE MINORITY MOVEMENT

1.   Details in **The Communist**, 28 October 1922.
2.   **The Communist**, 9 September 1922.
3.   **The Communist**, 9 September 1922.
4.   **Communist Review**, April 1922.
5.   **All Power**, December 1922.
6.   **All Power**, 7 April 1923.
7.   **Coventry Minority Movement Minute Book 1924–9**, in Sara Maitland Collection, University of Warwick.
8.   **Workers' Weekly**, 30 June 1923.
9.   **Workers' Weekly**, 28 April 1923.
10.   **Workers' Weekly**, 28 April 1923.
11.   **The Worker**, 20 December 1924.
12.   **Workers' Weekly**, 21 April 1923.
13.   **All Power**, August 1923.
14.   **All Power**, August 1923.
15.   **Workers' Weekly**, 4 July 1924.
16.   **Workers' Weekly**, 4 July 1924.
17.   **Workers' Weekly**, 4 July 1924.
18.   Woodhouse, page 281.
19.   Quoted in Woodhouse, page 317.
20.   **The Mineworker**, 15 March 1924.
21.   P Cairns, Scottish treasurer of the Miners' Minority Movement, in **The Mineworker**, 12 April 1924.
22.   **The Mineworker**, 13 June 1925.
23.   **The Mineworker**, 21 February 1925.
24.   **The Worker**, 29 September 1923.
25.   Beveridge Collection, section 3, item 5.
26.   **The Worker**, 9 February 1924.
27.   **Workers' Weekly**, 29 August 1924.
28.   **Communist Review**, October 1923.
29.   J MacFarlane, **The Communist Party: Its Origin and Development until 1929** (London 1966) pages 324–5.
30.   J R Campbell, writing in **Communist Review**, May 1924.

Chapter 10: TAILING THE LEFT LEADERS

1.   **Workers' Weekly**, 21 September 1923.
2.   **Workers' Weekly**, 12 October 1923.
3.   **Workers' Weekly**, 9 January 1925.
4.   **Labour Monthly**, volume 6, pages 268–9 (May 1924).
5.   **Labour Monthly**, volume 6, page 167 (March 1924).
6.   **Labour Monthly**, volume 6, page 467 (August 1924).

7.   **Labour Monthly**, volume 6, page 457 (August 1924).

8.   **Labour Monthly**, volume 6, page 464 (August 1924).

9.   **Labour Monthly**, volume 6, page 467 (August 1924).

10. J Klugmann, **History of the Communist Party of Great Britain** (London 1969) page 22.

11. **Labour Monthly**, volume 7, page 79 (January 1925).

12. **Workers' Weekly**, 26 December 1924.

13. **Workers' Weekly**, 12 December 1924.

14. Theses of the Moscow Committee of the Communist Party of the Soviet Union, quoted in Trotsky, **The Third International after Lenin** (London 1974) page 101.

Chapter 11: THE WRITING ON THE WALL:
THE COMMUNIST PARTY AND 'RED FRIDAY'

1.   Robin Page-Arnot, **The General Strike** (London 1926) page 34.

2.   Quoted in Page-Arnot, **The General Strike**, page 35.

3.   G A Phillips, **The General Strike: The politics of industrial conflict** (London 1976) page 54.

4.   TUC Library, GC Box 123, SIC 23 July 1926.

5.   Quoted in G M Young, **Stanley Baldwin** (London 1952) page 99.

6.   **The Worker**, 28 February 1925.

7.   **The Worker**, 4 April 1925.

8.   **Workers' Weekly**, 7 August 1925.

9.   **Report of Second Annual Conference of National Minority Movement** (London 1925) page 8.

10. **Report of Second Annual Conference of National Minority Movement**, pages 16–17.

11. Aitken Ferguson to the Enlarged Plenum of the Executive Committee of the Comintern on 26 February 1926, quoted in **Orders from Moscow?** (London 1926) page 25.

12. Ferguson, quoted in **Orders from Moscow?**, pages 25–6.

13. **The Worker**, 20 February 1926.

14. **Orders from Moscow?**, page 32.

15. **Orders from Moscow?**, pages 38–9.

16. **Workers' Weekly**, 18 September 1925.

17. G Hardy, **Those Stormy Years** (London 1956) page 175.

18. Leading article in **Workers' Weekly**, 4 September 1925.

19. J R Campbell in **Workers' Weekly**, 9 October 1925.

20. **Workers' Weekly**, 9 October 1925.

Chapter 12: THE LEFT-WING MOVEMENT

1.   **Second Congress of the Communist International**, volume 2, pages 183–4.

2.   **Second Congress**, volume 2, page 188.

3.   **Communist Unity Convention**, pages 39–40.

4.   **Second Congress**, volume 2, page 183.

5.   **The Communist**, 12 August 1922.
6.   **Communist Review**, March 1923.
7.   **Workers' Weekly**, 8 February 1924.
8.   **Workers' Weekly**, 15 February 1924.
9.   **Workers' Weekly**, 28 May 1925.
10.   **Sunday Worker**, 27 September 1925.
11.   **Sunday Worker**, 20 December 1925.
12.   **Sunday Worker**, 20 December 1925.
13.   **Sunday Worker**, 18 October 1925.
14.   **Sunday Worker**, 25 October 1925.
15.   **Sunday Worker**, 29 November 1925.
16.   **Sunday Worker**, 26 February 1926.

Chapter 13: VIEWS FROM OUTSIDE: TROTSKY AND THE COMINTERN

1.   **International Trade Union Unity** (London 1925) page 19.
2.   **Protokoll über den Dritten Kongress der Roten Gewerkschafts Internationale, Moscow 6–21 July 1924** (no place of publication given) page 45. (Report of RILU Third Congress.)
3.   **International Trade Union Unity**, page 18.
4.   Trotsky, **Writings on Britain**, volume 2, page 119.
5.   Trotsky, **Writings on Britain**, volume 2, page 122.
6.   Trotsky, **Writings on Britain**, volume 2, page 136.
7.   Trotsky, **Writings on Britain**, volume 2, page 141.
8.   Trotsky, **Writings on Britain**, volume 2, pages 138–9.
9.   Trotsky, **Writings on Britain**, volume 2, page 192.
10.   Trotsky, **Writings on Britain**, volume 2, page 192.
11.   Trotsky, **Writings on Britain**, volume 2, page 191.
12.   Trotsky, **The Third International after Lenin**, page 97.

Chapter 14: TIME RUNS OUT FOR THE COMMUNIST PARTY

1.   **Communist International**, number 9, pages 12–13.
2.   **Communist Review**, October 1925.
3.   **Workers' Weekly**, 31 July 1925.
4.   **Communist International**, number 16, pages 81–2.
5.   **Communist International**, number 8, pages 31–3.
6.   Leading article in **Workers' Weekly**, 15 January 1926.
7.   Leading article in **Workers' Weekly**, 15 January 1926.
8.   **Workers' Weekly**, 12 March 1926.
9.   **Workers' Weekly**, 26 March 1926.
10.   **Workers' Weekly**, 9 April 1926.
11.   T H Wintringham, writing in **Workers' Weekly**, 30 April 1926.
12.   **Workers' Weekly**, 30 April 1926.
13.   **Orders from Moscow?**, pages 50–51.
14.   **Sunday Worker**, 25 April 1926.

Chapter 15: THE TUC BLUFF IS CALLED

1. R R James, **Memoirs of a Conservative: J C C Davidson's Memoirs and Papers 1910–37** (London 1969) pages 178–9.
2. James, page 180.
3. J Symons, **The General Strike** (London 1957) page 19.
4. British Government Cabinet Papers, CP390 (25).
5. CP390 (25).
6. CP390 (25).
7. CAB 23/50 44 (25) 2 (7 August 1925).
8. W M Crook, **The General Strike** (Chapel Hill 1931) page 356.
9. Page-Arnot, **The General Strike**, pages 48–54.
10. British Government Home Office Papers, HO 45 12336/2130.
11. CAB 81/26.
12. Quoted in A Bullock, **Ernest Bevin** (London 1960) volume 1, page 281.
13. Bullock, volume 1, pages 289–290.
14. TUC General Council, **Report of Proceedings at a Special Conference of Executives**, 20 January 1927, page 10.
15. **Report and Minutes of Evidence of Samuel Commission on the Coal Mining Industry** (Cmnd 2600, 1926) page 236. (Samuel Report.)
16. **Samuel Report**, pages 228 and 294.
17. Hutt, pages 123–4.
18. **The Record**, May–July 1926.
19. Bullock, pages 295–6.
20. Bullock, page 295.
21. Page-Arnot, **The General Strike**, page 104.
22. Page-Arnot, **The General Strike**, page 107.
23. TUC Library, GC 123, 13/6/13a, SIC 21 April 1926.
24. T Jones, **Whitehall Diary** (London 1969) volume 2, page 15.
25. Jones, page 15.
26. **The Times**, 19 April 1926.
27. Jones, page 13.
28. Jones, page 16.
29. Page-Arnot, **The General Strike**, page 133.
30. Page-Arnot, **The General Strike**, page 133.
31. Page-Arnot, **The General Strike**, page 132.
32. A J Cook, **The Nine Days** (London, June 1926) page 9.
33. CAB 23/52 21 (26).
34. CAB 23/52 23 (26).
35. Cook, page 11.
36. Cook, pages 12–13.
37. Cook, page 13.
38. **Hansard**, 2 May 1926. (Minutes of proceedings in the British parliament.)
39. **Hansard**, 3 May 1926.
40. **Hansard**, 3 May 1926.
41. J H Thomas, **My Story** (London 1937) page 104.
42. J R Clynes, **Memoirs** (London 1927) pages 75–6.
43. Clynes, page 78.
44. Clynes, page 82.
45. Thomas, page 104.

46. Quoted in the **Daily Herald**, 4 May 1926.
47. Citrine, **Men and Work** (London 1964) page 173.
48. Hutt, page 134.

Chapter 16: REVOLUTIONARY MASS STRIKE
OR BUREAUCRATIC NIGHTMARE?

1. M A Waters (editor), **Rosa Luxemburg Speaks** (New York 1970) page 171.
2. Rosa Luxemburg, **Ausgewählte Reden und Schriften** (Berlin 1955) volume 1, pages 227–8.
3. Luxemburg, **Ausgewählte**, pages 201–2.
4. Luxemburg, **Ausgewählte**, page 274.
5. Luxemburg, **Ausgewählte**, page 187.
6. Rosa Luxemburg, **Gesammelte Werke** (Berlin, no date) page 457.
7. Page-Arnot, **The General Strike**, page 162.
8. **British Worker**, 7 May 1926.
9. Raymond Postgate, 'Inner History of the General Strike' in **Locomotive Engineers Journal**, July 1926.
10. **The Story of the ETU: An official history** (London 1952) page 119–120.
11. TUC library, Box HD 5366, SOC 11 May 1926.
12. Page-Arnot, **The General Strike**, page 161.
13. M Morris, **The General Strike** (London 1976) page 35.
14. R Postgate, R Horrabin and E Wilkinson, **A Workers' History of the General Strike** (London 1926) page 25.
15. Morris, page 34.
16. TUC Library, Box HD 5366.
17. Morris, page 36.
18. J B Jefferys, **The Story of the Engineers 1800–1945** (London 1946) page 232.
19. S Benton, 'Sheffield' in Morris, pages 431–2.
20. Benton, in Morris, pages 432–3.
21. Benton, in Morris, page 438.
22. Robin Page-Arnot, 'The General Strike in the North East', in L M Mundy (editor), **The Luddites and other essays** (London 1971) pages 270 and 279.
23. S Bhaumik, 'Glasgow', in Morris, page 401; and P Carter, 'The West of Scotland', in J Skelley, **The General Strike 1926** (London 1976) pages 131–2.
24. H Fyfe, **Behind the Scenes of the General Strike** (London 1926) page 62.

Chapter 17: A SOLID STRIKE KEPT PASSIVE

1. Symons, pages 61–2.
2. Page-Arnot, **The General Strike**, page 175.
3. **British Worker**, 6 May 1926.
4. TUC Library, Box HD/5366.
5. CAB 27/331.
6. CAB 27/331, Supply and Transport Bulletin number 9.
7. P S Bagwell, **The Railwaymen: The History of the National Union of Railwaymen** (London 1963) pages 472–3.

8.   Bagwell, page 475.

9.   Quoted in Bagwell, pages 475–6.

10.   Calculated from figures in CAB 27/332, Supply and Transport Bulletin, 13 May 1926.

11.   Crook, page 390.

12.   Phillips, page 213.

13.   Postgate, Horrabin and Wilkinson, pages 25–6.

14.   TUC Library, Box HD 5366.

15.   E and R Frow, 'Manchester Diary', in Skelley, page 163.

16.   J Attfield and J Lee, 'Deptford and Lewisham', in Skelley, pages 263 and 265.

17.   Morris, page 37.

18.   Carter, in Skelley, page 115.

19.   Jefferys, page 233.

20.   Morris, page 33.

21.   TUC Library, Box HD 5366.

22.   Postgate, Horrabin and Wilkinson, page 37.

23.   HO 45/12336.

24.   HO 45/12336/2130, 11 May 1926.

25.   A Mason, **The General Strike in the North East** (Hull 1970) page 48.

26.   K Jeffery and P Hennessy, **States of Emergency** (London 1983) page 114.

27.   Merseyside Council of Action Strike Bulletin, number 3, in TUC Library, Box HD 5366.

28.   General Council circular of 5 May 1926, quoted in Postgate, Horrabin and Wilkinson, page 36.

29.   Fyfe, page 33.

30.   Fyfe, page 39.

31.   Symons, pages 171–2.

32.   W R Garside, **The Durham Miners 1919–1960** (London 1971) page 193.

33.   Phillips, page 169.

34.   **British Worker**, 5 May 1926.

35.   TUC Library, Box HD 5366.

36.   TUC Library, Box HD 5366.

37.   Emile Burns, **General Strike: Trades Councils in Action** (London 1975) pages 102, 132, 136, 137, 168 and 181.

38.   TUC Library, Box HD 5366.

39.   Postgate, Horrabin and Wilkinson, page 59.

40.   Christopher Farman, **The General Strike** (London 1974) page 229.

41.   Morris, page 55.

42.   **British Worker**, 9 May 1926.

43.   Burns, page 160.

44.   Symons, page 142.

45.   Farman, page 228.

46.   **General Strike in Sheffield**, with an introduction by Bill Moore (Sheffield 1981) page 24.

47.   **Police Review**, 21 May 1926.

48.   **Police Review**, 28 May 1926. Our emphasis.

49.   **Police Review**, 28 May 1926.

50.   **Police Review**, 21 May 1926.

51.   **Hansard**, 2 and 10 June 1926.

52. Alex Callinicos and Mike Simons, **The Great Strike: The miners' strike of 1984–5** (London 1985) page 223.
53. R Mace, 'Battersea', in Morris, pages 388–9.
54. TUC Library, Box HD 5366.
55. TUC Library, Box HD 5366.
56. Postgate, Horrabin and Wilkinson, pages 42–3.
57. Trotsky, **Writings on Britain**, volume 2, page 166.
58. Phillips, page 162.
59. **British Worker**, 9 May 1926.
60. **British Worker**, 9 May 1926.
61. TUC Library, Box HD 5366.

Chapter 18: CONTROLLING FOOD SUPPLIES

1. CAB 27/331, Supply and Transport Committee Daily Bulletin number 1, 3 May 1926.
2. Mason, page 18.
3. Quoted in Cook, page 9.
4. **Hansard**, 3 May 1926.
5. Morris, page 59.
6. Postgate, Horrabin and Wilkinson, page 34.
7. TUC Library, Box HD 5366.
8. Philips, pages 198–9.
9. TUC Library, Box HD 5366.
10. TUC General Council, **Report of Proceedings at a Special Conference of Executives**, 20 January 1927, page 72.
11. **Report of Special Conference**, page 43.
12. CAB 23/52 28 (26), 10 May 1926.
13. Burns, pages 55–6.
14. **British Worker**, 6 May 1926.
15. **British Gazette**, 8 May 1926.
16. **British Worker**, 9 May 1926.
17. **British Worker**, 10 May 1926.
18. **Hansard**, 6 May 1926.
19. Mason, pages 55–8.
20. Jefferys and Hennessy, pages 125–6.
21. C L Mowat, **Britain between the Wars 1918–1940** (London 1983) page 314.
22. 'B W' in **Sheetmetal Workers' Quarterly**, October 1926, quoted in Postgate, Horrabin and Wilkinson, pages 34–5.

Chapter 19: LOCAL ORGANISATION OF THE STRIKE

1. Mason, pages 22–3.
2. Letter from Darlington Trades and Labour Council to Walter Citrine, 9 May 1926, in TUC Library, Box HD 5366.
3. Postgate, Horrabin and Wilkinson, pages 46–7.
4. Burns, pages 15, 123, 154 and 171; A Clinton, **The Trade Union Rank and**

File: **Trades Councils in Britain 1900–1940** (Manchester 1977) pages 217–9; and Phillips, page 197.

5. Morris, page 46.

6. R P Hastings, 'Birmingham', in Skelley, page 212.

7. J Corbett, **The Birmingham Trades Council 1866–1966** (London 1966) page 125.

8. Mason, page 25.

9. Page-Arnot, in Mundy, page 277.

10. Benton, in Morris, page 438.

11. Burns, page 146.

12. Burns, page 139.

13. J Jacobs, **London Trades Council 1860–1950** (London 1952) page 129.

14. Bhaumik, in Morris, pages 397 and 409.

15. Bhaumik, in Morris, page 401.

16. Peter Kerrigan, 'From Glasgow', in Skelley, page 324.

17. Kerrigan, in Skelley, page 322.

18. Bhaumik, in Morris, page 400.

19. Bhaumik, in Morris, page 410.

20. Kerrigan, in Skelley, page 316.

21. Carter, in Skelley, page 130.

22. Bhaumik, in Morris, pages 402 and 410.

23. Phillips, pages 205–6.

24. Clinton, page 75.

25. J Mendelson, W Owen, S Pollard and V Thornes, **The Sheffield Trades and Labour Council 1858–1958** (Sheffield 1958) page 67.

26. James Hinton, **The First Shop Stewards Movement** (London 1973) page 138; and W Kendall, page 140.

27. Hinton, pages 223, 237, 248 and 263.

28. 'Theses on the Lessons of the General Strike', adopted unanimously by the Executive Committee of the Communist International on 8 June 1926, **Communist Review**, volume 7 (1926), page 126.

29. Murphy, **The Workers Committee**, page 23.

30. **The Socialist**, 6 May 1920.

31. Document issued by the London Committee of the Red International of Labour Unions in 1922, written by Harry Pollitt and quoted in Pollitt, **Serving my Time** (London 1940) page 161.

32. Tom Quelch, 'The Trades Councils: The need for the extension of their scope and work', in **Labour Monthly**, March 1922, quoted in Clinton, page 94.

33. **All Power**, March 1922.

34. See Tom Quelch's articles in **The Call** of 28 June 1917, 14 February 1918, and 16 October 1919, for example.

35. **Workers' Weekly**, 22 May 1925.

36. **Workers' Weekly**, 22 May 1925.

37. D E Baines and R Bean, 'The General Strike in Merseyside 1926', in J Harris (editor), **Liverpool and Merseyside** (London 1969) pages 242–4.

38. Baines and Bean, in Harris, page 254.

39. Baines and Bean, in Harris, page 258.

40. Symons, page 85.

41. Baines and Bean, in Harris, page 265.

42. **Police Review**, 28 May 1926.
43. Reported in the **Bootle Times**, 14 May 1926, quoted in Baines and Bean, in Harris, page 273.
44. Baines and Bean, in Harris, page 275.
45. Minute Book, 8 May 1926, in TUC Library, quoted in Phillips, page 343.
46. Patrick Renshaw, **The General Strike** (London 1975) page 18.
47. Mowat, pages 317–8.
48. Mason, page 66.
49. **Hansard**, 2 June 1926.
50. Bagwell, page 481.
51. Burns, page 176.
52. TUC Library, Box HD 5366.
53. Quoted in I MacDougall (editor), **Militant Miners** (Edinburgh 1981) page 91.
54. MacDougall, page 92.
55. Postgate, Horrabin and Wilkinson, pages 43–4.
56. MacDougall, page 92.
57. Symons, pages 111–112.
58. Symons, page 111.
59. Symons, pages 193–4.
60. **British Worker**, 9 May 1926.
61. **British Worker**, 10 May 1926. Emphasis in the original.
62. **British Worker**, 6 May 1926.
63. Crook, pages 422–3.
64. Crook, page 422.

Chapter 20: CONSPIRING FOR A DEFEAT
1. Bullock, page 323.
2. Citrine, page 185.
3. Citrine, page 184.
4. Jones, volume 2, pages 39–40.
5. Jones, volume 2, page 40.
6. Jones, volume 2, page 43.
7. Osbert Sitwell, **Laughter in the Next Room** (London 1950) page 228.
8. **British Worker**, 10 May 1926.
9. **British Worker**, 9 May 1926.
10. **British Worker**, 11 May 1926.
11. **British Worker**, 11 May 1926.
12. Citrine, page 188.
13. **The Times**, 10 May 1926.
14. Farman, pages 276–8.
15. **British Worker**, 7 May 1926.
16. Citrine, page 186.
17. Cook, pages 18–19.
18. Citrine, page 194.
19. Citrine, page 195
20. Citrine, page 199.
21. Citrine, page 203.

22. CAB 23/52 27 (26) 1, 8 May 1926, 6pm.
23. TUC Library, Box HD 5366.
24. Cook, page 22.
25. **Sunday Worker**, 23 May 1926.
26. **British Worker**, 12 May 1926.
27. Cook, page 20.
28. Cook, page 21.
29. **British Worker**, 13 May 1926.
30. Hutt, pages 158–9.
31. Farman, page 291.
32. TUC Library, Box HD 5366.
33. TUC Library, Box HD 5366.
34. Farman, pages 295–6.
35. CAB 23/53 31 (26) 3, 13 May 1926.
36. **Hansard**, 13 May 1926.
37. Symons, page 216.
38. Page-Arnot, **The General Strike**, page 239.
39. Postgate, Horrabin and Wilkinson, page 90.
40. Postgate, Horrabin and Wilkinson, page 243.
41. Crook, pages 462–3.
42. Morris, page 101.
43. **The Times**, 13 October 1926.

Chapter 21: THE ENDING OF THE STRIKE — FACT AND FICTION

1. Bagwell, page 479.
2. Bagwell, page 479.
3. Bagwell, page 479.
4. TUC Library, Box HD 5366.
5. **British Worker**, 11 May 1926.
6. TUC Library, Box HD 5366.
7. CAB 27/332.
8. Morris, page 264.
9. Bullock, pages 353–4.
10. Quoted in Cook page 7.
11. Crook, page 468.
12. **Locomotive Journal**, July 1926, quoted in S Nearing, **The British General Strike** (New York 1927) pages 108–9.
13. Citrine, page 204.
14. **Sunday Worker**, 13 June 1926.
15. **Sunday Worker**, 13 June 1926.
16. Cook, page 24.
17. **The Times**, 24 June 1926.
18. **The Miner**, 26 June 1926. Emphasis in the original.
19. **Report of the TUC at Bournemouth**, September 1926, pages 388–90.
20. **Report of the TUC at Bournemouth**, page 392.
21. **Report of the TUC at Bournemouth**, page 392.
22. **Hansard**, 1 May 1926.

23.   **British Gazette**, 6 May 1926.
24.   **British Gazette**, 10 May 1926.
25.   **Hansard**, 5 May 1926.
26.   **Hansard**, 8 May 1926.
27.   Aneurin Bevan, **In Place of Fear** (London 1952) pages 20–21.
28.   Jones, volume 2, page 53.
29.   **Hansard**, 13 May 1926.
30.   TUC General Council, **Report of Proceedings of a Special Conference of Executives**, 20–21 January 1927, page 58.

Chapter 22: THE LEFT PARTIES AND THE STRIKE

1.   **Manchester Guardian**, 4 August 1925.
2.   **Socialist Review**, June 1926, page 8.
3.   M Cole (editor), **Beatrice Webb's Diaries 1924–32** (London 1956) pages 90 and 92–3.
4.   Cole, page 98.
5.   Cole, page 102.
6.   Cole, page 113.
7.   Cole, page 122.
8.   David Coates, **The Labour Party and the Struggle for Socialism** (Cambridge 1975) page 137.
9.   Ralph Miliband, **Parliamentary Socialism** (London 1961) page 21.
10.   Quoted in L Panitch, **Social Democracy and Industrial Militancy** (Cambridge 1976) page 10.
11.   Panitch, page 53.
12.   Miliband, page 13.
13.   Quoted in Miliband, page 34.
14.   CAB 37/110 (1912) number 62, S Buxton, 'Industrial Unrest', pages 4–5, quoted in J M Winter, **Socialism and the Challenge of War** (London 1974) page 25.
15.   Quoted in Miliband, page 38.
16.   Miliband, page 69.
17.   J R Clynes, **Memoirs 1924–37** (London 1937) pages 95–6.
18.   Cole, page 281.
19.   **Workers' Weekly**, 22 October 1926.
20.   **Workers' Bulletin**, number 1, 4 May 1926.
21.   **Workers' Bulletin**, number 2, 5 May 1926.
22.   **Workers' Bulletin**, number 2, 5 May 1926.
23.   **Workers' Bulletin**, number 8, 12 May 1926.
24.   **Special Strike Bulletin**, issued by the Sheffield District Committee of the Communist Party, number 6, 11 May 1926, in B Moore (editor), **The General Strike in Sheffield** (Sheffield 1983) page 47.
25.   Hardy, page 185. Our emphasis.
26.   Fyfe, pages 68–9.
27.   **Workers' Weekly**, 21 May 1926 and 28 May 1926; TUC Library, Box HD 5366; Klugmann, page 154; MacFarlane, page 165; and R Martin, **Communism and the British Trade Unions 1924–33** (London 1969) page 72.

28.   **Report, Theses and Resolutions of the Eighth Congress of the Communist Party of Great Britain**, Battersea, 16–17 October 1926, page 7.

29.   Klugmann, page 160.

30.   Mason, page 26.

31.   Klugmann, page 156.

32.   Burns, page 146.

33.   Burns, pages 147–8.

34.   Jacobs, page 129.

35.   **Eighth Congress of CPGB**, page 64.

36.   Hardy, page 188.

37.   **Workers' Weekly**, 21 May 1926.

38.   **Workers' Bulletin**, 13 May 1926.

39.   **Eighth Congress of CPGB**, page 12.

40.   **Eighth Congress of CPGB**, page 65.

41.   **Eighth Congress of CPGB**, page 68.

42.   **Eighth Congress of CPGB**, page 74.

43.   **Eighth Congress of CPGB**, page 71.

44.   **Imprecor**, 30 December 1926.

45.   **Eighth Congress of CPGB**, page 72.

46.   MacFarlane, page 302; and Hugo Dewar, **Communist Politics in Britain** (London 1976) page 85.

47.   Trotsky, **Writings on Britain**, volume 2, page 253.

Chapter 23: THE END OF AN ERA

1.   **Report of the Annual Conference of the Miners Federation of Great Britain**, Southport, 25 July 1927, page 111.

2.   **Conference of MFGB**, page 39.

3.   **Report of Trades Union Congress**, Edinburgh, September 1927, page 151.

4.   **Report of TUC**, pages 320–1.

5.   **Report of TUC**, page 336.

6.   Bullock, page 392.

Chapter 24: IN CONCLUSION

1.   Trotsky, **Writings on Britain**, volume 2, page 248.

INDEX